Monographs of the Hebrew Union College

1. Lewis M. Barth, *An Analysis of Vatican 30*
2. Samson H. Levey, *The Messiah: An Aramaic Interpretation*
3. Ben Zion Wacholder, *Eupolemus: A Study of Judaeo-Greek Literature*
4. Richard Victor Bergren, *The Prophets and the Law*
5. Benny Kraut, *From Reform Judaism to Ethical Culture: The Religious Evolution of Felix Adler*
6. David B. Ruderman, *The World of a Renaissance Jew: The Life and Thought of Abraham ben Mordecai Farissol*
7. Alan Mendelson, *Secular Education in Philo of Alexandria*
8. Ben Zion Wacholder, *The Dawn of Qumran: The Sectarian Torah and the Teacher of Righteousness*
9. Stephen M. Passamaneck, *The Traditional Jewish Law of Sale: Shulhan Arukh Hoshen Mishpat, 189–240*
10. Yael S. Feldman, *Modernism and Cultural Transfer: Gabriel Preil and the Tradition of Jewish Literary Bilingualism*

Monographs of the
Hebrew Union College,
Number 10

Modernism and Cultural Transfer
Gabriel Preil and the
Tradition of Jewish Literary Bilingualism

Modernism and Cultural Transfer

Gabriel Preil and the Tradition of Jewish Literary Bilingualism

by

Yael S. Feldman

Hebrew Union College Press

Cincinnati 1986

Published with the assistance of
the Alexander Kohut Memorial Fund of
the American Academy for Jewish Research

Library of Congress Cataloging in Publication Data

Feldman, Yael S.
Modernism and cultural transfer.
(Monographs of the Hebrew Union College; no. 10)
Includes index.
1. Preil, Gabriel—Criticism and interpretation.
2. Bilingualism and literature.
3. Hebrew literature, Modern—Yiddish influences.
4. Yiddish literature—History and criticism.
I. Title. II. Series
PJ5054.P7Z68 1985 892.4'16 85–1757

ISBN 0–87820–409–1

Designed and produced by Special Edition, Inc., Columbus, Ohio.

Manufactured in the United States of America.

Distributed by KTAV Publishing House, Inc.,
900 Jefferson Street, Box 6249,
Hoboken, New Jersey 07030–7205.

לאמא —
אשר בכוחך הגעתי עד הנה.

Table of Contents

Acknowledgments

Like any study that has evolved from a doctoral project, this book has been long in the making and I have incurred many obligations. Teachers, friends, colleagues, and students have all contributed, directly and indirectly, of their professional expertise, intelligent insights, and moral support. The entire list is too long to be included here, but my thanks go to all of them, and particularly to the schools and scholars who welcomed me upon my arrival in this country. Their understanding and confidence made possible everything that has followed.

Special thanks go, first and foremost, to my advisors at Columbia University: Professor Isaac Barzilay, whose erudition and broad historical perspective were invaluable in shaping this study, and Professor Robert Austerlitz, whose linguistic and prosodic insights were instrumental throughout. I am thankful to both of them not only for the balanced share of guidance and freedom they generously gave me, but also for their friendship and for providing a warm working atmosphere. I also wish to thank the members of my doctoral committee for their valuable comments and criticism: Professor Avraham Holtz, for his meticulous suggestions and constant support; Professor David Sidorsky, for his thought-provoking arguments; and Professor Sacvan Bercovitch, for his appreciation and recommendations that gave me the courage to turn the thesis into a book. Parts of the manuscript were also read by Professors Robert Belknap and Arnold Band, for whose helpful insights I am greatly indebted. Finally, I owe the publication of this book to the generous readings of Professors Robert Alter and Ezra Spicehandler, without whose enthusiasm it would have never materialized.

Methodologically, this study is informed by several different approaches. I wish to thank their propagators in the hope that I have not compromised their teachings: Professor Michael Riffaterre of Columbia University, and Professors Benjamin Hrushovsky and Itamar Even-Zohar of Tel Aviv University. Last, but not least, my deep gratitude to Professor Dan Miron, whose instruction, both formal and informal, has been an inspiration throughout.

Research for this study was partially conducted at the libraries of the Hebrew Union College, Jewish Theological Seminary, YIVO Institute for Jewish Research, and the New York Public Library. My thanks are extended to the staff of each of these institutions for their time and patience. I am also indebted to the National Foundation for Jewish Culture, whose doctoral grant enabled me to complete the initial research in 1981, and to Columbia's Council for Research in the Humanities for two summers (1983, 1984) that provided me with the time necessary for revision and rewriting.

The final shape of the book is the result of the combined efforts of several people, all of whom I gratefully thank: my former student Lee Siegel, who graciously performed the preliminary editing; Professor Yehiel Hayon and his staff at Special Edition, who devotedly and painstakingly edited and produced this book; and, above all, Professor Michael A. Meyer, Chairman of the Publications Committee of HUC-JIR, whose interest and support did not fail throughout the long period of gestation of this book, and whose meticulous reading was instrumental in giving it its present form.

On a more personal level, this book owes its existence to the life work of its subject, the poet Gabriel Preil. I wish to extend my thanks to him for his friendship and help, and particularly for the gift of his verse. As he approaches his 75th birthday, may this book join his numerous literary awards in spurring him to many years of continued games with "the wandering words."

To the many unnamed close friends who always lent me their ears, I am profoundly indebted for their moral support and their illuminating chance comments.

Earlier versions of chapters IV and V appeared in *Prooftexts: A Journal of Jewish Literary History* (1982) and the *Association for Jewish Studies Review* (1981), respectively, and I thank both publications for the permission to reuse them here. Parts of chapters III and VII were published in Hebrew in *Moznaim* (January 1984) and *Jerusalem Studies in Hebrew Literature* (1983), respectively. A portion of chapter IX was presented at the Second International Conference for Research in Yiddish, held at the Oxford Centre for Postgraduate Hebrew Studies (July, 1983).

My final thanks are the hardest to formulate in writing. This book is dedicated to my mother, Clara Keren-Or, whose life-long and unbounded love, strength, and confidence—even across the ocean—have brought me to this moment. No words can express my debt. All that is mine is from her and hers. Finally, to my husband Peter, for his wit and humor, irony and kindness; for his patient listening to bungled first drafts and his unmatched ear for wrong pitch; for his being there just when it really counted—all my gratitude and boundless thanks.

Preface

אֵין מָנוֹס מִן הַזְּמַן שֶׁלִּי.
הוּא לִיטָא, הוּא אֲמֶרִיקָה, הוּא אֶרֶץ־יִשְׂרָאֵל.
אֲנִי הֶעְתֵּק מְיֻחָד שֶׁל אֲרָצוֹת אֵלּוּ;
אֵיכְשֶׁהוּ הֵן קָלְטוּ מִמִּזְגֵי אֲוִירַי.

No escaping of my time.
It is Lithuania, it is America, it is *'Eretz Yisra'el.*
I am a unique copy of these countries;
Somehow they absorbed my weathers.

ס׳איז ניטאָ קיין אַנטלויף פֿון מײַן צײַט.
ס׳איז ליטע, ס׳איז אַמעריקע, ס׳איז ארץ ישראל.
איך בין אַ ספּעציעלער אָפּדרוק פֿון אָט די לענדער;
ווי עס איז האָבן זיי אײַנגעזאַפּט מײַנע וועטערן.

("Another Time," *Poems from End to End,* 1976:10)

Born in Estonia (1911) and raised in Lithuania, the poet Gabriel Preil nevertheless has a rightful claim on both America and Israel. At age 11, he emigrated with his mother to the United States, where he has been subsequently living and writing in New York and environs. Although his first visit to Israel did not take place until 1967 (with two more recent trips in 1977 and 1983), his Hebrew verse, written mostly in America, has long puzzled Israeli poetry readers by its genuine use of the contemporary vernacular. For American Hebrew circles, Preil fulfilled the role of the "modernist" right from the beginning. In fact, the emergence of his imagistic free verse in the American-Hebrew periodicals of the 1930s and 1940s was quite unexpected. While in the new Hebrew center of the time (Palestine of the 1930s) Bialik's romantic tradition had already been challenged in the name of a variety of new "-isms," on the American periphery the very same tradition was being reinforced by its encounter with English Romanticism. Against the backdrop of this prolonged adherence to the romantic heritage, Preil's free forms were felt as a bold departure from the norm. The first critical responses labeled him as "modernist," "painter," "American," "nature poet," and "Robert Frost's disciple." Later critics related his work to various schools (mostly American!) of painting and writing. Most, however, neglected to consider (either on ideological grounds or out of sheer ignorance) two basic facts: (a) Preil made his début as a Yiddish (rather than Hebrew) modernist and (b) his early Hebrew verse presented him as a self-declared *romantic*—in complete contrast to his later image and fame.

This contradiction assumes special importance when seen against the background of the different poetic traditions of Hebrew and Yiddish. Hebrew poetry in modern times represented a fusion of romantic themes and attitudes with a classical, elevated style. Conversely, Yiddish, the language of the folk culture, inspired a literature marked by colloquialism, intimacy, and vitality. Moreover, the two languages differ not only in their heritage, but also in their recent evolution. While Hebrew was still struggling to liberate itself from "old forms" (e.g., the Shlonsky-Bialik debate on the question of modernism in Palestine in the 1930s), Yiddish literature had already reached an apex in its finest modern verse in America (the *Inzikhistn* [Introspectivists]). The earlier modernization of Yiddish poetry was no doubt enhanced by its ties with the innovative Anglo-American poetic movements of the time. (The *In Zikh* manifesto [1920] clearly resembles both F.S. Flint's "Imagisme" [1913] and Ezra Pound's "Vorticism" [1914].) A parallel effort among Hebrew poets in Palestine at that time was less successful. It merely resulted in another kind of highly stylized verse, mostly rhymed and in meter (Shlonsky and Alterman).

In view of these differences, Preil's début as a Yiddish poet is indeed instructive. His participation in the last issues of the periodical *In Zikh* (1936–1939) well explains his inclination towards imagism, free verse, and the use of common speech in poetry. Just as significant is his practice of autotranslation (Yiddish to Hebrew) by which he helped to prolong a long-standing tradition of Jewish literary bilingualism, which at that time was already on the wane. By the mid-1930s, when young Preil joined the Jewish literary scene in New York, the lines between the two languages and their literatures were clearly drawn. Thus, Preil remained the only writer of his generation to continue a dialogue of sorts between the two cultures.

The results of his dialogue are of special interest for historical poetics: Preil's modernism preceded, in fact, the liberating tendencies that became a governing principle in Israeli poetry of the 1950s and 1960s, when young Israeli poets began to reexamine the roots of their poetic heritage. Not unlike T.S. Eliot, they revolted against their immediate predecessors and reached back to the peripheral, "minor" poets of the beginning of the century (D. Fogel and A. Ben-Yitzhak). In these poets they found precedents for their kind of poetry—personal poems of free forms, common speech, and stark imagery. It was in this newly discovered poetic lineage that Preil's verse assumed an honorable central position. It constituted, indeed, an American link between those early attempts at Hebrew Modernism (mostly of European provenance), and its flowering in Israel three decades later.

Just as intriguing is this case of bilingual creativity for literary theory: Preil's formative years, and his practice of autotranslation in particular, may offer new insights into the mechanics of literary transfer and demonstrate the constraints operative in cultural contacts. Thus, for example, his early verse attests to his struggle with the long tradition of elevated style of Hebrew poetry and to his effort to liberate it, with the help of Yiddish models, from its romantic themes and its classical diction, rhythm, and form. No less fascinating, however, is the diametrically opposite move, the one underlying Preil's later verse—the attempt to save his modernism from the risky limitations of "pure" Imagism, by infusing it with newly modified romantic concerns.

It is in the above theoretical and historical perspectives that Preil's work is placed in the present study. Part One offers a bird's eye view of the different modernizing effects of the literary transfer from Yiddish to Hebrew during the revival period, when it affected mostly prose-fiction (chap. I), as opposed to the post-revival period when poetry was the main beneficiary of this process (chap. II). Chapter III reviews the critical reception of Preil's verse from the problematic perspective of his bilingualism, and chapters IV and V trace his dual roots in the Hebraic as well as the Yiddish traditions. Part Two is devoted to the description of Preil's poetics. Special attention is given to his formative years, when the struggle between his Hebrew romantic impulses (chaps. VI and VII) and the opposing Yiddish imagist drives (chap. VIII) can be best observed in his autotranslations (chap. IX). Finally, Preil's "metapoetic" journey to the borders of Imagism and back concludes our study of this breakthrough of Hebraic modernism "on American soil."

All translations were made by the author of this study, unless otherwise stated. Transliterations follow three different systems: (1) The *Encyclopedia Judaica* was consulted for the proper names of people and places; (2) Hebrew transliteration follows (with minor deviations) the "American National Standard Romanization of Hebrew," which was approved by the American National Standards Institute (January 22, 1975); and (3) Yiddish transliteration follows the system of the YIVO Institute for Jewish Research (see Weinreich's *Modern English-Yiddish Dictionary*, New York, 1968, p. xxi).

Part One

Literary Modernism and the Tradition of Jewish Bilingualism

Introduction

1. *The Historical Perspective*

Belletristic multilingualism was put back on the literary map by the counter-Romantic revolt of the twentieth century.[1] General distrust of language as a valid means of communication resulted in violation of linguistic order, on one hand, and in overstepping of the boundaries of distinct languages, on the other.[2] Thus, modern polyglot writers seem to undo the closely knit bond that eighteenth-century Romantics believed to exist between language and nationality.[3] This post-Romantic turn, the roots of which can be traced back to nineteenth-century French *symbolisme*, was described by Northrop Frye as an "ironic gesture of turning away from the world of the marketplace.... They renounce rhetoric, moral judgement and all other idols of the tribe..." (1957:60). By the turn of the century, this renunciation took the form of an overt opposition between the literary nationalists and the *avant garde* modernists. Later on, the impact of the Great War "finally undermined the fabric of the national past and led the way into total cultural nihilism" (Cahn, 1976:163). Central to this "nihilism" was the idea that "the really serious artist must be as international, *polylingual* and professional as a scientist" (Homburger, 1976:158; emphasis added). This polyglot writing is interpreted by some as a search for individualistic expression, which sanctions the use of common idiom on one hand, and multilingual experiments on the other (Forster, 1970:64,87, *et passim*). Precisely this practice, however, can be seen as the manifestation of a diametrically opposite aspiration to recreate an all-embracing universalized literature (Pound's *Cantos* and Joyce's *Finnegans Wake*, for instance). As such, it may finally be viewed as an ironic reversal of the long process of national and linguistic individuation by which European vernaculars detached themselves from their Latin common heritage and established their respective unilingual identities.

Viewed against this general scene, the linguistic predicament of modern Hebrew literature constitutes a rather different phenomenon. The literary revival of Hebrew in the past hundred years[4] exhibits a mélange of conflicting features: While the impetus behind the Hebrew renaissance was clearly romantic, i.e., nationally oriented (cf. Rabin, 1983), its linguistic medium was a classical, highly stylized and unspoken idiom, a language of three millennia of writing. Consequently, while Wordsworth and his peers could, at least in theory, just open the doors to a viable "people's" tongue and mode of expression, Hebrew romantic nationalists had to create the illusion of a vernacular out of their literary sources, simulating in Hebrew daily exchanges that had actually taken place in Yiddish, Russian, or Polish.

In a sense, the stylistic predicament of Hebrew modernists at the turn of the century was not unlike that encountered by the first European vernacular writers. In each case there had arisen a need to break away from the classical separation of styles inherent in Hebrew literary tradition and in Latin letters, respectively. This correspondence has been observed often, but the ensuing divergence was not. While the fusion of styles and the concomitant emergence of realism took place outside Latin letters, i.e., in the branching vernaculars (see Auerbach, 1953; cf. Frye, 1963), the analogous Hebraic process finally took place within Hebrew itself (although not without the mediation of the vernacular, as we shall soon see). The fact that today, only a century since its *modern* rebirth, Hebrew letters functions as a thoroughly independent and balanced literary system points to a rapid and multifaceted process of modernization. In this process, Hebrew was transformed from a literary language to a modern vernacular, the idiom of the State of Israel. When we remember, however, that spoken Hebrew did not fully come into its own until the 1940s, we cannot but wonder at the stylistic feat performed by its exponents at the turn of the century.

Indeed, the literary implications of the absence of a spoken model cannot be overemphasized. It is obvious that the modern Hebrew writer was operating under conditions quite different from those of his European counterpart. Had he been loyal to the idea of a national revival, he would have had to abstain from using the prevalent Jewish vernacular, Yiddish, thus risking his accessibility to wider ranges of society. Had he written in the vernacular, he would have felt cut off from the long Hebraic literary tradition, precisely the one he wished to rejuvenate. Consequently, Jewish writers were forced into a literary diglossia—a bilingual situation in which each language is used for different yet often complementary needs.[5]

Just as diglossia is evident in other languages (cf. ancient and modern Chinese, Greek, and Arabic), its existence is not something new in the history of post-biblical Hebrew. Until modern times Hebrew had always enjoyed the status of a classical literary idiom, while the vernacular changed from Aramaic to Arabic, Ladino, Yiddish, or other local languages.[6] However, it was not until modern times that a vernacular (namely, Yiddish) slowly developed its own independent belletristic system. Thus, at the end of the nineteenth century, Jewish literary activity was simultaneously taking place on two fronts. More often than not, it was one and the same writer who concurrently advanced the cause of Yiddish while modernizing Hebrew. Clearly, this state of affairs can give rise to rich literary cross-fertilization; nevertheless, later ideological developments strained this intimate relationship and clouded even the purely artistic interaction between Hebrew and Yiddish. As a result, early Hebrew literary historiographies excluded the Yiddish output of Hebrew authors, thus overlooking a vital part of their creative oeuvre.[7]

This attitude was finally reversed by Professor Dov Sadan of the Hebrew University. He was the first to insist, in both theory and practice, on the totality of what he labeled *Sifrut Yisre'elit* (literature of the people of Israel or Jewish literature). Sadan's insistence left its mark on contemporary Israeli research. Even though "Jewish" literature in other languages is rarely treated, Yiddish literature has been subjected to historical and literary studies.[8] Several of these studies deal with the interaction between Yiddish and Hebrew, particularly in the Revival period (1880–1920). Special attention has been given to authors who not only wrote in the two languages but also translated (or were translated) from one to the other. The work of such writers raises questions concerning the socio-linguistic aspects of their practice, since their bilingual activities were aimed at different audiences; yet this issue is hardly separable from questions of *literary* import, namely, the stylistic[9] and generic effects that such an interaction exerted on the literary traditions themselves.

Answers to questions of this kind require an inclusive theoretical perspective, one that will treat both Hebrew and Yiddish as members of the same system and that will be capable of probing into the dynamics of their "historical poetics." With this purpose in mind, we turn now to the theories of Russian neo-Formalism (as Victor Erlich labeled it, [1955] 1981:134–135) and its contemporary offshoots. It is in these theories that issues of literary change and cultural contacts have been greatly elaborated. Because these very concerns are also at the heart of the historical poetics of Hebrew (and Yiddish) literature, we should not be surprised to find Israeli scholars deeply involved in the current endeavor to redefine the Formalist notion of the literary system. It is precisely one of these redefinitions, the hypothesis of the literary "polysystem," that offers an appropriate frame of reference for the subject at hand, and it is, therefore, this theory that commands our attention in the following section.[10]

2. *The Theoretical Perspective: Literature as a Polysystem*

The Polysystem Hypothesis is a recent elaboration of the later Russian Formalists' theory of culture as "a system of systems," advanced as early as 1928 by Roman Jakobson and Jurij Tynjanov.[11] Inasmuch as it grew out of the Formalists' concern for literary evolution, its main thrust is the description and explanation of the dynamics of the emergence and decline of literary forms in both intra- and inter-cultural contacts.[12]

The fundamental assumption underlying this theory is that language (and by implication also literature or any other secondary-order system of signification such as art, film, etc.) "is not an aggregate of isolated facts, but a system, 'a coherent whole in which all parts interact upon each other' " (Erlich [1955] 1981:160).[13] This premise enables us to consider all levels of literature, "official" belles lettres as well as "unofficial" popular culture, as integral parts of the same complex system, despite their obvious differences. Consequently, culture is viewed as a multi-layered structure, whose strata are conceived hierarchically by consumers and manipulators alike. Furthermore, by introducing diachronic aspects into a synchronic structure of any given moment, the systemic model can account for seeming disparities caused by the constant flow and change of historical evolution.[14] Thus, the disappearance and reappearance of genres or stylistic devices from the literary arena is explained as one step in a circular, "organic" process. Overfamiliarity with old forms causes a loss of their effectiveness. In order to revitalize them, a breach of the readers' horizon of expectations is needed. This leads to literary "revolts" or deviations from the expected norms, whether linguistic, stylistic, or generic.

It was this dynamic aspect of literary evolution that fascinated the Formalists, who, therefore, focused on the mechanisms by which change is effected. They noticed, for instance, that many literary novelties were, in fact, devices formerly prevalent in folktales (Gogol), sentimental novels (Dickens and Dostoyevsky), or other semi-literary texts. On the other hand, once these devices have been exhausted by their use in the "canonized" literary center, they "do not disappear, they just move forward (or down, if you wish) from the canonized system for adults to other literary systems." This point, originally suggested by Tynjanov, was greatly elaborated and emphasized by the Israeli scholar Even-Zohar (1978:19,32–35,85–87), who consequently came to the conclusion that the literary polysystem is governed by a double movement of innovation and preservation. This movement is attributed to the center and periphery (or canonized and non-canonized systems), respectively, at least in modern cultures.[15] However, he makes every effort to fend off any possible value judgment regarding the function of the "conservative," non-canonized system:

> The canonized system got its popularity, flexibility and appeal by a constant and positive struggle with the non-canonized system. Dostoyevskij and Dickens would be inconceivable without the popular sensational and sentimental literature of the time (1978:17; cf. 1979: 296).

Implied in this statement, though never explicitly verbalized, is the cyclic nature of literary evolution. In this cycle, subculture serves not only as the storehouse for worn-out forms, but also as the indispensable reservoir of the new ones.

Curiously enough, this notion is supported from unexpected quarters. Although proceeding from a different point of departure, Northrop Frye arrives at a similar conclusion:

> Popular art is normally decried as vulgar by the cultivated people of its time; then it loses favor with its original audience as a new generation grows up; then it begins to merge into the softer lighting of "quaint," and cultivated people become interested in it, and finally it begins to take on the archaic dignity of the primitive.[16]

What seems even more surprising, however, is the fact that the polysystem hypothesis discloses some parallels to Jung's psychological theories (which clearly lurk in the background of Frye's archetypal modes). When it is claimed that subculture is practically the inventory from which literary novelties are borrowed, and when, furthermore, the dynamism and vitality of high culture are attributed to their constant struggle with the subculture, we are treading very close to Jungian concepts of the unconscious. Unlike Freud, Jung treats the unconscious positively, as a repository of culturally collected symbolic forms.[17] In his psychological scheme, the unconscious is the refuge into which psychic energy withdraws when current social (i.e., conscious) symbols lose their effectiveness. The new symbols that one recovers from the unconscious are actually of old tradition, but they are now used in another guise. Likewise, Jung defines a well-balanced and healthy personality as one growing out of the conflict and struggle between the conscious, social symbols (cf. high, canonized culture) and the unconscious ones (cf. low, popular subculture).[18]

This unexpected overlapping lends a psychological, subjective dimension to the historical, objective mechanism of literary change as it was observed by the Formalists and their disciples. It is, therefore, not difficult to imagine the impact of the absence of an intrinsic spoken subculture on a newly developed literature, as was modern Hebrew in the nineteenth century. Psychologically speaking, it meant an unfortunate dissociation between the conscious (Hebrew) and unconscious (Yiddish) layers of the writers' psychic activity.[19] Culturally, it implied the lack of a stimulating competition usually offered by a popular subculture. Linguistically, it entailed the complete reliance on ancient scriptural sources. With no recourse to a viable Hebrew vernacular, the literature tended to be highly stylized, even bookish. Thus, Hebrew developed its marked "mosaic" style—a jigsaw puzzle of literary allusions, truncated verses, and scriptural collocations (bound phrases). The shortcomings of such a synthetic language as an artistic medium are self-evident, particularly when employed in the service of realistic prose. In addition, the traditional sources were suffused with pious and religious overtones, which somewhat restricted their effectiveness in conveying the modern secular experience.

Its inherent deficiency notwithstanding, Hebrew preserved its vitality by linguistic and literary appropriations from neighboring cultures.[20] In recent times, life on Russian soil naturally triggered a dependence on Russian literature, just as Jewish contacts with Greek, Arabic, or Italian did in Hellenistic Palestine, medieval Spain, or Renaissance Italy, respectively. However, a special role was reserved for the close contacts with Yiddish the actual vernacular. As a folk culture, Yiddish was naturally endowed with colloquial intimacy and flexibility, precisely the traits so conspicuously absent from Hebrew. Yiddish, however, lacked the prestige enjoyed by Hebrew as the language of the canonized literature. Thus, the two languages complemented each other in their respective socio-linguistic functions. This complementary relationship is defined by Even-Zohar as a "symbiotic polysystem" (1978:79–80). The scope and limits, as well as the validity, of this suggested concept are the subject of the next two chapters.

Chapter I

The Revival Period (1880-1920): A Bilingual Symbiosis?

> "No poet, no artist of any art, has his complete meaning alone. His significance, his appreciation is the appreciation of his relation to the dead poets and artists. You cannot value him alone,...I mean this as a principle of aesthetic, not merely historical, criticism."
>
> T.S. Eliot, "Tradition and the Individual Talent" (1919)

If Hebrew and Yiddish literatures functioned, indeed, as a singular symbiotic polysystem, each of them should exhibit certain, expected features. The polysystem's socio-linguistic implications are quite easy to demonstrate. Even-Zohar does just this when he interprets the practice of translation that was common at the turn of the century: "Even the most important of Yiddish writers tried to achieve canonization via translation into Hebrew (e.g., Sholem Aleikhem)" (Even-Zohar, 1978:79). Elsewhere he states that "for centuries Yiddish texts functioned as the non-canonized system of Hebrew literature..." (*op. cit.:* 58). It is clear, then, that when Yiddish writers had their works translated into Hebrew, these works attained the permanence and the acclaimed status of canonized literatures. By the same token, though, Jewish writers, when choosing to write in Yiddish, were obviously seeking immediate access to and contact with wider ranges of Jewish folk. Thus, their works enjoyed the informality and popularity of non-canonized literatures.

More difficult to prove is the share each of the systems had in the process of revitalization (deautomatization) of literary forms, which is so central in the polysystem hypothesis. This difficulty stems, in part, from the overlapping of interliterary relations. Both Yiddish and Hebrew maintained contacts of dependence with Russian or German simultaneously with their symbiotic relationship with each other. Consequently, it may be impossible to sort out the exact sources of various literary appropriations.[1] Even-Zohar himself refrains from any substantiation of this aspect, claiming that "we lack even basic information on various aspects of the symbiotic existence" (1978:78). Nevertheless, there are several inquiries into the heritage of the acclaimed master of the bilingual tradition, S.J. Abramovitsch (1835–1917), better known by his literary persona, Mendele Mokher Seforim.[2] It is true, though, that other bilingual writers have just begun to attract proper scholarly attention.* This delay may be due to the prevalent view, recapitulated by Even-Zohar (1978:58, 79), that the symbiotic polysystem did not last beyond the collapse of the East-European center after World War I and the Russian revolution. In other words, the bilingual symbiosis is roughly equated with the Revival period (1880–1920).

According to this view, the change had been fashioned by intrinsic ideological forces, which upset the cultural symbiosis from within and instigated open rivalry. The ideological split between nationalists and socialists also took the form of a culture conflict, when Yiddish and Hebrew openly competed for the allegiance of Jewish writers.[3] Translating this socio-cultural struggle into purely literary terminology, we could agree with Even-Zohar that, as Yiddish literature came into its own, it liberated itself from the status of non-canonized literature (1978:80). In addition, the center of Hebrew moved from Russia to *Eretz Yisra'el*, where writers slowly created an intrinsic literary substratum from the Hebrew vernacular that was finally emerging there.[4]

However, this is not the whole picture. It would seem that the widely accepted outline of the literary symbiosis delineated above principally follows the interaction between Hebrew and Yiddish *fiction* only. Admittedly, the greater achievements and impact of bilingualism during the Revival period, the "official" symbiotic existence, were indeed in the realm of fiction. As we shall see later, bilingual *poetic* activity was surprisingly limited and without any enduring consequences. After World War I, however, the reverse is true. Despite the official estrangement of the two literary systems, there were a number of poets who perpetuated the bilingual paradigm of the Revival period. Not unlike their novelist predecessors, some of these poets introduced into Hebrew aspects of modernization that were first tried out in Yiddish and later transferred to Hebrew.

The poetic innovation of Gabriel Preil is the most recent link in this bilingual chain. Following T.S. Eliot's premise that "no poet... has his complete meaning alone" (1919; see epigraph of this chapter), we give first an overview of the bilingual tradition to which he is heir and of which he is perhaps the last exponent.

*As this book goes to press, a study of the (early) bilingual verse of U.Z. Greenberg has been published in Israel (Lindenbaum, 1984; and see chap. II below).

1. *The Modernization of Hebrew Fiction: (Auto)Translation from Yiddish*

Typical of the Hebrew-Yiddish symbiotic polysystem was the practice of autotranslation. Therefore, if a direct interaction between two literary systems is to be detected, the investigation should begin with the writings of self-translated authors. We should not be surprised, then, that scholars felt attracted by the life-work of the autotranslator par excellence—Mendele Mokher Seforim.

The history of Mendele's threefold evolution (Hebrew-Yiddish-Hebrew) is well documented and need not be repeated here; Mendele's example definitely bears out our polysystem argument. His role as the revitalizer of Hebrew fiction in both genre and style is indisputable, but it would have been inconceivable without his earlier experimentations in Yiddish. His transition from the didactic genres of the Enlightenment—the sentimental novel or the Romance (represented best by the biblical novels of Abraham Mapu [1807–1867])—to the new realistic satire had actually taken place in his interim Yiddish writing.[5] Only in Yiddish could he summon the figure of his "little Jew" to act out before his mind's eye the lively colloquial exchanges that later found their way into the dialogues of his fictional figures.[6] In Hebrew this option was, of course, not available. There, the writer's consciousness was probably divorced from his innermost, unconscious well of linguistic creativity—an insurmountable difficulty for a mimic artist as Mendele obviously was. The attempt to escape this threatening dissociation must have led, then, to the non-canonized system of the vernacular.

Emerging from this creative process was a new Mendele, now transferring his innovations to Hebrew. This, however, was easier said than done: The "little Jew" simply did not speak or gesticulate in Hebrew! The result was a conscious search for suitable Hebrew *equivalents* to replace the idiomatic vernacular used by Mendele's living protagonists. Typically enough, the first step taken by Mendele greatly resembled the stylistic changes evidenced by the emergence of Realism, which Erich Auerbach identifies in the early literature of European vernaculars (Auerbach, 1953:159–162, 183–185, 190–191, 271). Not unlike medieval innovators, Mendele did away with the time-honored veneration for the separation of styles. Biblical purism (the Hebrew equivalent of classical high style), which by the time of the Enlightenment had become a literary norm, was replaced by a calculated fusion of all Hebrew diachronic layers, thus compensating for the synchronically "defective system" (Even-Zohar, 1970a, and Shaked, 1977:43–48,83–89). Consequently, Mendele was credited with creating a new "low" style, unprecedented in Hebrew fiction (Shaked, 1965, 1977:83–89; Miron, 1973, 1979a:296–301).[7] Notwithstanding this stylistic feat, the greatest linguistic challenge was in the translation of colloquial idioms. Here Mendele's linguistic ingenuity, as well as its inherent limitations, are revealed. His utmost efforts were devoted to culling semantic equivalents from the diverse Hebrew sources that had been sanctioned by tradition in their own right (*ibid.*; also Zeitlin, 1943). Very rarely would he surrender to *literal* translation, either lexical or syntactic, which he considered a violation of good, balanced Hebrew style. Consequently, his Hebrew protagonists sounded more literate and literary than their Yiddish counterparts. Precisely this, however, was the source of the aesthetic attraction that Mendele's Hebrew fiction held for his contemporaries. It stemmed, at least in part, from a certain interaction between two different sets of idiomatic phrases—the Yiddish colloquialisms and the Hebrew literary idioms that represented them. Thus, there is today something of the ironic in Mendele's artistic achievement: Because much of the effect of the quasi-vernacular he had coined depended on bilingual readers, this very effect is often lost on the contemporary reader, for whom Yiddish is becoming a rarity.

This contemporary input should not detract, however, from our essential argument; Mendele's practice of autotranslation supports the claims of the polysystem hypothesis. In this case, both generic and stylistic innovations in Hebrew (the canonized system) were actually a transfer from Yiddish (the uncanonized system).[8] With Mendele, a new set of norms was established in Hebrew fiction, one that turned the fusing of historically different layers of Hebrew into a method. However, although the impetus behind this norm was the need to create a Hebrew vernacular as a means for a new realistic style, this goal was not actually attained. Mendele was still inhibited by what he considered the inherent literary constraints of the language. These checks and balances were transmitted to his faithful disciples, who perpetuated his prose style and his mode of translation (Shaked, 1977:84–89; Miron, 1979a:298–301).

That this innovative mode soon turned into a prescriptive norm can be attested to by the ambiguous epithet that was suggested by Bialik and has been widely accepted ever since: Mendele—the initiator of the *Nusach* (namely, 'the formulaic version' or 'the established path') ("*Yotzer ha-Nusach*," in 1974:170–175). Bialik's extolling intentions notwithstanding, this term connotes not only a conventional style of prayer, sanctified by tradition, but also the overfamiliarity of a well-trodden path. We should not be surprised, then, that the drive for defamiliarization did not lag behind. But before we examine its relevance to our argument, a few words by way of a summary are in order.

The preceding discussion leads to a twofold conclusion: (1) The modernization of Hebrew fiction revolved around the generic transition from the "high-mimetic mode" (i.e., romance, sentimental novel) to the "low-mimetic mode" of Realism, and by implication to a lower narrative style, incorporating the vernacular (cf. Frye, 1957:33–34); and (2) Its actual achievements notwithstanding, the Hebrew *Nusach* stopped short of completion: Though unquestionably "lower" than its antecedents (the Enlightenment novel of Abraham Mapu and his peers), its style is still quite literary and demonstrates a strong reliance on textual sources, both biblical and post-biblical.

As mentioned before, the deficiencies of the new norm did not pass unnoticed. As early as the turn of the century, it was challenged by writers who rejected its confining armor. For them, the liberties Mendele took with the linguistic heritage of Hebrew were not daring enough. In addition, his mimetic-representative mode was criticized in the name of individual expressiveness. The "little Jew's" typical speech patterns and external gesticulations were not in the limelight any more; the stress now shifted to inner struggles of individualized characters, and with this to the idiosyncracies of the idiolect.[9] In order to meet these demands, the exponents of the new trend embarked on diverse stylistic experimentations, which were later bound to revolutionize Hebrew style.[10]

Most prominent among those rebels was Y.H. Brenner (1881–1921), whose literary achievements bear directly upon our discussion. Although Brenner is traditionally counted among Mendele's stylistic opponents, he was actually a dialectic follower of the "master"; not unlike him, Brenner was motivated by a drive for artistic realism. However, his mimetic ambition reached deeper and further; he consciously tried to equip his protagonists with differentiated narrative voices and individualized speech patterns. For this purpose Brenner unhesitatingly borrowed from Russian, English, or Arabic.[11] This means that he continued Mendele's lexical expansionism, while ignoring the prescriptions set by the latter. In Brenner's works we would not find Mendele's so-called "well-made" sentence, replete with its synonymic and rhythmic repetitions (inspired, no doubt, by the biblical model of parallelism). By the same token, literary allusions are used sparingly, only for special effects. It would not be erroneous to claim, then, that Brenner got as far away from literary stylization as was possible in his time.

Yet, what seems to lurk behind his syntactic idiosyncracies is the model of colloquial Yiddish (and, as some claim, Russian[12]), which he *literally* transposed into Hebrew. True, we lack decisive evidence in this matter, because he did not leave us any autotranslation (even though he wrote copiously in Yiddish; see Bacon, 1975:130–168); but we do have his unpublished translation of Sholem Aleikhem's *Tevie the Milkman.* A comparison between the "canonized" Hebrew translation, made by Y.D. Berkowitz (in collaboration with the author), and the one made by Brenner is indeed edifying (see Bacon, 1972:217–219). Since Berkowitz's rendition follows Mendele's *Nusach*, all Tevie's utterances are rounded into well-balanced Hebrew phrases and bound idioms. Brenner, on the other hand, faithfully "copies" the Yiddish original, with all its awkward syntactical stops, lexical redundancies, and broken structures. The effect is one of rough, unpolished, conversational tone, recreating in Hebrew Tevie's original Yiddish monologues. This very same effect, however, is the hallmark of the speech patterns of Brenner's own Hebrew protagonists.

The fact that Brenner avoided publication of his translation is also instructive. It would seem that his notions of style and his norms of translation (issues still hotly debated in Israel today[13]) were far too audacious for his contemporaries. Mendele, as the literary arbiter of the time, and Bialik, as a senior editor, frowned on young Brenner's experiments. They considered him stylistically negligent and demanded compliance with their prescribed norms. Indeed, Brenner's attempt at deautomatization of Hebrew fiction style may have been premature for a literary system that had instated its own *Nusach* (norm) just two decades earlier. In addition, his attempt at avoiding literary allusions was hardly possible for the members of a generation that appropriated Hebrew mainly via its sacred texts, which they had studied and memorized throughout their childhood.

The further development of Hebrew realism as genre and style would lead us to the new center in Palestine, where Hebrew was slowly assuming the function of a vernacular, which naturally affected the literary polysystem. But this stage, precarious and fascinating as it was, lies beyond the scope of the present inquiry. There is no doubt, however, that the imprint of Yiddish colloquialisms on the language of prominent Hebrew novelists like S.Y. Agnon (1888–1970) and Hayim Hazaz (1893–1973) is unquestionable and calls for further investigation.[14]

2. *The Modernization of Hebrew Verse: The Russian Connection*

In retrospect, Hebrew verse of the Revival period (1890–1920) differed from its counterpart in prose in two ways: (1) Poetic innovations, unlike prose innovations, were *not* preceded by experiments in Yiddish; instead, they relied on norms that had been principally borrowed from the Russian.[15] (2) The established poetic norms were not *openly* challenged from within, as was Mendele's prose style by Berdichevsky, Gnessin, and Brenner.[16] Thus, the spectacular achievements of the era produced their own epigonic literature without having the benefit of a literary counter-trend to revitalize it. These two factors combined may account for the essential features of this body of verse as well as for the nature of the modernization it introduced. The latter will be best demonstrated by the work of H.N. Bialik (1873–1934), modern Hebrew poet laureate.

As a writer of prose, Bialik is usually considered the somewhat unorthodox disciple of Mendele. In the main, he followed Mendele's *Nusach*, despite the (limited) liberties he took with his master's linguistic prescriptions (such as direct translations of Yiddish idioms, or lexical calques [appropriations] from Yiddish or from Russian). Hebrew poetry, however, confronted him with a longer and even more deeply rooted convention of biblical purism. In the verse of the Golden Age in Spain (tenth to thirteenth centuries) and of the early and late Enlightenment in both Germany and Russia, it was mainly biblical Hebrew that was deemed fit for poetic expression.[17] Thus, Bialik was the first poet to transcend the limitations imposed by his predecessors. Following Mendele's example, he sanctioned all historical resources of Hebrew as "proper" poetic media. This later developed into a conscious cultural policy, resulting in an immense enterprise of compilation, part of which he carried out himself. Nevertheless, the major effect of his linguistic expansion was generally (that is, excluding his "folk" poems and his children's verse) not that of lower poetic diction and tone. For, while Mendele assumed the public position of a satirist, Bialik's public poetic guise was that of the prophet. In this persona, biblical tradition merged well with the romantic ideals inherent in his Russian models. Thus, his elevated rhetoric was not alien to his home-tradition (the prophetic diatribe with its heightened diction and tone), while it was also able to vie with norms appropriated from external sources.[18]

The prophetic genre, however, was just one facet of Bialik's poetry. Thematically and poetically, his major modernization of Hebrew verse was in establishing a new mode of the lyrical poem. From his time on, personal experience has been considered the principal source and the only worthy motivation of poetic expression.[19] Furthermore, the poetic representation of this experience had to be anchored in concrete descriptions, whether biographical or natural.[20] Still, even this new bent toward the concrete and the personal did not entail a complete stylistic shift. For Bialik, even personal experience was a state of heightened consciousness, and even the concrete deserved elaborate imagery, quite distinct from the realities that had triggered it. It is clear that both thematically and stylistically Bialik, the personal lyricist, was not divorced from Bialik, the prophet-seer. As a result, he was bound to be torn between national and individual concerns. No wonder that his personal poems are marked by a dramatic tension (Sandbank, 1976:9–45; Ha'ephrati, 1976:168–171). This tension is evidenced in his verse topically as well as structurally and stylistically. It underlies the poems' semantic structure and is operative even on the figurative level.[21]

The dramatic effect is achieved, in part, by Bialik's masterful employment of literary allusions. It seems that with no other poet was there such a compatibility between subject and medium: Classical Hebrew, with all its linguistic burden of a national past (allusions, connotations, associations) was an ideal tool to express the inner conflict of a poet who was bending under the yoke of the national role he had taken upon himself even contrary to his most innate inclinations.

We should not be surprised, then, to find that the absence of Hebrew vernacular was not acutely felt in Bialik's art. At the time when English verse, for example, was developing its conversational (free rhythm) poetry, Hebrew's poet laureate was immersed in building up romantic imagery and elevated rhetoric. This was accompanied by prosodic experimentations that ran the gamut of all possible meters (to the exclusion of quantitative meter). The hallmark of Bialik's prosody was, however, his rich syllabo-tonic versification.[22] Even though he was not the first to introduce it to Hebrew, it assumed natural (aural) flexibility and musicality only in his hands.[23] This was made possible because of the simultaneous transition to the employment of Ashkenazi pronunciation; its sonic proximity to the stress-system of Yiddish, the spoken idiom, rendered it more musical. (The Ashkenazi pronunciation is penultimately stressed, as is Yiddish; the Sephardi is ultimately stressed.) Bialik's unique prosodic achievements, and his dependence on Russian versification, have been recently described and evaluated (Shavit, 1978). Of interest for our discussion, however, is the light his prosodic techniques can shed on the effect Yiddish had on his poetics.

Unlike Mendele, Bialik did not have much use for Yiddish in his poetic work. His Yiddish activity was quite brief and limited (1899–1906); it consists of sixteen poems, some of them translations from Hebrew and German (Sadan, 1965). A wider area of interest is suggested by his translations in the opposite direction—from Yiddish to Hebrew. Here we have a self-contained group of poems—folk verse—which Bialik treated as an autonomous poetic genre. Together with his lyric and epic verse, this genre was incorporated into his official volume, which was to constitute his poetic canon.[24] Most of these simulated folk-songs, although traceable to original collections of Yiddish folk-songs (published around the turn of the century), are not direct translations. Rather, they were meant to be artistic representations of the popular folk genre. Their artistic reworking is attested to by their prosody (Shavit, 1978:179–183). It seems that Bialik meticulously and consistently avoided the original cadences of Yiddish songs;[25] instead he recreated this genre in the more disciplined syllabo-tonic meter, following, it would seem, the Russian artistic folk poem (Zhirmunskii, 1966:230–237). When he finally gave up the melodious syllabo-tonic versification, he did it in specific genres—the prophetic diatribe (or the poem of wrath) and the autobiographic epics (Shavit, 1978:228–342). But these poems, as mentioned before, were far from approaching any lowering of high style. Despite their violation of the strophe structure and their illusion of free rhythms (achieved, in part, by reverting to quasi-biblical parallelism), their pathos and heightened tone were upheld throughout by the choice of biblical rhetoric, diction, and imagery, which were obviously appropriate for the occasion.

We can conclude, then, that in pursuing his artistic intentions Bialik did not have much use for the liberating properties found in Yiddish folk-songs. In recreating the genre that was closely related to them, he deliberately shied away from their original freer rhythm (the same applies also to his children's poems). It appears that of the two home-traditions that anticipated modern free verse—the elevated biblical rhetoric and the lower conversational Yiddish folk-song—Bialik chose the former and thus opened the way for the high variation of free rhythms.[26] This prosodic choice was, of course, compatible with his romantic poetics; however, it did not go along with the prosodic tendencies of twentieth-century Western verse—the speaking prose rhythms of the personal lyric.[27]

Consequently, we could perhaps establish a certain correlation between bilingualism and lower style in the literature of the Revival period. The heightened norms set by Bialik were observed by a whole generation of poets who showed no traces of bilingual creativity. The only bilingual writer (Zalman Shne'ur [1887–1959]) was also the one who showed the strongest interest in free rhythms. Whether this is a coincidence or not is still to be investigated. (For more about this, see chap. II, below.) What is beyond any doubt is the fact that, despite some opposing tendencies, Bialik's poetics governed the scene, and his poetic standards later became the target of the rebellious post-war generation that was to follow.

However, we cannot turn to the post-Revival period before pointing to other phenomena pertaining to the issue of low poetic style. A limited lowering was effected by Saul Tchernichowsky (1875–1943), the only Hebrew classicist (in the Greek sense). Translating copiously from Greek, he introduced into Hebrew classical epic versification. The serene narrative tone of his idylls is coupled by his relative freedom from the traditional device of literary allusions (resulting from a rather mundane reason—growing up in a Russian village, his traditional education was not as intense as that of his contemporaries; his mother-tongue was Russian rather than Yiddish or Hebrew). Still, epic style is a far cry from an intimate, personal low style. In his lyric verse, Tchernichowsky was as dramatically romantic as Bialik and adhered to the same heightened poetic norms. In order for a new, personal genre to develop, the Russian territory had to have been left behind. Thus, we must move from the literary center of the Revival period to its western peripheries—Warsaw and Vienna. There, under the influence of German Modernism, literary innovations were being hatched.

The pioneer of this new trend was the poet Avraham Ben-Yitzhak (1883–1950), whose verse is more personal, whose diction is relatively humble, and whose versification is mostly free from traditional constraints. However, such a minor poet was not the right person to challenge tradition. Thus, his artistic work passed unnoticed. On the whole, it did not leave its mark on Bialik's generation, nor on the one following it. The modernization of Hebrew verse (if by "modern" we mean the conversational variation of free rhythms) had to wait for two more poetic generations and for the ascendency of a new center as well as new literary models. Nevertheless, the line modestly begun by Ben-Yitzhak had its tenuous heirs in the following generations and finally culminated in the "new" poets of the State of Israel. However, as we shall soon see, this stylistic line, in which Gabriel Preil holds a central position, had yet to struggle with the post-Bialik modernizers, whose reign was marked by resistance to Yiddish as much as to free verse.

Chapter II

Beyond the Bilingual Symbiosis: Between Russian and Central-European Modernist Models (1920–1940)

The first stage in the evolution of modern Hebrew verse was justifiably labeled "Bialik's Era." There is room, of course, for reservation and qualification concerning the homogeneity of the poetic output of the era (see Miron, 1961a); but there is no doubt concerning Bialik's central position as the initiator of a wide range of poetic innovations that became the dominant norms for his *pléiade*. This centrality could be extended readily to include geographical interrelations within the Hebrew literary polysystem of the time. Hebrew poetry of the Revival period was clearly dominated by the Russian center (mainly Odessa); new poetic roads, modestly paved by poets in the two geographical peripheries of the time—Central Europe (Vienna and Warsaw) and Palestine—remained largely marginal. It was not until the intervention of extra-literary forces (World War I and the Russian Revolution) that the balance between center and periphery was upset, both geographically and culturally. With the physical destruction of the East European center, the two former provinces came to the fore. The pioneers of the third *aliya* (immigration) gave rise to a new range of local themes, celebrating the Zionist-Socialist enterprise in *Eretz-Yisra'el*; Jewish cosmopolitans in Central Europe gave expression to European individualism and nihilism. Even though both trends had their pre-war antecedents,[1] it seems that the war acted as a funnel: It absorbed the accumulating changes and let them explode in the following decade. The best exponents of this revolutionary explosion are Uri Zvi Greenberg (1896–1981) and Avraham Shlonsky (1900–1973). To describe the convergences and divergences of these two multifaceted careers is well beyond the scope of this chapter. We will, therefore, limit ourselves to their respective positions on the issue of Jewish bilingualism and to the effect these positions had on the nature of their poetic innovations.

1. *Shlonsky's Russified Modernism*

The poetic modernism of Shlonsky[2] and his school has been typically associated with an open challenge of the older literary establishment, epitomized by the authority of Bialik. Shlonsky called for a poetic recognition of the new experience in *Eretz-Yisra'el,* in themes as well as in language. Attention to the local landscape (so different from its European counterpart), echoes of current ideologies and hopes, and the rough actualities and frustrations of the pioneers' life—all were added to the older (diaspora) inventory of Bialik and his peers.

This thematic modification was accompanied by a phonetic transition: The so-called Sephardi pronunciation slowly superseded the Ashkenazi European pronunciation.[3] This meant a change in both stress (from penultimate to ultimate) and vowel qualities, which by itself constituted a tragic threat for the prosody of Bialik and his contemporaries. The tonic musicality of Bialik's versification, including his folk-songs and children's songs, would eventually be lost to the generations that would be raised on the new pronunciation. We would expect, though, that Bialik's free-biblical poems could survive the dramatic change in language. But these were threatened from another quarter: Wrapped in the introduction of the spoken accent was a declaration of war on Bialik's diction. The new poets announced their intent to incorporate the Hebrew vernacular—then only in its infancy—into their modern verse. Most notorious was Shlonsky's frontal attack on the rhetorical tropes (*Ha-Melitza,* 1923):

> Civil marriage, free love among words—without stylistic matchmakers, without genealogies and a dowry of associations, and mainly—without a signed contract! (Too much familial purity in our language!)... This is the rule: liberty. A match just for a suitable moment. War against dogma, in order to avoid routine and habit.

Later, the same artistic goal drove Shlonsky to a severe critique leveled at one of Bialik's last poems (Shlonsky, 1931):[4]

> Is there any meaning to a stylized "I"?... Bialik gave us a poem of wrath—but it consists mostly of quotes. Every verse—"And he said"; every expression—"And it is written." This is a nice mosaic of sayings, artistic craftsmanship attesting to mastery of the language, but not a personal expression, drawing upon the innermost personal wrath of a *speaker in a specific era.* (Emphasis added.)

The theoretical intentions thus displayed by Shlonsky actually recapitulated the stylistic program exhibited earlier by the wave of anti-*Nusach* prose at the beginning of the century. It would seem that in verse the drive toward poetic realism and the need to replace the aesthetics of the sublime with the spoken idiom took longer to formulate than they did in prose. As mentioned before, elevated stylization was well entrenched in Hebrew poetry and it did not easily succumb to modern approaches. It took a poet who had actually experienced Hebrew as his daily spoken language even to *suggest* a change in poetic diction, lexical inventory, and syntactic structures.

Paradoxically enough, this suggestion remained mostly theoretical. Contrary to the prevalent notion (and obviously also to the poet's own declarations), Shlonsky's main contribution was not in the area of the vernacular. Despite his initial liberated prosody (using lines of different lengths in a-strophic structures) and his metaphoric freedom (and perhaps because of the latter), the main body of his poetry does not yield the impression of a lowered style, conversational tone, or free rhythms. On the contrary, Shlonsky's verse actually reached new heights of stylization, achieved by a carefully (and often conceptually) constructed imagery and by precisely measured syntax, meter, and rhyme. The occasional use of lexical colloquialisms is overshadowed by his neologisms, which doubtlessly contributed to the heightened effect of artistry conveyed by his verse.[5] These neologisms were mistakenly taken for colloquialisms, because Shlonsky relied more on the intrinsic options of derivation inherent in the morphology of Hebrew than on calques from foreign sources.

In view of the obvious gap between Shlonsky's declared intentions (to "lower" poetic Hebrew) and his actual practice, it is perhaps not surprising to learn of his determined reaction to Yiddish as a literary vehicle. Clearly, the cultural climate of the 1920s and 1930s was not amenable to a literary bilingualism of the kind that fertilized Hebrew prose of the Revival period. This reversal is dramatized by its own historical irony: Bialik, whose own poetic use of Yiddish had been limited, was not attacked by Shlonsky for allegedly supporting the rival camp (Yoffe, 1966:44–51; Z. Shavit, 1983:173-180). Indeed, the rejection of any of the artistic aspects of the former generation exemplifies the deeply felt need for deautomatization, for shaking the old norms. At the same time, the lack of self-confidence on the part of the newly created spoken language brought about a complete negation of anything that even smacked of the rival camp. Thus, the old way of deautomatization via the uncanonized literary layer (Yiddish) was barred. Spoken Hebrew was called upon for total self-reliance, yet was still too young to rise to the occasion. As we now know, it took two more decades for the spoken idiom to become a viable artistic medium. No wonder, then, that Shlonsky and his followers again fell—against their better judgment—into the footsteps of their predecessors, for they had to rely on foreign models. Shlonsky's earlier metaphoric and prosodic freedom could be traced back to his Russian contemporaries—the Futurists' *Imagenism* and particularly Mayakovsky's revolutionized rhythms. After his travels in Europe (1930, 1932), traces of the more restrained French symbolism colored his later poetry; his imagery became more centrally focused, and he reverted to a more disciplined and musical prosody, which largely underlined his subsequent verse.

To sum up, Shlonsky could be said to have aroused in Hebrew verse a self-awareness of its stylized heritage, coupled with a drive for change. In practice, he and his other Russian-born peers and disciples[6] continued the Russian (and French) connection in their prosody and imagery, thus perpetuating the tradition of elevated stylization or normative versification.

2. *Greenberg's Yiddish Connection*

The controversial poet U.Z. Greenberg[7] was somewhat of an outsider among the Russian Hebrew poets in their new center. Born in Galicia (1896), Greenberg migrated to *Eretz Yisra'el* at the age of 28, and was the first Hebrew poet whose background was other than Russian to achieve prominence there. Indeed, Greenberg's poetic apprenticeship took place in the Central European wing of Hebrew literature (Warsaw and Vienna), where the inspiring models were German and Polish rather than Russian. Not less outstanding was Greenberg's active participation in World War I in the Austrian army, an experience that left its clear mark on his imagery and poetic vision. Finally, Greenberg was the only one to come to *Eretz Yisra'el* as a published *bilingual* author: He began by publishing in Hebrew and Yiddish simultaneously.

This poetic bilingualism, practiced well beyond the supposed time limits of the Hebrew-Yiddish literary symbiosis, might serve as a test-case for the question of the interaction between Hebrew and Yiddish verse. A cursory overview of the main direction of Greenberg's artistic development will suggest an intriguing clue: His modernistic breakthrough took place first in his Yiddish verse and was later transferred to Hebrew. In the early 1920s, Greenberg was an active member of the avant-garde Yiddish circles in Warsaw, cooperating with Peretz Markish (1896-1952) and publishing his own modernistic poems and periodicals, not accidentally entitled *Mefisto* (1921) and *Albatross* (1921-1923). The general tenor of these periodicals was clearly in the vein of German Expressionism (of the loudly protesting variety).[8] Here one can follow young Greenberg's painful search for his Jewish identity, and the process of his ideological change. It did not take him long, however, to realize that the cosmopolitanism and nihilism expounded then in Vienna by both German and Yiddish writers did not hold any tangible solution for the Jewish problem. Arriving at this ideological conclusion, he turned to Jewish nationalism and even to Messianism; in 1924 he migrated to *Eretz-Yisra'el*, there reverting to Hebrew verse.[9]

But despite this conspicuous change in themes, concerns, and ideology, Greenberg's early Hebrew poetry shows all the expressionistic features of his Yiddish verse. Indeed, he established a new visionary mode, unprecedented in Hebrew. He soon found out that he was alone on the poetic front; his Russian-born contemporaries continued to perpetuate the poetic conventions of traditional European versification. For Greenberg, however, poetic, even linguistic, order exploded from within. His long Whitmanesque lines and strophic chains, which have since become the hallmark of his verse, clashed with the carefully constructed cadences of his peers.[10] In Greenberg's view, despair, as well as new hope, justified a search for a new poetic idiom. No more the melodious, musical, well-rounded stanza; now the ideal became a rough texture, the adequate expression of harsh realities of human and Jewish existence. This effect was created by breaking down all possible limits of stylistic distinctions and "good taste." The revolt against the classical separation of styles here reached an extreme manifestation. Sacred and secular, Scripture and vernacular, Yiddish (Germanized and Russified) and Aramaic, and, of course, the whole gamut of Hebrew diachronic levels—all were equally and indiscriminately welcomed into his poetic workshop. The audacity of his metaphorical technique reveals a similar tendency to transcend any delimitations, as do his masterful syntactic innovations.

If Shlonsky's rebellion against the generation of the fathers took the form of a war against rhetorical tropes and biblical allusions, Greenberg's no less vehement revolt symbolically centered around the issue of prosody—of rhyme and meter.[11] In one of his early Yiddish mock-poems, he dramatizes his scorn for the banality of poetic conventions in a way that defies translation:

S'nudyet, nudyet: lider-vaser, sentimentn-lakrits;
Gramen-shtramen: lib un trib un harts mit shmarts un kh'veys vos!
Meydl—kleydl, malekh—galekh, zind und blind un gas hint!

The mocking euphony and rhythm speak for themselves.[12] Yet later, the poet launched an explicit, full-scale attack against the other "99 poets" (or 99 percent of poets, excluding himself) who were writing Hebrew in the traditional way:

> You can skewer me alive, yet I will not stop asking: How can a Hebrew writer compose sonnets and idylls? Petrarch—yes! Longfellow—Yes! A Hebrew poet—No! We, Jews that we are, and art for art's sake? Artistic structures just for literary purposes? (*Kelapei Tish'im ve-Tish'a*, 1928:6).

Greenberg's nationalistic ideology comes through quite clearly. Aesthetic changes are often part and parcel of ideological transitions, and nobody illustrates this better than U.Z. Greenberg. In fact, his stylistic achievements, complex and contradictory as they are, successfully reflect the intricacy of his thematic message: The elating sense of a prophetic vision is concomitantly anchored in the actual realities of the moment. Thus, for example, his daring metaphoric and lexical liberty is controlled by an overriding elevated tone and rhetorical devices (anaphoras, catalogues, repetitions). This results in the paradoxical impression of a daily diction and of a visionary pathos at one and at the same time.

Less conspicuous and more paradoxical is Greenberg's prosodic art. Here, again, history displays one of its ironic twists. Reading Greenberg's verse today, in our Sephardi pronunciation (ultimate stress), we can readily be convinced by his own offensive against traditional versification, and see him as a propagator of free rhythms. After all, was that not the intention of his manifesto in verse?

מְשׁוֹרֵר יְהוּדִי הֲיָרֹן בְּיַמְבּוּס רוֹמָאִי? וְטִפַּת הַדֶּמַע שֶׁלָּנוּ כְּכֹבֶד הַגְּלוֹבּוּס!
חֲרוּזִים רְחָבִים! חַתְחַתִּים בַּחֲרוּזִים! — מָשָׁל לְדַרְכֵי יִשְׂרָאֵל בָּעוֹלָם.

Meshorer Yehudi ha-yaron be-yambus Roma'i? Ve-tipat ha-dema' shelanu ke-choved ha-gelobus!
Charuzim rechavim! Chatchatim ba-charuzim!—Mashal le-darchei Yisra'el ba-'olam.

(Ha-Gavrut ha-'Ola, 1926:31)

A Jewish poet, would he versify in Roman iambs? When just one of our teardrops is as heavy as the globe!
Expansive verse! Bumpy rhymes!—Thus to exemplify the ways of [the people of] Israel in the world.

Indeed! "Expansive verse," or "the rhythm of the sea," as he labels his style elsewhere (*Kelev-Bayit*, 1929:30)—why, then, was Greenberg's pioneering free verse not recognized as such in his own time? For a very simple reason: Like most poets of the 1920s, he still used the Ashkenazi pronunciation (cf. Shlonsky's early verse). Scanned along the lines of this phonetic system, all the above-quoted lines fall into a perfect syllabo-tonic meter (even amphibrachs):

Mĕshōrĕr Yĕhūdĭ hă-yārŏn bĕ-yāmbŭs Rŏmā'ĭ?[13]

Still, even in Ashkenazi accentuation, Greenberg's verse creates the illusion of free rhythms, despite the carefully measured line. This was effected by the subordination of metrical units to long syntactic units. As Hrushovski convincingly demonstrated (1978:41), one of Greenberg's lines (equalling a complete sentence) could sometimes contain eight or ten amphibrachs, which would easily constitute a whole stanzaic unit in Bialik's lyric verse.

However, this fascinating prosodic technique depends, it would seem, on Ashkenazi reading—the one close to Yiddish, Greenberg's mother tongue. As he moves towards Sephardi pronunciation he reverts, not unlike Shlonsky, to more traditional line-length and stanzaic forms, regularly metered and rhymed.

To sum up, like Mendele before him (in prose) and, as we shall see, like Gabriel Preil after him, Greenberg used Yiddish to shape his poetic innovations. *Yiddish was, I shall argue, more amenable to "unpoeticizing" orientation because of its natural colloquial characteristics.* Against the background of Shlonsky's rejection of bilingualism on the one hand, and his adherence to a prosodic "*Nusach*" on the other, Greenberg's position in poetry resembles that of Brenner in prose;[14] he actually veered toward a kind of anti-*Nusach* in verse. And like Brenner, his endeavor did not attract a following.

From another point of view, Greenberg continued the line of Bialik's elevated free rhythms. Though they utilized different prosodic techniques, the respective results of their enterprises were similar. The illusion of free verse was employed in both cases in the service of the prophetic vision with its heightened tone and diction.[15]

Greenberg and Shlonsky, on the other hand, shared a common thematic and moral interest. In their early years, at least, both were involved in public issues, and thus set up the identification of verbal art with *littérature engagée.* None of the personal lyricists of the era, neither of the older generation nor of the younger one, could gain prominence. Public, national, and ideological concerns were at the center of attention. Typical of this atmosphere was the unsuccessful *aliya* (immigration to Israel) of another modern poet from Central Europe—David Fogel (1891-1944).

3. *Fogel's Minor Lyricism*

David Fogel's case was one of extreme personal and poetic individualism. Without manifestos or declarations of departure from existing norms, he paved a new path of his own in Hebrew verse. Writing mostly in Europe, he steered clear of the central lines of Hebrew poetic tradition and cleaved to its peripheral, minor writers, his older contemporaries, the poet Ben-Yitzhak, and the individualistic novelist U.N. Gnessin (1879-1920).

Fogel's unique style is unprecedented in Hebrew verse. He lowers and thins out his diction, imagery, and syntax. He recoils from literary allusions and from fixed meters. His short poems are generally strings of loosely linked images, governed by the flowing rhythm of syntactic units. Still, some claim that Fogel was *not* familiar with German Expressionism (its minor, individualistic varieties like Trakl [1887-1914] and Rilke [1875-1926]) before developing his own style (Pagis, 1966:42-45). However, from the little we know, it is evident that he was close to Yiddish circles, first in Vilna (*op. cit.*:42) and later in Vienna. In 1920, two of his poems were translated into Yiddish from manuscript (*op. cit.*:43), and it is plausible that he was familiar with Greenberg's *Albatross*, which was published in Warsaw (1922) and Berlin (1923).

Though the source of Fogel's innovation is obscure (and is likely to remain so), there is ample evidence of his own view about his poetic enterprise. He is reported to have said: "I wrote just a little, but you would have to admit that until now nobody wrote in Hebrew like me! I am somewhat different, am I not?" (*op. cit.*:27). A script of a lecture he gave in 1936 (found only a decade ago) reveals his aversion to those "linguistic virtuosi" who "bombard us with verbal shells which do not explode at all ... they jump ahead pretending to be literary guides, so-called innovators and revivers" (*op. cit.*:36)[16]

These few pronouncements suffice to illustrate the extent to which even the most personal and least public of all Hebrew writers of the era was consciously involved in stylistic issues. The need for a change was felt by all; the ways in which this need was expressed took different forms. Shlonsky addressed himself to the question of poetic diction and rhetorical tropes; Greenberg concerned himself with issues of prosody, meter, and rhyme; and Fogel talked about "The Language and Style of Our Young [Modern] Poetry" (the title of his lecture).

The three diverging solutions suggested by these young poets each had its own development. As early as 1936, Shlonsky's norms received legitimization by critical public opinion. For the next two decades the center of Hebrew poetry was occupied by Shlonsky's school. His disciples, as is customary, were not always orthodox; nevertheless, they carried on the stamp of his new *Nusach*. Successfully competing for public attention, U.Z. Greenberg alone continued to change and develop his prosody. In his later book (*Rechovot ha-Nahar*, 1951) he came quite close to free verse.[17] Only Fogel followed in the footsteps of his admired predecessors. Continuing to write Hebrew verse on the continent until the bitter end (he perished in the

Holocaust), he was relegated to the periphery of the world of Hebrew poetry.

In the 1930s and 1940s it looked as if the individualistic variety of modern free verse had had a tenuous breakthrough with Ben-Yitzhak and Fogel, but had no future among Hebrew poets. Confronted with the epigrammatic virtuosity of Shlonsky and Alterman and the thundering rhetoric of Greenberg, whispering Hebrew lyricism was all but silenced.[18] A reversal of this situation took place, predictably, in the early 1950s. It seems that only then did Hebrew feel vital enough to break the barriers of the allusive or literary expression. This process was, no doubt, encouraged by new contacts with Anglo-American modern poetry, which replaced the Russian-French models of the former generation. As a result of this change, young Israeli poets tried to redefine the contours of their poetic heritage. Not unlike T.S. Eliot, they reacted against their immediate predecessors and reached back to the peripheral, "minor" poets of the beginning of the century.[19] This was the first generation of Hebrew poets that did not have to rely only on foreign models in their attempts at deautomatization. This time, the new poets unearthed and canonized so-called marginal poetic "grandfathers" (Ben-Yitzhak) or "uncles" (Fogel) to help them drive aside (for a while, at least) the central (Russified) axis of Bialik-Shlonsky-Alterman. To this new lineage, a third link was soon added—a younger uncle, from a still-farther periphery—the American poet Gabriel Preil, who started to publish his individualistic free verse in 1936, just when, in *Eretz-Yisra'el,* traditional modes of versification reached a new apex.

Chapter III

Preil's Bilingualism: The Critical Reception[1]

> No poetry, of course, is ever exactly the same as speech that the poet talks and hears: but it has to be in such a relation to the speech of his time that the listener or reader can say "that is how I should talk if I could talk poetry."
>
> T. S. Eliot, "The Music of Poetry" (1942)

There is something of the ironic in the attempt to render into English the unique effects of the Hebrew poetry of Gabriel Preil. Indeed, it is hardly possible. The fact is that Preil's artistic achievements, as well as his poetic charm, stem, at least in part, from his surprising mastery of the new Israeli vernacular. And surprising indeed it is, because, geographically speaking, the American resident Gabriel Preil has been doubly distanced from Israeli soil. Born in Estonia in 1911, he spent his childhood in Lithuania and escaped post-war Europe with his mother, Clara Preil (née Matzkel), migrating to the U.S. in 1922. New York has been his home ever since, and New England his favorite countryside. (Both New York cityscapes and New England landscapes figure greatly in his verse.) Only in 1968 did Preil visit Israel for the first time, with two more recent trips in 1977 and 1983, but by then he had already published four volumes of verse and had already been recognized and embraced by Israeli poets and critics, modernists and conservatives alike. Special attention has been given—and justly so—to his "Israeli Hebrew." The poet Natan Yonatan, after a visit to New York, during which he met Preil for the first time, writes: "How does he speak such Hebrew, fresh and lively, and how does he fashion such Hebraic verse (*shira 'Ivrit kazot*), surrounded as he is by alien speech sounds and literary echoes?" (1968:67). The same amazement is expressed by an Israeli interviewer (Stavi, 1977): "How do you do that? How does one become an Israeli poet in the U.S.?" And then: "The Hebrew you write and speak is so lively, it is simply miraculous. New [Hebrew] words, which we in Israel have not yet wholly digested, are already used in your poems and also in your conversation. How does this happen?" (*ibid.*). Another poet (and critic), Ben-Shaul, adds (1977): "His Hebrew is so Israeli; it draws upon the contemporary language, both written and spoken, which is constantly being changed and renewed, as if he is always here, aware of whatever is going on."[2]

One could say that Preil's life and art are a manifestation of two diametrically opposite movements: His physical biography led him further away from Israeli soil, but, through his artistic activity, he tenaciously bridged the distance and successfully approached the contemporary sources of his poetic medium. In order to do this, he had to cross two language barriers: Yiddish, his European mother tongue, which continued to be the language spoken at home throughout his life, and English, the language he acquired in his new home-country and which soon became a rich literary source for young Preil, the avid reader.

These two barriers not withstanding, Preil was confronted by still a more complex one, i.e., the gulf between classical, or literary, diaspora Hebrew, used by his fellow poets in America, and modernized Israeli Hebrew, which was slowly branching out into differentiated "registers" (as does every living language), for example, the literary, the journalistic, the spoken and the colloquial.[3] This last transition, even though intra-linguistic, may have been the most difficult. As was outlined above, literary bi- (or even multi-) lingualism has always been the lot of Hebrew writers. No Hebrew writer, until recently, had ever used Hebrew as his spoken mother-tongue. In this respect, Preil was no exception. He was, however, one of the few poets who managed to break away from the elevated rhetoric and stylization, as well as from the classical diction and versification inherent in modern Hebrew verse. Instead, he developed his conversational poetic mode, employing free verse and common speech, even before this mode was adopted by avant-garde poets in Israel.[4]

When his poems first reached Israeli readers (in the late 1930s or early 1940s), the need to lower the poetic style and to incorporate the vernacular into the poetic domain had long been recognized but, on the whole, had not yet been attained. In Israeli verse, the ringing rhyme schemes and meticulous metrics of the Shlonsky-Alterman school were still competing with the visionary pathos and political rhetoric of U.Z. Greenberg. The personal free verse of Ben-Yitzhak and Fogel did not yet constitute a school by itself. No wonder, then, that from the very beginning reviewers on both sides of the ocean acclaimed Preil as a new modernist voice.

Preil's first volume, *Nof Shemesh u-Chefor* [*Landscape of Sun and Frost*], was published in New York in 1944, and was warmly received by his American contemporaries as well as by Israeli poets.[5] Yet, there is a marked difference between the critical responses of the respective parties. While in Israel Preil's innovation is vaguely felt as "American modernism" (Lea Goldberg, Shin Shalom, and Shmuel Bass, 1945–1949), the first American reviews pinpoint the novelty much more accurately; they draw attention to his conversational tone (T. Carmi, 1945) and his prose-like rhythm (Ribalow, Bavli, and Silberschlag, 1943) and describe his verse as a departure from "Hebrew classical tradition" (Epstein and T. Carmi, 1944/5). This divergence should not surprise us: Much as Preil's new style was a daring deviation from the mainstream of Hebrew verse in its new Israeli center, it constituted an even bolder departure from the norms of Hebrew poetry in America. Indeed, in order to appreciate fully the new ground he broke, we have to judge his verse not against the setting of the Israeli center, of which he was not even fully aware at the time,[6] but against his immediate environment. Namely, we will not be able to follow the dynamics involved in the reception and the effect of Preil's free verse, if we do not place it in the perspective of the tradition of American Hebrew verse.[7]

American Hebrew poets were untouched by the modernizing ideas (if not practice) informing the Israeli center from the 1920s on. Writing on the periphery farthest removed from the center of the newly organized Hebrew literary system, they were still perpetuating the poetic and prosodic norms of Bialik's era. The leading figures of the second generation of American poets—Hillel Bavli (1893–1961), Israel Efros (1890–1981), Abraham Regelson (1896–1981), and Simon Halkin (b. 1899)—were all born in Europe and were raised in the classical norms of the Russian center. The poetic genres mainly dominant in their work were the narrative epic (treating intrinsically American topics—the life of American Indians, for example) or the long, philosophically laden lyric. This last genre may attest to another source of inspiration: English Romanticism. Halkin, for example, translated Shelley's "Defence of Poetry" ([1928] 1969, III:271–300), and his poems reveal traces of Wordsworth and Keats, as well. Regelson, on the other hand, wedded the indigenous mysticism of Ibn-Gabirol with that of William Blake. He was also inspired by Milton, Shelley, and Keats.[8] There is no evidence, however, for any contacts with contemporary American verse, particularly of the imagist free-verse varieties. Clearly, whether they took their cue from their own Hebrew predecessors or from extrinsic sources, American Hebrew poets preserved in their early output a former stage of classical Hebrew, a kind of belated Revival poetry.[9] Naturally, their literary output was marked by high diction and tone and by conventional metric and strophic forms.

It should be clear by now how unexpected was the appearance of Preil's short and compact poems, with their stark imagery and understated individualism. No wonder their emancipation from the traditional constraints of rhyme and meter was acutely felt—by American Hebrew standards in particular—as a departure from all accepted norms. This unpredicted breach of the horizon of expectations of the Hebrew literary circles in New York, and to a lesser degree in *Eretz-Yisra'el* as well, set readers on the detective trail. For a long time, critical responses focused on defining Preil's modernism and on tracing its sources. Using this focal interest as a parameter, the critical reception of Preil's modernism may be divided into three topical groups. Although this division is basically synchronic, it partly corresponds to certain diachronic processes, which attest, as will be shown, to intrinsic historical developments in the Hebrew belletristic polysystem.

1. *Early Views: American Modernism*

In their attempts to account for Preil's new style, his first reviewers (1945) attributed his innovation to the influence of American culture. The poet Lea Goldberg (1911–1970) detected in Preil traces of Whitman and Sandburg and went on to welcome this import from "another language" as a counter-balance to the provinciality of Hebrew verse. The poet Shin Shalom perceived in Preil's verse glimpses of Edgar Allan Poe's America, and S. Bass added a list of American poets as diversified as Robert Frost, Edgar Lee Masters, Amy Lowell, Edna St. Vincent Millay, and H.D. (Hilda Doolittle). American critics were less generous: Silberschlag mentioned some resemblance to Frost, and Epstein brought up Walt Whitman, Robinson Jeffers, and Carl Sandburg (1952:229).[10] Epstein was also the only one to mention another influential figure, the Yiddish poet Jacob Glatstein (1896–1971): "Particularly was he [Preil] influenced by the Yiddish modernist Jacob Glatstein in his Inzikhist period" (1952:229).

Why and how this "particular influence" took place we are not told; this single statement is never elaborated on, and subsequent reviewers ignore it altogether. That the young Preil was not only close to Yiddish circles in New York, but actually made his début in Yiddish periodicals, seems to have passed unnoticed. Nowhere, including Epstein's review (which was published in Yiddish as well!), is there any mention of Preil's contributions to the last issues of the Yiddish modernist periodical *In Zikh*, nor of his translations (into Hebrew) of Glatstein's poems.[11] Most importantly, no one accords any significance to Preil's bilingual creativity, although many of Preil's early poems were concurrently published in both Hebrew and Yiddish. Whether or not they had also been simultaneously composed is another problem, not always easy to settle.

Be that as it may, we are here once more confronted with the Jewish literary paradigm of *autotranslation.* A close examination of Preil's bilingual activity reveals that in his early stages he translated himself from Yiddish into Hebrew, and only later reversed the procedure. A few of his first Yiddish poems were not translated at all, and one was translated into Hebrew only after a conspicuously long interval, and not accidentally so.[12] Furthermore, there is a striking difference, in form and style, between the first Hebrew poems and the earlier Yiddish poems. Predictably, the early Hebrew originals are *not* as innovative as their Yiddish counterparts. Of course, they were quite novel in the framework of Hebrew verse in America, but not yet as daring in their departure from the governing norms as they later became, or as some of the Yiddish verse had been from the start.

There is room to argue, then, that a close look at Preil's bilingual activity *in toto* may shed more light on the genesis of his poetic modernism than the attempts to locate his inspiration in interliterary contacts. If we place his autotranslation in the perspective of the bilingual tradition of Jewish literature, we are likely to understand his growth in terms of intraliterary symbiosis. We might be surprised to find that, even in the America of the 1930s, half a century after Mendele's enterprise, Yiddish still afforded the poet an appropriate experimental medium. Not unlike his great predecessor, Preil used Yiddish as a workshop in which he learned to lower and tone down his poetic medium. What had been done in Hebrew prose around the turn of the century had to wait longer to take roots in Hebrew verse, because of the long tradition of high poetic style delineated above. It should not seem accidental, therefore, that this transition was made possible once more through the mediation of Yiddish. This interaction, however, must have been significantly different from the one in prose, due to the divergence between the respective developments of Hebrew and Yiddish poetry in America. While Hebrew assumed the peripheral activity of preservation and "automatization" (see Introduction, section 2), Yiddish plunged into a fast process of modernization and deautomatization. This was no doubt enhanced by the colloquial nature of Yiddish—a feature that Modernism adopted as one of its new dominant principles.[13]

Still, all this was clearly ignored by young Preil's contemporaries. Epstein's brief mention of Preil's Yiddish contacts was soon forgotten. When Preil's second volume was published, this time in Israel (*Ner mul Kochavim* [*A Candle Against the Stars*], 1954), more Israeli writers applauded his novelty. The novelist Moshe Shamir (1954) rightly described his verse as "lyrical objectivism," attributing it to American influence. Others observed his successful fusion of Hebrew and alien (American) elements (Lander; M. Yoffe, 1955) or again stressed his departure from the tradition of Bialik and his disciples (Lander, 1955; Shamir, 1954). Later, a new critical approach emerged—a more analytic reading, attempting to describe Preil's particular techniques (mainly Zach, 1959 and 1961, but also Lubin and T. Shlonsky, 1958). In America, responses continued to be thematically inclined (Ivry, 1955), and the publication of Preil's third volume, *Mapat 'Erev* [*Map of Evening*, 1960] was celebrated by a series of essays obliquely debating his Americanism. Friedland (1960) welcomed it as the first successful Hebrew Americanism, while Zeitlin (1960) stressed the Jewish shades of Preil's Americanism—his perennial yearnings and misgivings.

2. *A Derivative Misconception: The Homogeneity Fallacy*

From the 1960s on, the main weight of literary interest and critical response naturally shifted to Israel (most of the American Hebrew writers had moved to Israel, whereas a younger generation had not emerged). This decade was a turning point in the poetics of Israeli writers. Natan Zach led a frontal attack against the mechanical versification of Shlonsky's school.[14] The criticism was levelled not against the master, but rather against his disciple, Alterman, since by then he had usurped the throne and become the poet laureate of the State generation (see Miron, 1980, especially 337, 373–374). Concurrent with this change were the publications of Preil's third and fourth volumes (*Mapat 'Erev*, 1960, and *Ha-'Esh ve-ha-Demama* [*Fire and Silence*], 1968), as well as his visit to Israel in 1967. The new poetic atmosphere in Israel was just ripe for applauding Preil's verse. His arrival was signaled by Zach's appraisal of *Mapat 'Erev* (1961), and was followed by numerous articles, which, for all their distinctive features, continued the major argument outlined by early reviewers. Despite the occasional new critical idiom—Sandbank (1962) discussed the stylistic deautomatization in Preil's use of Hebrew, Moked (1961) mentioned metaphysical poetry, and Shabtay and Hanaami (1965) evoked existentialism and the absurd—there remained a consensus that what distinguished Preil's verse was its American Modernism, or its *Imagism*, as it was often called.[15]

Accompanying this critical view was the growing notion that Preil's verse had not changed with time. Bertini's statement that Preil's third book added no new elements to the earlier poems (1961) seemed to be the accepted notion as late as 1977 (cf. Hanaami). This tendency may have derived from a typical feature of the criticism on Preil: Most reviews were written on the occasion of the publication of each new volume and, as it so often happens, critics generally limited their evaluation to the volume they were reviewing. Thus, they may have lost the perspective of Preil's growth as a poet and the development of his stylistic techniques, attitudes, and concerns. This did not change with the publication of a short selection of his verse (introduced by Shabtay, 1965), nor with the emergence of a new kind of analytic approach—the close reading of a single poem (Alter, 1965; Hanaami, 1969; Perry, 1972; Komem, 1977). It would seem that the reviewers of the later books wrote as if neither Preil's earlier works were in existence (see, for example, the reviews of *Fire and Silence* by Dor, 1968, Kremer, 1968, and Rabinowitz, 1969),[16] nor his poems in Yiddish, which by then had already been collected into a book entitled *Lider* (1966).

The only exception to the rule was Bertini, in his later essay, 1971, who explicitly raised the issue of development and change in Preil's verse. Still, he preferred to deal not with variables, but rather with the constant features of this oeuvre. Characteristically, Bertini mentioned that Preil was at home with Yiddish poetry (cf. Keshet, 1963). Bertini was also the only one even to mention Preil's translations of his poems into Yiddish. Parenthetically, he wondered whether Preil also translated the other way around. In other words, both the fact that Preil started out writing in Yiddish and was immersed in autotranslation, and the effect that this practice may have had on his Hebrew verse, were completely unknown to most of his Hebrew reading public.

If Israeli critics, however, could enjoy the benefit of ignorance, their American counterparts could not. It is hardly conceivable that Preil's bilingualism was unknown to them, inasmuch as his Yiddish poems were all published in New York periodicals, as was his Yiddish book. Nevertheless, even in the close Hebrew and Yiddish literary community of New York, Preil was judged by his Hebrew verse alone. His Yiddish verse was disregarded even by the bilingual writer A. Zeitlin (1960) and was completely ignored by the staunch Hebraist Silberschlag. In 1962, the latter delivered a comprehensive address in honor of Preil, on the occasion of a literary award granted to him. Silberschlag's insightful analysis was prefaced by an elaborate biographical sketch, outlining the influential figures in Preil's life, both literary and familial. Following Preil's own verse statements, Silberschlag concluded that "it seems that Preil was never a young man. Consequently there is hardly any change from his first book of poems to the following ones" (p. 281). Along with this familiar argument, he went on to point out the poet's affinities with diverse Hebrew and American poets. His contribution to this old notion was in the convincing textual references by which he bolstered his argument. Preil's Yiddish ties, however, were nowhere mentioned. Since Silberschlag explained that he had based his address on an "autobiographical letter" which Preil had sent him, it is hard to determine whether the Yiddish factor was ignored by the speaker or by the poet himself. More instructive, however, is the way in which, just a few years later, this factor finds its way into Preil's public and private pronouncements. In his first interview with the Israeli press (Hanaami, 1965) Preil mentions his Yiddish ties only in passing, without any elaboration (in contrast to his interview of a decade later, as we will soon see). The reason for this reticence may be found in a letter, sent the following year to the Israeli poet, and for many years the secretary of the Israeli Writers Association, Avraham Broides:

> ...An important "by the way": the renowned Yiddish poet Jacob Glatstein had his 70th birthday and I haven't found anywhere even a mention of the fact! (And at the same time we keep applauding and celebrating all sorts of foreign writers who are not of the first rank.) I do not understand this attitude to

> Yiddish literature. After all, it is more intimately ours than all those *Hotentotim* and *Bashebazukim** with whom our journals and papers are preoccupied.[17]

This deep concern speaks for itself: Even the changing climate of the 1960s did not affect the attitudes toward Yiddish, as they had been established by Shlonsky and his school in the 1920s. On the whole, the Hebrew-Yiddish symbiosis, which saw its heyday in Europe at the turn of the century, ended in post-World-War-I Vienna (U.Z. Greenberg). Thus, by the 1930s, when Preil was just starting out, the ideological alliances that came to be represented by each of the languages also drew a cultural dividing line between their respective adherents (cf. Weinreich, 1953:99–104).

However, the calamity of World War II and the establishment of Hebrew as the official language of the new state of Israel naturally changed the social and demographic balance between the two camps. Even before the war was over, an attempt at a cultural rapprochement was initiated in New York. In 1943, Hebrew and Yiddish men of letters, headed by Menachem Ribalow (1895–1953) and Samuel Niger (1883–1955), collaborated in the publication of *'Achi-Sefer* (meaning "Book-Brethren" or "Brotherly Book"), which included translations into Hebrew of American Yiddish verse and fiction and general surveys of both Yiddish and Hebrew letters in America. Sincere as the endeavor may have been, it was met by the biting irony of Jacob Glatstein, the leader of Yiddish belles lettres. In a long sardonic poem, "On Reading *'Achi-Seifer*" (*Sevive* 7, New York, April-May 1944:25–29), he described the translations as the funeral of Yiddish, and mockingly suggested that they "turned him over" into Jacob Kdorleoymer:

> Gib a zets dem Glatshteyn iber
> Oyf Yakov Kdorleoymer.

This hardly translatable sarcasm is generated by Glatstein's masterful manipulation of both Hebrew and Yiddish features. Characteristically, it is a Scriptural allusion in the case of Hebrew (*Kdorleoymer* being the name of the king of Elam, in Genesis 14, who first terrorized his neighbors and then was taken over by Abraham "the Hebrew" [verses 13, 17]); yet in the case of Yiddish, it is a linguistic witticism: *iberzetsn*, one of the Yiddish words for "translate," literally means to "trans-pose" or "put in another seat" (Weinreich, 1968:32). Glatstein not only pulls apart the semantic components of this composite word; he also utilizes the polysemy of the

*A folkloristic Yiddish synonym of *Hottentots*, the figurative meaning of which is defined by the Oxford Dictionary as "person of inferior intellect or culture."

component *zetsn*. Although as a verb it means "to seat, place," as a noun it takes on the meaning of a "blow, slam, punch" (*op. cit.*:181). Thus, the literal double-entendre of the above verse would be:

> Give Glatstein a push-over/trans-position
> into Jacob Kdorleoymer.

The translation from Yiddish into Hebrew is viewed by him as a detrimental transposition, a literal pushing-over, in which Jacob Glatstein assumes the position of the alien enemy who had been vanquished by "the Hebrew."

Glatstein's sense of loss and finality[18] even in the face of the attempts at rapprochement proved prophetic. Despite the mediating activities of some bilingual writers,[19] the bilingual symbiosis was practically over. Consequently, the bilingual aspect of Preil's verse was not properly perceived, perhaps even intentionally ignored. The fact that he was the only poet to revive the practice of autotranslation and to use it as a deautomatizing device altogether eluded his Hebrew readers.

Summing up more than thirty years of criticism (from the late 1930s to the early 1970s), we can conclude that Preil's Hebrew oeuvre was considered a homogeneous body of verse and was viewed as a departure from the existing norms. The roots of this departure were believed to be in American modern verse; and his Jewish bilingualism and its possible effects on his development were completely overlooked.

3. *The Developmental Approach*

Only by the late 1970s did the consensus described above begin to be disrupted. In 1976, Preil published a slender volume entitled *Shirim mi-Shenei ha-Ketzavot* [*Poems from End to End*]. It included his then most recent poems (1971–1976) and some of his earliest ones (which had never been incorporated into his books), written mainly between 1938 and 1947. Judging from the reviews of this slim volume, the structural and thematic ranges of Preil's verse appear to have been finally understood. Perhaps the juxtaposition of the two "ends" under the same roof, so to speak, illustrated more vividly what had previously been suspected only by a few. In the new reviews the earlier assertion of homogeneity is occasionally replaced by a developmental approach, yet even now this was linked only once to Preil's Yiddish roots.[20] Shortly thereafter, however, in his second interview with the Israeli press (Stavi, 1977), Preil himself stressed this point. Asked about the effect American Hebrew poets had on him, he surprisingly said that when he first started out, he wrote only in Yiddish: "Here and there I published under the influence and with the encouragement of the renowned Yiddish poet, the late Jacob Glatstein." After humorously describing their first encounter, Preil explains that through Glatstein's group, *In Zikh*, he absorbed Anglo-American Imagism, and subsequently wrote in that style. Interestingly enough, the author's interpretation of his ties with Yiddish poets differs somewhat from the critic's view. While the former stresses Imagism as his connecting link with Yiddish, the latter emphasizes Introspectivism (Miron, 1977)—the two seemingly opposing but somehow complementary forces that indeed shaped Preil's mature poetry.

Yet, there is more to Preil's reply in this interview. The report of his Yiddish ties unexpectedly leads in another direction (Stavi, 1977):

> Later on I began to search for Hebrew poets whose writing resembled the Imagist style. Thank God, I found one in Poland—the poet Ber Pomerantz. I read his few poems and right away found the points of contact between us. I was very happy to find another poet—in Europe—who was close to me. I did not want to be an only child in Hebrew poetry. I looked for a peer, and I found one.

This confession is very instructive. It attests to the writer's self-awareness of being a *Hebrew* author. It points out a sense of belonging and obligation to the tradition and continuity of Hebrew letters. Preil's frame of reference emerges here as Hebrew literature, despite his personal and professional indebtedness to such a prominent Yiddish figure as Jacob Glatstein.

It is quite likely that a deep-seated clash of loyalties is to be found in the creative persona of Gabriel Preil. Writing in America from the 1930s through the 1960s, he could not have enjoyed the naive bilingual symbiosis of Grandpa Mendele. Though he started out bilingually, his Hebrew world did not take cognizance of this fact. Furthermore, while names of Hebrew poets crop up abundantly in his verse, neither Glatstein nor any other Yiddish poet is mentioned before the 1970s. As we have seen, a similar difference exists between his two interviews. This was no coincidence; apparently, only in the 1970s did Israeli Hebrew (language and literature) feel sufficiently secure to endure the burden of the rediscovered Jewish bilingualism of the past. In fact, it was also in the 1970s that Sadan's teaching finally resulted in intensive research in this area (see note 8 of the Introduction).

Preil's bilingualism belongs to the very near past. Actually, it borders on the present. He is probably *the last link* in a literary chain that began more than a century ago. In addition, his bilingualism is doubly significant because it involves the *modernization* of Hebrew verse.[21] However, the fact that in his youth Hebrew actually lagged behind Yiddish in America raises the question of Preil's double loyalty: Why did he choose to shift from Yiddish to Hebrew? And if he decided on Hebrew, why did he stay in America? Answers to these questions require an understanding of the special nature of Preil's Hebraism, and it is with this aspect that we begin our journey into his poetic world.

Chapter IV

A Family Romance: Preil's Exilic Hebraism

פִּרְקֵי זְמַן: שֶׁלִּי־שֶׁלּוֹ

רְאוּ אֶת סָבָא צָעִיר בַּעֲיָרָתוֹ הַלִּיטָאִית.
הוּא נָהַג לְהַשְׁכִּים בַּבֹּקֶר־בַּבֹּקֶר
וּלְאַחַר תְּפִלָּה רָשַׁם לוֹ חִדּוּשֵׁי תּוֹרָה
הֵכִין מַאֲמָר לְ״הַמֵּלִיץ״ וְגִלָּה טִיב מָן
בְּפַת חֲרֵבָה וְכוֹס מַיִם רוֹתְחִים.
הוּא הָיָה אָדָם הַמַּעֲלָה.

רְאוּ אוֹתִי צָעִיר עַל הָאֲדָמָה הָאֲמֶרִיקָנִית.
לֹא בְּדִיּוּק אֵיזֶה יְצוּר יוֹצֵא־דֹּפֶן
הַכּוֹתֵב אֶת שִׁירָיו בְּעִבְרִית. אָדָם
הַמִּתְפַּלֵּל מִתּוֹךְ אֵלֶם, שׁוֹתֶה עִם צָהֳרַיִם
סֵפֶל־בֹּקֶר פּוֹשֵׁר וּמִשְׁתַּכְנֵעַ שֶׁמָּצָא בּוֹ
אֶת טַעַם הַנָּדִיר הֶחָלוּם.

כָּל אִישׁ לְמַנּוֹ בִּזְמַנּוֹ;
זוֹ גְּלוּלָה אוֹטוֹבִּיוֹגְרָפִית
הַמֻּתֶּרֶת לִבְלִיעָה עַד הָנֵץ
הָרֶבַע הָאַחֲרוֹן לְמְאַת הָעֶשְׂרִים.
הַיָּמִים מִכָּאן וְאֵילָךְ — מוּקְיוֹנִים
מַחֲלִיקִים בְּהִסּוּס עַל קֶרַח־לֹא־קֶרַח.

קָשֶׁה לְשַׁעֵר מֶה הָיָה אוֹמֵר סָבָא עֲלֵיהֶם —
מִכָּל־מָקוֹם הָיִיתִי רוֹצֶה לִחְיוֹת אֶת זְמַנּוֹ.

Chapters of Time: His and Mine

Take a look at Grandpa, young in his Lithuanian town.
Early in the morning he would rise,
and after prayer jot down his new comments on the Law,
then prepare an essay for *Hamelitz*,
and discover qualities of manna
in stale bread and hot water.
He was a great man.

Take a look at *me*, a young man on American soil.
Not exactly an anomalous creature
writing poems in Hebrew. A man
whose prayer is mute, sipping at noon
a tepid morning-cup and convincing himself
he'd found in it a taste of something rare, dreamt.

To each man his manna in his own time.
This is an autobiographical pill
approved for consumption only until the budding [dawning]
of the last quarter of this century.
From now on—days are clowns
dubiously skating on very thin ice.

It's hard to imagine what Grandpa would have said about them—
I, however, would have liked to have lived in *his* time.

(*Poems from End to End*, p. 11)

The familial-biographical tone of this poem from the 1970s is surprising.[1] Most of Preil's poems are anchored in the concrete world of nature and avoid biographical detail. With the exception of a few early poems about his parents and his two grandfathers,[2] his biographical background is rarely used as material for his work. Even poems with such misleading titles as "*Biyografia*" [Biography] (1960:52; 1972:99), "*He'ara Biyografit*" [A Biographical Note] (1968:75; 1972:56), or "*Deyokan 'Atzmi*" [Self-Portrait] (1968:54; 1972:46) are not what the reader would expect. These personal themes are treated in an extremely metaphorical way, denying the least hint of a presumed reality behind the language. It seems that the writer preferred to hide behind his "self-portrait" rather than reveal details of his extraliterary existence.[3] However, this a-biographical tendency underwent a change in the past decade. The 1976 volume, *Shirim mi-Shenei ha-Ketzavot* [*Poems from End to End*], included several poems of reminiscence that hardly amount to a full autobiographical account, but which do conjure up family scenes that go back as far as the nineteenth century.[4]

The poem cited here, "*Pirkei Zeman: Sheli-Shelo*" [Chapters of Time: His and Mine] obviously is in keeping with this new trend. With a few strokes of the pen the poet describes the figure of a grandfather, whom he has known by hearsay only.[5] Yet, what is remarkable about "Chapters of Time" is less its biographical concreteness than its attempt to turn a family history into a literary tradition. Reaching back to the figure of his grandfather, the poet tries to establish a direct line between their respective spiritual worlds, thus justifying his eccentric Hebraism on American soil. The conspicuous dissimilarities—religion vs. secularism—are easily glossed over with the help of an age-old analogy: poetry is equivalent to (mute) prayer. The similarities, on the other hand, are stressed by a partial stanzaic parallelism (situational and in places also morpho-syntactic).[6] Both grandfather and grandson share a materially limited existence (hot water instead of tea corresponds to a tepid morning-cup at noon); yet for both of them, this existence is redeemed by spiritual idealism, their dedication to Hebrew letters in exile, whether in the form of essays or poems. This very equivalence is restated in another poem in the same collection (1976:54):

לִפְעָמִים מַאֲבִיב, פְּסוּקֵי שִׁיר
מְרַחֲפִים בָּאֲוִיר וְיָדִי
נִמְשֶׁכֶת לְתָפְסָם כְּאִלּוּ
הָיוּ נִצְנוּצֵי סוּגְיָה
בְּמֹחוֹ שֶׁל סָבָא.

Sometimes it turns spring, lines of verse
hover in the air and my hand
is drawn to catch them, as if
they were flashes of a *sugya*[7]
in Grandpa's mind.

Direct comparison replaces the parallelism of the first poem, but the effect is similar: full identification with the grandfather figure. The newness of this identification is attested by an earlier version of the same analogy, in which, however, the shift is not yet complete. In "*Sava ve-Tidhar*" [Grandpa and an Elm Tree] (1954:97), the grandfather's rabbinic knowledge and his concern for Jewish matters are contrasted (rather than paralleled) with the handsomeness of an old elm tree as it changes its colors in the fall. The grandson naively sees himself as partaking of the characteristics of both:

אָנֹכִי הַנֶּכֶד, בִּבְחִינַת תִּדְהָר וְזָקֵן הִנְנִי:
בֵּין יָפְיוֹ שֶׁל אֶחָד וְחָכְמָתוֹ שֶׁל שֵׁנִי אָתוּר שְׁבִיל.

I, the grandson, resemble both elm and elder/grandfather:
Between the one's good looks and the other's wisdom I will seek a path.

Significantly, this thematic fusion is linguistically concretized by a submerged allusion to the Rabbinic collocation *zaken ve-ragil*, which is a quasi-synonymic expression literally meaning "old and experienced." Since *zaken* stands also for "sage" *and* "grandfather," the collocation used here, *tidhar ve-zaken*, could be read as a deautomatization of the bound phrase, replacing the "experience" of the old/sage/grandfather with its antonym, the beauty of nature. However, deautomatized as it is, the synonymic Rabbinic phrase is still present between the lines, conjuring up the lost harmony of tradition, which the grandson no longer shares.

The longing for this submerged past openly erupts in the later poem, "Chapters of Time." A partial explanation for this shift is obliquely supplied by the poem itself:

רְאוּ אוֹתִי צָעִיר עַל הָאֲדָמָה הָאֲמֶרִיקָנִית.
לֹא בְּדִיּוּק אֵיזֶה יְצוּר יוֹצֵא־דֹּפֶן
הַכּוֹתֵב אֶת שִׁירָיו בְּעִבְרִית...

Take a look at me, a young man on American soil.
Not exactly an anomalous creature
writing poems in Hebrew . . .

A paradoxical exilic existence inflicts a severe sense of eccentricity and loneliness, and it is this feeling that is counteracted in the poem by the attempt to establish a continuity of a literary family line.

The motif of cultural-linguistic seclusion is not new in Preil's writing. Still, it is not found in his earliest poems; it did not make its appearance until the 1950s—precisely when Hebrew was flourishing in the new state of Israel. If we recall, in addition, that by the 1950s, the poet's older peers had already migrated to Israel,[8] we will better understand the timing of a group of poems which expressed an acute and tangible sense of "separateness," and which were published in *Mapat-'Erev* (1960).[9] Most eloquent among these is the poem "*Tzayar 'Ivri*" [A Hebrew Painter], which closes the collection (1960:111):

צַיָּר עִבְרִי

תּוֹךְ גַּעַשׁ וְרַחַשׁ צְבָעִים אֶתְעַנֶּה יְחִידִי,
צַיָּר עִבְרִי שֶׁעֲדַיִן לֹא רָאָה בְּמוֹ עֵינָיו
אֶת הַשָּׁמַיִם הָעִבְרִיִּים בָּהֶם נִכָּרִים עוֹד
עִקְּבוֹת אֵל עֶלְיוֹן דּוֹרֵךְ עַל כּוֹכָבָיו.

בֵּינְתַיִם אֲנִי יוֹשֵׁב בְּחֶבֶל הַמִּגְדָּלִים הָאֲפֹרִים
שֶׁעַל חוֹף הַנָּהָר הָאָפֹר.
יוֹשֵׁב וּמוֹצֵא אֲמַתְלוֹת אֲפֹרוֹת
עַל שְׁאֵלָה נִנְעֶצֶת כְּמַחַט אֲפֹרָה, —

עַד תָּבוֹא שָׁעָה וּבָרָק יְפַלַּח לֵב הַכְּפִיר וְהַצְּבִי:
אֶהֱפֹךְ בִּצְבָעַי תַּחַת אֵשׁ־שֶׁמֶשׁ שֶׁבִּכְנַעַן,
לְשִׁלְגֵי הַחֶרְמוֹן יַעֲלֶה פֵּרוּשׁ מִכְחוֹלִי.

אֶהְיֶה נֶאֱמָן לִשְׁעָתִי שֶׁתָּבוֹא.
וְהַצָּהֳרַיִם יַעַמְדוּ גְּבוֹהִים מְאֹד.

A Hebrew Painter

Through the rumble and rustle of paints, lonely, I agonize:
A Hebrew painter, whose own eyes have not seen
the Hebrew sky on which still linger
footsteps of a Supreme God, spanning the stars.

Meanwhile, I sit in the region of grey towers,
along the shores of the grey river.
Sit and think up grey pretexts
for a question that pierces like a grey needle,—

Until an hour comes when lightning will split the hearts of lion-cub and deer:
I'll stir my paints under a sun-fire in Canaan,
my brush producing commentaries on the snows of mount Hermon.

I will be loyal to my hour when it comes,
and noon will rise, very tall indeed.

On the surface, the two poems ("A Hebrew Painter" and "Chapters of Time") are quite different from each other. They differ in tone and texture (the latter poem is much more restrained and less metaphorically laden), as well as in their overt subject. What they have in common, however, belongs to a deeper psychological level: Both poems are motivated by the poet's sense of isolation and loneliness, expressed in one as the distance from the "Hebrew sky" and in the other as the oddity of writing Hebrew "on American soil." But the solutions offered in the poems diverge significantly. One veers towards the future, while the other harkens back to the past. The guilt that was still evident in the early poem ("think up grey pretexts") has been dissolved by nourishing high hopes for the future, when "the hour comes." However, by the 1970s, these hopes seem to have faded. The poet's first brief visit to Israel (1968) must have aggravated the pain of physical dissociation from the living milieu of his chosen poetic language, while in America his continued production in Hebrew must have deepened the alienation he felt from his immediate surroundings. The future, too, holds little promise, as implied in the poem "*Ma'gal 'Artzi*" [My Country's Orbit] (1976:14):

My Country's Orbit	מַעְגַּל אַרְצִי
My hand is writing on a desk	יָדִי כּוֹתֶבֶת עַל שֻׁלְחָן
somewhere upon this continent	בְּאֵי־מָקוֹם עַל הַיַּבֶּשֶׁת הַזֹּאת
while I am all ablaze	כְּשֶׁאֲנִי כֻּלִּי בּוֹעֵר
within my country's orbit	תּוֹךְ מַעְגַּל אַרְצִי
listening to her clocks	וּמַאֲזִין לַשְּׁעוֹנִים שֶׁלָּהּ
that speak in my room	הַמְדַבְּרִים בְּחַדְרִי
while I edit with care	כְּשֶׁאֲנִי עוֹבֵר בִּקְפִידָה
another galley, [written]	עַל עוֹד הַגָּהָה
in my tongue, in hers,	בִּלְשׁוֹנִי־לְשׁוֹנָהּ
and thinking in a flush of arrogance,	וְחוֹשֵׁב בְּמֵעֵין יָהֳרָה
of books that I am yet to plant	עַל סְפָרִים עוֹד אֶטַּע —
as if Time were not simply	כְּאִלּוּ הַזְּמַן אֵינוֹ סְתָם
a dishevelled scroll	מְגִלָּה מְדֻבְלֶלֶת
through which may pass sometime a storm,	בָּהּ עוֹבֵר פַּעַם סַעַר
like that of Gabirol,	כָּזֶה שֶׁל גַּבִּירוֹל
or a verse, starlit with serenity,	אוֹ פָּסוּק כְּכוּב שַׁלְוָה
may sing in its folds.	שָׁר בֵּין קִפּוּלֶיהָ.
I merely dare	אֲנִי רַק מֵעֵז
at times to bridge	לְגַשֵּׁר לִפְעָמִים
the gaps	אֶת הָרְוָחִים
between wisdom and innocence	שֶׁבֵּין חָכְמָה וּתְמִימוּת
in my tongue, within my country's orbit	בִּלְשׁוֹנִי, תּוֹךְ מַעְגַּל אַרְצִי
even though my hand is writing	אִם־גַּם הַיָּד כּוֹתֶבֶת
on a foreign desk.	עַל שֻׁלְחָן זָר.

The poet's existence, as depicted in this poem, is one of alienation from the immediate present (the "foreign desk," "somewhere on this continent" clearly corresponds to "an anomalous creature writing poems in Hebrew" "on American soil" in the poem "Chapters of Time"); furthermore, there is a disillusionment with the possibilities inherent in the approaching future. Indeed, the poet still nourishes thoughts of "planting books," but this is ironically undermined by the sad realization that Time is nothing but a "dishevelled scroll," prey to the storm or calm of a capricious climate, or, as in "Chapters of Time," hovering over "very thin ice."[10]

This sober assessment of present and future possibilities naturally leads to the past. In "Chapters of Time," the past selected by the poet is the one growing out of a family history, but it also represents an idealized Hebraic existence on European soil. The covert need to justify his own existence in exile and the oddity of being perhaps the last Hebrew writer in America, is clearly the "generating nucleus" of this poem.[11] The equivalence between himself and his grandfather enables the poet to relive—at least in his creative psyche—a heroic-idealistic past of Hebrew letters, of which his forefather had been an exponent. This equivalence, moreover, is finally resolved into an hierarchic order: "I, however, would have liked to have lived in *his* time." The poet's preference is rather intriguing: In grandfather's chapter of time it was possible to be loyal to Hebrew in a Lithuanian village, *without* the guilt feelings which arise in the American situation. The option for realizing one's commitment to Hebrew, made possible by the establishment of the State of Israel, may not, after all, be such a welcome reality for the persona speaking in these poems. The poet's devotion to Hebrew may therefore be viewed as a *romantic* mission, an unrequited love, which is rather enriched by its distance from the object of its yearning.

It is probably no accident that Preil's first attempt at establishing a literary lineage reaches as far back as the first half of the nineteenth century. His earliest literary model is not even a poet, but the first Hebrew novelist—Avraham Mapu (1807–1867), also a Lithuanian—who composed biblical romances. The rationale behind his "Lines to Avraham Mapu" ("*Shurot le-'Avraham Mapu*," 1954:34; 1972:149) is very much the same as in "Chapters of Time," although the poetic technique employed is less sophisticated. Here the analogy is explicitly stated rather than demonstrated imagistically:

שׁוּרוֹת לְאַבְרָהָם מַאפּוּ

אֲנִי כָּמוֹךָ יְהוּדִי לִיטָאִי,
אֲשֶׁר נִסָּה לְהוֹצִיא מֵאֲדָמָה סְתָמִית
עֵצִים פִּכְּחִים בָּהֶם מִשְׁתַּלְהֵב הַחֲלוֹם.

Lines to Avraham Mapu

I, like you, am a Lithuanian Jew
who tried to bring forth from bland soil
sober trees in which a dream is ablaze.

The yielding of realistic sobriety to dreamlike imagination is what Preil recognizes as the literary legacy bequeathed to him by his great *landsman*. Unfortunately, he himself is surrounded by a different reality, less conducive to romantic dreaming:

וַאֲנִי, אֲנִי יוֹשֵׁב בְּאֶרֶץ אַחֶרֶת מִתְחָרָה בַחֲלוֹם, מַמְצִיאָה מְצִיאוּת;
אוּלָם בֵּית־הַקָּפֶה לְעוֹלָם לֹא יְכַבֶּה תַבְעֵרוֹת הַבְּדִידוּת.

But I—I dwell within another land which vies with dreams, invents reality;
and yet the coffee-house will never quench the fires of solitude.

A place where reality "vies with dreams" and imagination "invents reality" is clearly not the suitable milieu for our poet.[12] No wonder he recoils from this existence and actually envies the ancient world of Mapu's biblical romantic materials, "peopled with shepherds and kings, abounding in palm and olive trees, singing with birds." This early preference for Mapu's idealized literary world is quite compatible with the one later granted to grandfather's idealized existential reality. The fact that the biblical past, so romantically depicted in Mapu's novels, has slowly become a reality in Israel is of no consolation to the poet, who would rather live in the nineteenth century:

אַשְׁרֶתָּ, רַבִּי אַבְרָהָם, עַל שֶׁיָּצָאתָ מַזְהִיר לִקְרַאת עָבָר
מְאֻכְלָס רוֹעֶה וָמֶלֶךְ, עוֹלֶה בְּתָמָר וּבְזַיִת, מְזַמֵּר בְּקוֹל־צִפֳּרִים:
בִּזְמַנִּי וַדַּאי נִפְלָא הֹוֶה עַמֵּנוּ מֵעָפָר הֶעֱלֵיתָ, נִשָּׂא מֵהָרִים, —
אַךְ נִמְעֶדֶת עוֹד רֶגֶל בְּעֵמֶק אָדִישׁ וְגֶשֶׁם יָגֵעַ מְתוֹפֵף.

Happy you are, Reb Abraham, for meeting with radiance a past
peopled by shepherds and kings, abounding in palm and olive trees, singing with birds;
In my time, marvelous indeed is our people's present that you conjured up from dust, loftier than mountains.
But the footstep still falters in an indifferent valley and a weary rain drums on.

One of Preil's most eloquent poems on this subject is, in fact, entitled, "The Nineteenth Century" (1954:100; 1972:203):

הַמֵּאָה הַתְּשַׁע־עֶשְׂרֵה...

הַמֵּאָה הַתְּשַׁע־עֶשְׂרֵה, שֶׁדֻּבַּר בָּהּ כֹּה הַרְבֵּה,
עַל הָאֱוִילוּת שֶׁלָּהּ וְעַל פְּשָׁעֶיהָ,
עַל זְמִירֶיהָ הַבַּיְרוֹנִים וְהַקִּיטְסִים,
הָיְתָה טוֹבָה וְרַחוּמָה כָּל כָּךְ:
הַיָּרֹק שֶׁבָּאֳפָקִים הָיָה אֵיתָן,
רַךְ הָיָה לַהַב הַשּׁוֹשָׁן
הַזּוֹרֵעַ הוֹצִיא לֶחֶם־אֲמִתּוֹ מִנִּיר,
וִיפִי מַלְכָּה וְחָכְמַת מֶלֶךְ הִזְרִיחוּ בָּעִיר.

The Nineteenth Century

The nineteenth century, so often talked about,
for its folly and sins,
for its Byronic and Keatsian nightingales,
was so kind and benign:
The green of its horizons was strong and firm,
tender was the lily's flame,
in the field farmers produced their true bread
and the city shone with queenly beauty, kingly sense.

This predilection for nineteenth-century Romanticism would later produce a peculiar blend of Hebrew and English Romantic poets: In Preil's imagination the poet Michal (Micha Joseph Lebensohn, 1828–1852) shares with Keats (1795–1821) a brief hour in which they both saw the eternity of Beauty ("*Be-Siman ha-Sha'a ha-Ketzara*" [Under the Sign of a Brief Hour], 1961:71; 1972:110), while Byron shares with Gabirol the fiery tidal-waves of their own inner torment ("*Nyu York: Be-Galgal ha-Kayitz*" [New York: In the Wheel of Summer], 1961:96; 1972:128).

The bond connecting young Preil in New York with nineteenth-century Europe in general, and with Mapu, Michal, and his grandfather in particular, is quite clear: It is a *commitment to Hebrew, conceived by the poet as a romantic ideal,* unhampered by changing realities, and perhaps even enhanced by the gaping distance between himself and the country where Hebrew has become a daily reality.[13]

This poetic lineage is not only a literary reality for the persona speaking in the poems. There is extraliterary evidence that it is also a psychological reality for the author himself. This is attested once again in Preil's interview (Stavi, 1977, see Chapter III, above). When asked if he remembered his first poem, Preil replied that he had written it when he was eight years old, and immediately volunteered the following information:

> Also, don't forget my family background. My grandfather was a Hebrew writer and a rabbi in a small town in Lithuania. He was a self-taught person and even learned Latin by himself and this over a hundred years ago. Nevertheless, he was a great rabbinical scholar, and polemicized in writing with M.L. Lilienblum concerning *Chibat Tziyon.*[14]

The importance the mature poet assigns to his familial heredity transcends strictly biographical details. In fact, he even twists them somewhat; in enumerating his grandfather's characteristics Preil actually exposes his own scale of preferences. His predecessor is portrayed as a Hebrew writer first and only secondly as a rabbi; his self-taught Latin is mentioned before his rabbinical expertise. In other words, the religious elements of his life, which have no points of contact with Preil's, are relegated to secondary status. Inadvertently thrown into relief are qualities that highlight the grandson's attitude toward his own life and vocation. From the vantage point of maturity, the poet unwittingly interprets the unfolding of his life through the image of the Lithuanian rabbi. Preil's life has been dominated by two passions, precisely the ones he attributes to his grandfather: writing in Hebrew and self-education.

Both of these passions had been implanted in Gabriel Preil from childhood. He was tutored privately in Hebrew from a young age, and soon tried his hand at verse. At the age of eight he was determined to edit and publish a Hebrew periodical, poetically entitled *Ha-Perach* [*The Flower*] (cf. Hanaami, 1965). This childhood activity was apparently greatly encouraged not only by his immediate family, but by the extended family as well. The mature poet is able to reminisce about an uncle who "rewarded" him for learning Hebrew, about aunts who applauded every "poetic" venture, and, of course, about his doting young parents, "lovers of Hebrew" both.[15] Evidently, young Preil was raised to live up to a family tradition, and accordingly soon developed a childhood aspiration to be a Hebrew writer.

All this came to an abrupt halt with his immigration to America after his father's premature death. Although the Hebrew atmosphere in his new home did not change drastically (his stepfather was a Talmudist of a Lithuanian background similar to that of the Preils[16]), his own Hebrew undoubtedly suffered from the necessity of having to compete with a new language and culture. Preil has avoided talking about these first years in America in his verse, prose, or oral pronouncements, but it is not difficult to guess the impact they had on his development. Speaking one language (Yiddish) and intent on learning and writing another (Hebrew), he was now facing the imminent need to master a third (English). This clash of interests obviously put his creative powers in temporary suspension. By his own admission (Stavi, 1977), his teens and early twenties were spent not at school, but in autodidactic activity. He read extensively, both fiction and poetry, and in English perhaps more than in Hebrew. Like the rest of American Hebrew poets, he made the acquaintance of the great tradition of English Romanticism. Yet, unlike them, his sympathies lay more with Keats and Byron than with Wordsworth or Shelley. Even then, the future Imagist clearly preferred sensuous imagery to philosophical verse.

The aspiration to become a Hebrew writer was clearly threatened by these circumstances. In a literary tradition of early beginners (most Hebrew poets of this century began writing between the ages of seventeen and twenty-one), Preil's début at the age of twenty-five would be considered a late start. This can be accounted for, however, by his linguistic circumstances. We may conjecture that Preil underwent a personal battle of languages. Hebrew must have suffered a setback while he was mastering English language and literature. Surprisingly, the battle between Hebrew and English resulted in the temporary victory of an unexpected third language—Yiddish. Preil's first poems were published in the Yiddish weekly *Nyu Yorker Vokhnblat* (Feb. 8, 1935).[17] To add confusion to surprise, these three short poems show no resemblance to any of the Hebrew poems that Preil published in the 1930s and 1940s, nor do they recall the writings of any of the poets, Hebrew or English, referred to in those poems. The Yiddish poems differ drastically from the Hebrew ones in both mode and style. They do not compare, juxtapose, or complain—actually they do not *say* anything (in the literal sense of a voice speaking). They rather paint, or draw, or imagine, i.e., conjure up images. These early attempts at verbal drawing would be best demonstrated by the poem "*Peyzazh*" [Landscape] (1966:14):

Landscape	פּייזאַזש
Sparks of calm scintillated	ס׳האָבן געמאַניעט פֿונקען פֿון רו
in cool-eyed mirrors;	אין קיל־אויגיקע שפּיגלען;
water arched in slender rings	ס׳וואַסער האָט גרין־גרויע שאָטנס
green-grey shadows;	אין רינגען דין געוועלבט;
gentle fingers spun	איידעלע פֿינגער האָבן געשפּונען
light-footed pranks;	לײַכט־פֿיסיקע שפּאַסן;
porcelain nirvana	אַ פּאָרצעלײַענע נירוואַנאַ
anchored the storm.	האָט פֿאַראַנקערט שטורעם.

Even without going into a detailed analysis, the distinctive quality of this poem is quite obvious. The voice of the poet (or of his poetic persona) is phased out; syntactic connectives and an overall thematic frame are also missing. An interpretation of the imagery is not even attempted. Instead, the poem consists of a string of four, seemingly disconnected, static pictures, so-called objective descriptions. True, the alleged objectivity is somewhat undermined by the prevalent metaphors of personification, but this is still a far cry from the subjectivity of the romantic tradition, both Hebrew and English. This style is reminiscent of some varieties of modern American verse, e.g., Ezra Pound in his early stages or "Objectivists" such as William Carlos Williams or Charles Resnikoff.[18] Even more intriguing is the fact that this style was later duplicated by other Hebrew poems of Preil that fall outside the boundaries of the present chapter.

We must conclude, then, that Preil's Hebrew romanticism was confronted by another kind of verse: Objectivism or Imagism, which he absorbed, by his admission, from American Yiddish verse. The personal style of his mature Hebrew verse seems to grow out of these two conflicting traditions. Preil's peculiar brand of restrained lyricism and imagistic romanticism could not have been attained without the interpenetration of these two forces. Because English verse embraces both, and—more importantly—because he did not use English as an active literary medium, we can determine that the seminal conflict took place within the boundaries of his own version of the Jewish polysystem, namely, between the literary traditions of Hebrew and Yiddish to which he had been exposed. This tension clearly marks the early period of Preil's verse, which is subjected to a close examination in the following chapters. But before undertaking such an examination, a brief description of the Yiddish context of his work is in order.

Chapter V

The Return of the Suppressed: Preil's Yiddish Sources (*In Zikh*)

Preil's romantic leanings are immediately signaled by an abundance of Romantic writers, both Hebrew and English, who populate his poems. By contrast the Imagist Yiddish models keep a rather low profile in his works; not one modern Yiddish writer had been mentioned throughout most of his verse, that from the 1930s to the 1970s. When this trend was finally reversed, it was the figure of Jacob Glatstein (1896–1971), the Yiddish modernist poet and one of the founders of *In Zikh*,[1] who was the first to be admitted into *Shirim mi-Shenei ha-Ketzavot* [Poems from End to End] (1976). The publication of this book concurred with Preil's interview (Stavi, 1977) in which he openly attributed his early imagistic techniques to the influence of Glatstein and his fellow-*Inzikhistn*. Nevertheless, this literary indebtedness is *not* the subject of the two poems into which Glatstein's figure was incorporated.

The first poem, "*Hartza'a*" [A Lecture] (1976:39), is a whimsical reconstruction of a lecture in which Glatstein is coupled with Mendele as the literary subject-matter that comes alive:

בָּאוּלָם מְאַבְחֵן הַמַּרְצֶה סוּגֵי סִפְרוּת
וְאֶת הַוְּרִידִים הָאַבְטוֹבִּיוֹגְרָפִיִּים
הָעוֹבְרִים בָּהֶם. מַעֲלֶה שֵׁמוֹת
מְהַבְהֲבִים בֵּין מִשְׁפָּט לְמִשְׁפָּט
כְּצִלּוּמֵי־פֶּתַע, כִּצְלִילֵי זִכָּרוֹן.
כָּךְ, לְמָשָׁל, בְּדֶרֶךְ־טִיּוּלוֹ סָר כָּאן
מֶנְדֶלִי־מוֹכֵר־סְפָרִים וּמֵעֵין בָּרָק
שֶׁל פְּלִיאָה נִתָּז מִמִּשְׁקָפָיו, אוֹ
גְלַטְשְׁטֵיין נִכְנָס כִּבְתוֹךְ שֶׁלּוֹ
וְחַכִּים כָּאוֹר מְחַיֵּךְ בְּעֵינָיו.

In the auditorium the speaker diagnoses literary genres
and the autobiographic veins
traversing them. He conjures up names
flickering between sentences
as instant photos, as echoes of memory.
Thus, for instance, Mendele Mokher Seforim
stops by while taking a walk and
something puzzling flashes off his spectacles, or
Glatstein enters as if into his own
and, wise like light, his eyes smile.

A more serious attempt is made in "*'Elul: Nisayon Avtobiyografi*" [Elul: An Autobiographical Experiment] (1976:40), which is dedicated to Glatstein. Here, Preil tried to span the distance of nearly forty years by recalling a meeting that had probably taken place some time in the 1930s. The concrete model for this poetic reconstruction may have been his "fateful" first encounter with Glatstein, which he humorously described in his interview (Stavi, 1977):

> I remember giving a few poems to Glatstein and asking for his critical opinion. He told me to come back a week later. I returned and since then I have been a miserable man, because he said I had talent and that I must continue.

Continuation is also the central thrust of our poem. As in the case of "Chapters of Time" (see above, p. 43), mimetic biography is used only as a springboard for establishing a literary continuity. The generic expectations aroused by the title ("Autobiography") are only partially fulfilled.[2] Of the meeting in that remote *'Elul* (the last month of the Jewish year and hence a month of soul searching preceding the New Year and the Days of Awe), just a few impressions have survived. The portrait of the sympathetic authority is broken down into disconnected parts (the head, hair, and eyes serving as synecdoches for the whole personality); whereas the gnawing doubts of the young, hopeful poet are metonymically transferred to a nearby witness—his cup of coffee:

Elul: An Autobiographical Experiment

For Jacob Glatstein

Since that day in Elul
more years have passed
than can be imagined.
His head, as if engraved,
shimmered with blond lights,
a kind of smiling blue seriousness
spoke in his eyes
as if to touch the leaves of my youth
scattered about a cup of coffee,
a kind of a cool, skeptic witness—

אֱלוּל: נִסָּיוֹן אַבְטוֹבִּיוֹגְרָפִי

ליעקב גלטשטיין

מֵאוֹתוֹ יוֹם שֶׁבֶּאֱלוּל
נָקְפוּ יוֹתֵר שָׁנִים
מִשֶּׁנִּתָּן לְשַׁעֵר.
רֹאשׁוֹ הָיָה אָז כִּמְגֻלָּף
נִצְנֵץ בְּאוֹרוֹת בְּלוֹנְדִינִיִּים
אֵיזוֹ רְצִינוּת חַיְּכָנִית
הִכְחִילָה, דִּבְּרָה בְּעֵינָיו
וּכְמוֹ נָגְעָה בַּעֲלֵי צְעִירוּתִי
שֶׁפֻּזְּרוּ עַל־יַד סֵפֶל קָפֶה
מֵעֵין עֵד צוֹנֵן וּמְסַפֵּק —

This description triggers the writer's attempt to evaluate his own artistic career as it has developed since that day in Elul. The former opposition between the young beginner and the seasoned authority is now resolved into an equality of artistic responsibility and a shared literary burden:

עַד שֶׁמִּמֶּרְחָק אוֹתוֹ יוֹם שֶׁבֶּאֱלוּל
נַעֲשֵׂיתִי אַחֲרַאי לְגַלִּים מְאֻחָרִים
שֶׁפּוֹעֲמִים בְּסֵפֶר מְגַלֶּה וּמְוַדֵּא
חֻלְשׁוֹת גְּדוֹלוֹת וּגְבוּרוֹת קְטַנּוֹת:
מִדִּמּוּיֵי זְמַן אוֹ נוֹף הֵן עוֹלוֹת, כְּשֶׁכּוֹתְבָן
מַחֲוִיר כְּיָרֵחַ בְּטֶרֶם נִפְגָּם.

Now, far removed from that Elul day
I've been put in charge of late waves
throbbing in a book, revealing and reaffirming
great weaknesses and small strengths:
From images of time or place[3] they rise, while their author grows
pale as the moon before waning.

Yet, as the poem unfolds, mimetic representation is gradually reduced. We will search in vain here for any clues to the Imagist bond between the two poets. "A sharp divergence" is mentioned but is never spelled out, whereas the listed similarities are of very limited referential value:

בֶּאֱלוּל מְסַכֵּם־פְּרָקִים זֶה
כָּרָגִיל מִתְעַנְּפִים בָּנוּ —
שְׁנִי חַד בְּמִקְצָת, קִרְבָה רַבַּת הֶקֵּפִים.
וּמִשּׁוּם־מָה צְמוּדִים אָנוּ
לָעִיר הַטְּרוּפָה וְקוֹדַחַת
שֶׁפִּזְּרָה לְכָל רוּחַ
אֶת עֲלֵי צְעִירוּתֵנוּ.
אֶלָּא שֶׁהוּא בִּסְפָרָיו, אֲנִי בִּסְפָרַי
הוּא בַּעֲיֵפוּתוֹ, אֲנִי בַּעֲיֵפוּתִי
כְּמוֹ אוֹמְרִים לְקַצֵּץ
בְּיַעֲרוֹת קוֹצִים וּתְלִיּוֹת,
לָטוּס כְּנִשְׁרֵי הַמְּלִיצָה
לָאָרֶץ אֵין שְׁנִיָּה לָהּ
וּכְמִתּוֹךְ כַּוָּנָה צְדָדִית
נִתְפַּלֵּל לְפַת־חָכְמָה
שֶׁלֹּא תִּשָּׁמֵט מִסַּלֵּנוּ —

עַד שֶׁיִּשָּׁמֵט מִמְּקוֹמוֹ הַיָּרֵחַ.

In this summing-up chapter of Elul
as usual there branch out within us—
a somewhat sharp divergence, a wide-ranging closeness.
Somehow, we are both attached
to this insane, feverish city,
that has scattered to the winds
the leaves of our youth.
Yet, he in his books, I in mine,
he in his weariness, I in mine,
somehow we mean to cut down
forests of thorns and gallows,
and take off like the eagles of rhetoric
to a land unlike any other
and, as if incidentally,
we pray that a loaf of wisdom
may not drop out of our basket—

until the moon itself drops down.

Unlike the correspondence with Grandfather's chapter of time, which permitted a clear encoding of its Hebraic roots (openly marked by *Ha-Melitz*), the analogy here either draws upon common general terms (city, books, fatigue), or is couched in figurative language. A close scrutiny nevertheless reveals that the figurative language represents a set of oppositions[4] that derive from a Romantic code—the city (negatively marked as insane) vs. the one and only promised land (aspired to, but never reached); the leaves of youth vs. the thorns and gallows of old age; the flight of rhetoric vs. the bread of wisdom. Indeed, nothing in the content of this poem addresses itself to the specific Imagism Preil supposedly learned from Glatstein. We might even doubt whether this set of values is as appropriate for Glatstein's poetry as it is for Preil's. In fact, the poet may have again grafted his own romantic code onto a poem describing the alleged source of his imagistic drive.

A similar, though less obvious, process of poetic "misrepresentation"[5] had taken place in Preil's Hebrew essay "On Jacob Glatstein," written for the latter's sixtieth birthday (1957). In this short article, Preil delineated the central role that Glatstein's poetry had played in the modernization of Yiddish verse. Characteristically his review is centered around Glatstein's daring beginnings in the 1920s and 1930s rather than around his later works as the spokesman of Jewish consciousness and of European Jewry after the Holocaust.[6] Preil describes the periodical *In Zikh* as "proving to the distrustful" that "Yiddish was also touched by the wings of Time"; namely, *In Zikh* put Yiddish on the contemporary literary map and Yiddish writers proved themselves to be on a par with their Anglo-American counterparts. Invoking the name of Ezra Pound, Preil placed Glatstein's verse in the perspective of post-World-War-I literature:

> Ezra Pound was then at the height of his power and influence. Poets in England and the U.S.A. followed in his footsteps. The Yiddish poet [J. Glatstein] did not follow the extremes of Pound's poetry, but he was familiar with its secrets and did not refrain from employing them. Directly and indirectly he [Glatstein] also tackled the Imagism perpetuated by John Gould Fletcher and Amy Lowell. Yiddish writers endeavored to adopt the immediate approach with all its blessings—the non-conventional image and free verse. Glatstein, I believe, would not have been able to reach his own colorful expression without this formula [*nusach*], the fruits of his era; he was one of the foremost creators of this style in Yiddish (Preil, 1957).

This evaluation is, no doubt, faithful to the historical facts of the inception of the *In Zikh* group and to the essence of their artistic credo, as it was formulated in the group's manifesto, "*Introspectivism*" (*In Zikh*, 1920:5–27, signed by J. Glatstein, A. Leyeles, and N.B. Minkoff). Despite the denial of Leyeles (1925), there was clearly a resemblance between the *Inzikhistn*'s poetic principles and the Imagist/Vorticist tenets of Flint (1913) and Pound (1913, 1914, 1915). The American Imagists were mentioned in the manifesto only in passing as "the most modernist school," but many years later Glatstein himself was to admit the effect those "American rhythms" had had on his poetics (1971).[7] However, what is missing in Preil's description is the emphasis on introspectivism (hence the name *In Zikh* [inward, into oneself]), which was the *Inzikhistn*'s rationale for their new poetic style:

> "*Introspectively*" means that the poet has to sincerely listen to his internal voice, has to observe his internal panorama—kaleidoscopic, contradictory, blurred or confused as it may be; out of this should be created the expression of the total union between the poet's soul and the phenomenon about which he writes [sings], simultaneously with the [specific] image or images which he sees *within himself* while so doing (*op. cit.*, p. 6).

Thus, *introspectivism* and *individualism* were the focal issue; all the rest—the unlimited, even "unpoetic," subject matter and language, the immediate imagery, and the rejection of formalistic constraints (the embracing of free verse)—were concomitant devices. Jewishness, on the other hand, was not considered an issue, nor a theme justified for its own sake (*op. cit.*, pp. 19–22). The mere fact of writing in Yiddish met this demand. Interest shifted from socio-cultural concerns to the ego of the individual. This entailed a close look at the poet's creative process, namely the mechanism of memory and association.[8] In practice, this resulted not only in linguistic experiments, but also in the unrestrained expression of an innermost, morbid disillusionment with a hostile, menacing world. Consequently, many of these introspective poems are marked by bitterness and mockery. Glatstein contributed his full share to this trend.[9] Nevertheless, this part of his poetry receives only a brief mention in Preil's review: "Glatstein reacted to this in a few interesting poems." The reviewer then hurries on to point out the *other* Glatstein, not the one anchored in his environment, but the one "escaping—like poets in all times—to his private realms—singing his own atemporal song." Evidently, this is where Preil identifies with Glatstein. After demonstrating his claim, he sums up:

> Here, too, the scheming external reality is felt, but is accompanied by a forgiving, *romantic* sadness [*tuga*]. It is as if the feeling of loss is compensated for by crystallized and premeditated imagery. Man is always in the center of a circle, from which he cannot get out unless he discovers *within himself* an opening into a *brighter world.* (Emphasis added.)

This formulation speaks for itself: Preil actually turned the introspective method topsy-turvy. The *Inzikhistn* followed Freud in their search for psychological truth and therefore braced themselves for the possibility of coming up with a morbid internal reality (*In Zikh*, 1920:10), while Preil romantically saw the self as a door to a brighter world. As for Glatstein's harsh and bitter poems, the writer evaluated them as "lip service paid by the poet to his times."

We can clearly see now that some aspects, at least, of Yiddish Modernism did not suit Preil's fundamental attitudes and leanings. Perhaps it is no accident that, in tracing his roots to Yiddish poetry (in his interview, discussed above, p. 41), he ignored its overall introspectivism and emphasized its imagistic technique. The fact is, however, that Glatstein's poetry does not abound in nature descriptions nor in purely imagistic poems of the kind with which Preil made his debut in Yiddish. Nor was Preil's poetry, in its early stages, conspicuously introspective. Most often his poems attempt to capture external realities by a series of concise photographic images; in others, he *reflects* about man in general rather than introspectively delving into his own mental processes.

So perhaps Preil was telling us more of the truth in his poetic indirection (see above, "Elul," pp. 57–58) than in his direct statement in the interview. Glatstein may have encouraged and inspired him, but apparently he was not Preil's immediate model.[10]

Our search must continue, then. In 1977, shortly after his visit to Israel, Preil published, in New York and in Israel simultaneously, an unusually long poem entitled "*Yehuda Leib Teller.*" In Israel the poem created quite a stir—the name was utterly unfamiliar. Anticipating this, a footnote was added: "Y.L. Teller (1912–1972) was one of the first Yiddish modernists, one of the outstanding younger poets of the Glatstein generation. He was a friend of the writer of this poem since youth." Admittedly, the footnote was not much help; apparently, Teller did not win the literary acknowledgment he deserved. In New York "Judd" Teller may have been better known as a journalist-publicist in his position as chief editor of the Independent Jewish Press Service. He was also the author of a handful of English books on Jewish socio-political subjects. His career as a poet, on the other hand, did not draw much attention. After publishing three slender books of verse (*Simboln*, 1930; *Miniaturn*, 1934; *Lider Fun der Tsayt* [*Poems of the Time*], 1940), he stopped publishing poetry altogether and did not resume until 1959 (in the periodicals *Di Tsukunft* and *Di Goldene Keyt*). A collection of his poems, entitled *Durkh Yidishn Gemit* [*In the Spirit of Yiddish*], was published posthumously in 1975.[11]

If interest in Teller's poetry was all but nonexistent, Preil's poem definitely helped change this state of affairs. Unexpectedly, Preil in this poem adopted a quasi-narrative style.[12] This enabled him to be more generous with the referential details of his story (1980:18):

יְהוּדָה לֵיב טֶלֶר

לדן מירון

א

יְהוּדָה־לֵיבּ גָּר בָּרְחוֹב הַשְּׁמִינִי מִזְרָחָה
בֵּיתוֹ הָרִאשׁוֹן אַחַר גַּלִיצְיָה, נִדְמֶה לִי.
אֲנִי הָיִיתִי הַנַּעַר הַלִּיטָאִי הָרִאשׁוֹן
שֶׁאָמַר לוֹ שָׁלוֹם כְּלָל־יְהוּדִי
(אֲשֶׁר לָאֲמֶרִיקָנִיּוּת — זוֹ הָיְתָה מוּבֶנֶת מֵאֵלֶיהָ).
כִּבְמִקְרֶה נִתְקַלְתִּי בּוֹ וְלָרִאשׁוֹנָה פָּגַשְׁתִּי
שִׁיר יוֹצֵא מִפִּי מְדַבְּרוֹ חַם וְקוֹדֵחַ —
עַד אָז הָיוּ אֲפִלּוּ חַיִּים־נַחְמָן וְהָאִישׁ שָׁאוּל
צוֹלְלִים תּוֹךְ עַרְפִלִּים בְּעָרֵי נָמֵל סוֹדִיּוֹת.
אֲנִי הָיִיתִי הַקּוֹרֵא הַתָּמִים, חוֹקֵר קְסָמִים
שֶׁלֹּא לִי נוֹעֲדוּ. אֲשֶׁר לִיהוּדָה־לֵיבּ —
מַחְבֶּרֶת הַשִּׁירִים שֶׁבְּיָדוֹ נֶפְנְפָה
בְּמֵעֵין אִירוֹנְיָה וּבִטְחָה־עַצְמִית וְלֹא בִּכְדִי.

"יֵשׁ מְשׁוֹרֵר אַנְגְּלִי־אֲמֶרִיקָנִי שֶׁשְּׁמוֹ אֶלְיוֹט
וְהוּא שׁוֹנֶה לְאֵין־שִׁעוּר מִמְּשׁוֹרֵר שֶׁשְּׁמוֹ סַנְדְבּוּרְג".
יְהוּדָה־לֵיבּ יָדַע אָז דְּבָרִים שֶׁאֲנִי לֹא שִׁעַרְתִּים.
פְּתִיחוּת הִבְהֲבָה בֵּין בַּיִת לְבַיִת
שֶׁל חֲרוּזָיו הַמְסֻגָּרִים וְחֹם וּפִקְחוּת מְעֻנֶּנֶת קְצָת.

פַּעַם כְּשֶׁמִּקְטַרְתּוֹ הָרַאַוְתָנִית מִתְנוֹדֶדֶת
בֵּין שְׁתֵּי שִׁנַּיִם מְחַיְּכוֹת, פָּלַט:
"גַּבִּי, אֲנִי חוֹשֵׁד בְּךָ, אוּלַי תְּנַסֶּה גַּם אַתָּה?"

ב

מִשְׁתָּעֲרִים
מִילִין־מִילִין שֶׁל זְמַן
וְאַתָּה מְנַסֶּה לַעֲצֹר בּוֹ יוֹם אֶחָד
עִם חָבֵר לְיַד סֵפֶל קָפֶה,
נִסָּיוֹן שֶׁחָזַרְתָּ עָלָיו אַלְפֵי פְּעָמִים, כַּמּוּבָן.

פַּעַם בִּשְׁעַת כְּתִיבָה רְחוֹקָה בְּאֵיזֶה בֵּית־קָפֶה אוּלַי
מָצָא לוֹ יְהוּדָה־לֵיבּ סִפּוּק בְּשִׁיר זֶה אוֹ אַחֵר
אַךְ כְּבָר חָמֵשׁ שָׁנִים הוּא לְיַד גְּלַטְשְׁטֵיין מוֹרוֹ
בְּבֵית־הָעָלְמִין בִּנְיוּ־גֶ׳רְזִי.
הָיִיתִי חוֹסֵךְ עֲבוּרוֹ כָּל מִיל מִן הַמִּילִין שֶׁלִּי,
מְוַתֵּר עַל מַה שֶּׁלֹּא נִתַּן לְוִתּוּר.
עַכְשָׁו סֵפֶר שִׁירָיו הַמְיֻתָּם בִּידֵי חָבֵר אַחֵר
וַאֲנִי מַתְחִיל לָחוּשׁ בְּקִיּוּמָהּ שֶׁל
אֵיזוֹ הַמְשֵׁכִיּוּת שֶׁעוֹבֶרֶת בֵּין זֶה לָזֶה.
הִיא הוֹפֶכֶת כִּמְעַט־לְוַדָּאוּת בִּרְאוֹתִי
אֶת עֵינֵי חֲבֵרִי מְטַיְּלוֹת עַל פְּנֵי־מִלִּים
בַּשּׁוּרוֹת הַצְּפוּפוֹת, עוֹצְרוֹת
וְאוֹמְרוֹת ״כִּי־טוֹב״.

וּכְשֶׁהֵחֵל עִטּוֹ לַחֲרֹשׁ וּלְפַעְנֵחַ פָּסוּק אַחַר פָּסוּק
לְתַרְגְּמוֹ לְלָשׁוֹן שֶׁנֶּעֶנְתָה כְּמִתּוֹךְ צִפִּיָּה אֲרֻכָּה
וְאַחַר הִתְפָּרְקוּת רִאשׁוֹנָה הִתְמַתְּנָה כָּאַיָּלָה
הָיְתָה פְּרִיחָה יְתֵרָה
וְהַזְּמַן נִחֵשׁ מְנוּחוֹת בְּסֵפֶל הַקָּפֶה.

ג
לְאַחַר שֶׁהוּת־מָה שֶׁשָּׁמַעְתִּי בְּקוֹלוֹ שֶׁל יְהוּדָה־לֵיבּ. חָדַלְתִּי
לְפַקֵּחַ עַל הַטִּירוֹת הַקְּטַנּוֹת שֶׁלִּי בַּמִּזְרָח הָאֶלֶגַנְטִי שֶׁבָּעִיר.
בַּיָּשָׁן יוֹתֵר מְנוּעָז, נוֹאָשׁ יוֹתֵר מְשַׂמֵּחַ
הִתְחַלְתִּי לְשַׂרְטֵט מִבְנִים בְּשׁוּלֵי הַשָּׁנִים
עַכְשָׁו הַשָּׁנִים בִּלְעָדָיו.
נִשְׁאַר הַיּוֹם הָאֶחָד שֶׁבּוֹ אַתָּה יוֹשֵׁב
לְיַד שֻׁלְחָן עִם יָדִיד,
עֵינָיו מְטַיְּלוֹת בַּסֵּפֶר הַמְיֻתָּם.

פַּעַם בִּשְׁנַת כְּתִיבָה רְחוֹקָה אָמַר יְהוּדָה־לֵיבּ אוּלַי
״כִּי־טוֹב״ לְשִׁיר זֶה אוֹ אַחֵר
אַךְ בְּוַדַּאי לֹא חָשַׁב שֶׁחָבֵר אַחֵר שֶׁל גַּבְרִיאֵל
יִפְתַּח רְחוֹב עִבְרִי צָעִיר לְדִמּוּיָיו הָעוֹמְדִים
מְחֻדָּדִים בְּטוּרִים חָפְשִׁיִּים כְּשֶׁאֵיזֶה פָּאתוֹס
מְכַרְסֵם דָּבֵק בָּהֶם.

Yehuda Leib Teller*

For Dan Miron

I.
Yehuda Leib lived on East 8th Street,
his first home after Galicia, I believe.
I was the first Lithuanian boy
to welcome him with a universally Jewish Sholem Aleikhem
(as for Americanism—this was taken for granted).
I ran into him as if by chance, and for the first time encountered
poetry feverishly coming out of its speaker's mouth—
Until then even Hayim Nahman and the man Shaul**
were sunk in mists of esoteric seaports.
I was the naive reader, investigating magic
not intended for me. As for Yehuda Leib—
The notebook of poems waved in his hand
in a kind of irony and self-confidence, and not for nothing...

"There is an Anglo-American poet named Eliot
and he is immeasurably different from a poet named Sandburg."
Yehuda Leib then had knowledge which I had not even imagined.
Openness and warmth and a somewhat melancholy cleverness
flickered between the stanzas of his enclosed verses.

Once, his pipe dangling for effect
between two smiling teeth, he spouted:
"Gabi, I suspect you. Perhaps you should try too?"

* Y.L. Teller (1912–1972) was one of the younger Yiddish modernists, an outstanding poet of the Glatstein generation. He was a friend of the writer of this poem since youth. [G.P.]

**H.N. Bialik and S. Tchernichowsky, the acclaimed Russian-born Hebrew poets.

II.
Miles upon miles of time
assail you;
with a friend over a cup of coffee,
you try one day to hold them back,
an experiment probably repeated time and time again.

Once, writing in a long-gone coffee shop,
Yehuda Leib had been pleased, perhaps, with this or that poem,
but five years have passed since he lies close to his mentor, Glatstein,
in a New Jersey cemetery.
I would have saved each of my own miles for him,
giving up the ungiveable.
Now his orphaned book of verse is in the hands of another friend
and I begin to sense the presence
of some continuity passing from one to the other.
It almost turns into a certainty when I notice
my friend's eyes travelling over words
in crowded lines, then stopping
to say: "It is good."

When his pen started to plow and decode phrase after phrase
translating into a language that responded as if after long anticipation
and, almost doe-like, slowed down after its initial release,
there was an abundance of flowering
and in a cup of coffee Time foretold a becalmed future.

III.
After a while, I followed Yehuda Leib's advice and no longer
supervised my little mansions on the elegant East Side.
More shy than daring, more despairing than content,
I began to draw structures on the margins of the years,
now years without him.
This day alone remains, when you sit
at a table with a friend,
his eyes traveling through the orphaned book.

Once, writing in a long gone year, Yehuda Leib may
have said, "It is good" about this or that poem,
but he most likely didn't foresee that another friend of Gabriel's
would open a youthful Hebrew street to his
sharp images set in free lines while some
gnawing pathos clings to them.

The conversational charm of this narrative poem should not mislead us. The biographical information offered in Part I is reworked in the following Parts II and III and leads, once more, to the central theme of literary continuity. It is the first time, however, that this very word surfaces in the lexicon of the poem:

עַכְשָׁו סֵפֶר שִׁירָיו הַמְיֻתָּם בִּידֵי חָבֵר אַחֵר
וַאֲנִי מַתְחִיל לָחוּשׁ בְּקִיּוּמָהּ שֶׁל
אֵיזוֹ הֶמְשֵׁכִיּוּת שֶׁעוֹבֶרֶת בֵּין זֶה לָזֶה.

Now his orphaned book of verse is in the hands of another friend
and I begin to sense the presence
of some continuity passing from one to the other.

Furthermore, this continuity is covertly expressed, as never before, in terms of a *bilingual* tradition. Teller's Yiddishism is not stated, except obliquely, via his better-known master ("but five years have passed since he lies close to his mentor, Glatstein, / in a New Jersey cemetery"). The poem concludes, however, with the explicit mention of Hebrew:

אַךְ בְּוַדַּאי לֹא חָשַׁב שֶׁחָבֵר אַחֵר שֶׁל גַּבְרִיאֵל
יִפְתַּח רְחוֹב עִבְרִי צָעִיר לְדִמּוּיָיו הָעוֹמְדִים
מְחֻדָּדִים בְּטוּרִים חָפְשִׁיִּים כְּשֶׁאֵיזֶה פָּאתוֹס
מְכַרְסֵם דָּבֵק בָּהֶם.

but he most likely did not foresee that another friend of Gabriel's
would open a youthful Hebrew street to his
sharp images set in free lines while some
gnawing pathos clings to them.

We are finally back to sharp images and free verse. At the same time, it is clear that this poem in particular is bathed in the most cherished memories of early youth and of the very first contact with both the practice and the knowledge of modern poetry. No wonder the earlier concepts that young Preil had of classical Hebrew poetry seemed dim, as if shrouded in a mist, when they were compared with the lively poetic know-how exhibited by his friend. It is not surprising, then, that Teller's Yiddish poems offer the best clue to Preil's imagism. This is particularly true for Teller's second book, *Miniaturn* (1934). Skimming through these miniature poems (a sample of which is given in Appendix 2), we are immediately struck by the features they share with Preil's early poems—their small format, some of their titles, and their purely imagistic technique.

Though the stark imagery of these short, lucid poems clearly followed the instruction of the *In Zikh* manifesto, they also betrayed a familiarity with the tenets of American Imagism.[13] Their brevity derived, in part at least, from the reaction against the verbiage of the long Romantic poem.[14] The Romantic poet's voice, commenting and interpreting nature, himself, and the relationship between them is superseded by a series of verbal paintings.[15] The organizing principle of these poems is the image itself; all other formal properties are subordinate to the image, and common speech and conversational syntax gain priority over poetic diction and measured line and stanza. The word *image*, however, does not imply visual dimensions alone; indeed, Teller's images are sensuous (and sensual), relying heavily on synesthesis. His use of auditory senses particularly affects his diction, inasmuch as he draws freely upon the rich welter of Yiddish onomatopoeic expressions (*krakhn, tseroyshte, rashike*).

The extent of the divergence between this anti-Romantic new genre, deriving from both English and Yiddish sources, and the initial romantic predilection of Preil's Hebrew roots cannot be overestimated. As we shall presently see, he began by proceeding simultaneously on two poetic fronts and in two poetic modes, writing pure imagistic poems in Yiddish and romantic free verse in Hebrew. Even more intriguing is the fact that in both cases he did not follow the leading literary figures. Just as his Yiddish model was Teller's imagistic miniature rather than Glatstein's introspectivist poem, he preferred Z. Shne'ur's "decadent" rhetoric to the "classic" romanticism of Hebrew poet laureate H.N. Bialik. Nothing could be more diametrically opposed than these two models: Teller's Yiddish understated miniature, in which the lyrical voice is hardly audible, over and against Shne'ur's highly rhetorical Hebrew verse, with its exhibitionist, self-dramatized "I".[16] Predictably, this is the very dichotomy that underlies Preil's own creativity in his early period. However, it is precisely out of the clash between these two modes (or norms) that Preil's Hebrew innovations were to be fashioned. Naturally, the struggle between these two forces as well as their interpenetration are nowhere as strongly felt as in his early bilingual experiments. Just like Mendele half a century before him, Preil used Yiddish as a workshop in which he practiced the demands of a new genre; and despite the obvious differences—fiction vs. poetry—a basic similarity does surface: The transition from the high-mimetic novel (or the romance) to the low mimetic novel (or the social satire) in the case of the prose writer; the transition from highly rhetorical romantic verse to "lower" (imagist) diction, syntax, and thematics, in the case of the poet.

The transfer of this new genre to Hebrew was not, however, immediately and directly accomplished. As has been recently claimed by translation theorists, it is often the norm of the target culture that determines the nature and direction of translational strategies.[17] In our case, this direction was already anticipated in the *intra*-literary transfer between Teller and Preil. Looking now at their representative poems, we can see the ways in which they are similar and, more importantly, how they differ.

Y.L. TELLER (1934)

ווינט

די האָר בלאָזן אין פּנים —
ווי האָגל, ווי רויך און
ווי רעגן.

זון בלאַנקט
מיט נאָענטע מעסערס פֿאַר די אויגן;
טײַכלעך גלוסטן דײַנע פֿיס.

ביסט יונג. שפּיגלען נעמען דיך
ווי אַ פֿרוי,
און הייסע זאַמדן לאָקערן
אַרום דײַן שאָטן.

G. PREIL (1935)

וווּנדער־שפּיגל

מיידל־גאַנג אין לבֿנה
מורמלט העלע רייד
אין טונקעלן סאַמעט.

זי בליצט אויף שפּיגלען,
שנײַדט סילועטן
אין פֿאַראַנקערטע אויגן.

זי טראָגט הייסן ווינט
איבער קילע שטערן,
אײַזיקן אָטעם
און זון.

Wind

Hair blows in face—
like hail, like smoke and
like rain.

Sun glitters
with knives close to eyes,
brooks desire your feet.

You are young. Mirrors take you
as a woman,
and warm sands lurk
around your shadow.

Wonder-Mirror

Girl's walk in moon light
murmurs bright words
in dark velvet.

She flashes off mirrors
cutting silhouettes
in anchored eyes.

She carries hot winds
over cool stars,
a breath of ice
and sun.

At first blush, the two poems share the miniature strophic format and fundamental imagistic techniques. In both of them the romantic poet's voice, commenting upon and interpreting his subject matter, is almost superseded by a series of verbal representations of a "slice" or a "moment" of reality. More specifically, "*Vint*" and "*Vunder Shpigl*" share a similar lexical/semantic range, the same "poetic world," in Lotman's terminology (1976). The lexemes *vint, shpigl, oygn, zun, heys* (wind, mirror, eyes, sun, and hot, respectively) are repeated verbatim. Other semantic fields have a different, sometimes antonymic textual actualization in each poem: sun or moon and stars; knives and cutting; glitter and flashes; young and girl; and finally warm vs. cool and ice. These similarities notwithstanding, the poems differ on two counts. Teller's is, and this may sound paradoxical, a *nominal* world of *action*. His nouns are mostly devoid of overt attributes. They act, they are not sensed. Sensory impressions are rendered indirectly, via objects whose characteristics may be inferred but are not explicitly stated. Conversely, Preil's extensive use of adjectives and colors shifts the emphasis from the objective reconstruction of reality to a grid of relations imposed on it. This is done by the oppositional organization of each stanza (bright vs. dark, mirrors vs. silhouettes, hot vs. cool, ice vs. sun). This organization controls the thematic encoding of the presentation, thus undermining its ostensible objectivity.

Evidently, our two poets demonstrate the power of the idiolect to fashion individual poetic pronouncements even when using common basic lexicons, styles, and generic modes. As George Steiner has asserted, "No two localities use words and syntax to signify exactly the same things, to send identical signals of valuation and inference. Neither do two human beings" (1975:45). This is all well and good as long as we accept the mystique of subjective idiosyncracy as the ultimate explanation. If we venture one step further, however, there is room to argue that, unlike his close friend Teller, Preil could not adopt fully the "poetics of hardness," which the *Inzikhistn* inherited from the Imagists, because of his *double literary loyalty*. The "softer" treatment of his materials, his surrender to the so-called "additional" words, may be viewed as an interference of his Hebraic, Shne'urian romantic rhetoric.[18]

It is precisely this rhetoric that later became the target of Teller's severe criticism. In 1945, while reviewing Preil's first Hebrew book, Teller offered this penetrating insight into the historical poetics of Hebrew verse:

> Because the greatest Hebrew writer of recent times, H.N. Bialik, was a great declamatory poet (*plakat-poet*), an exalted folk-preacher (*folk prediker*), who utilized the rhetorical image which cannot be seen but affects you by the power of speech alone—this very device has become the classical model in

> modern Hebrew verse. With Shne'ur, for example, the rhetorical image is used to convey erotic and other purely introspective experiences—an unbearable practice for sensitive poetry lovers. Whatever was a natural instrument for Bialik's themes is just as unnatural when used for introspective ones. In erotic poetry, declamation and rhetoric are unaesthetic, and [they] too strongly recall the operatic mis-en-scène (not its music!) (Teller, 1945:135–136).

Inasmuch as this was written in 1945, Teller's literary-historical insight is indeed fascinating. He was the only critic who, while writing in *Yiddish*, evaluated Preil's *Hebrew* innovations from the perspective of the internal stylistic evolution of Hebrew literature itself.[19] He immediately sensed the conflict between Preil's way of writing and the governing norms of classical Hebrew poetry, as it was then represented by Zalman Shne'ur. By poignantly defining the drawbacks of Shne'ur as Bialik's heir, he correctly interpreted the difficulties of Hebrew poetry when confronted with the demands of Modernism.

As for Preil's poetics, Teller saw as his greatest contribution the introduction of the "mood image," which is "a very delicate instrument, bridging between the poetic word and the *melitse* ('embellished diction' or 'trope'), and by which one can immediately recognize the difference between a real poet and a rhymster." After describing the organic cohesiveness effected by the use of the visual image, he concludes that

> this alone is a contribution to Hebrew verse, which for the last twenty years has been involved in a struggle (in its homeland as well) to free itself from the rhetorical vulgarity which debased Bialik's wonderful rhetoric, just as Freud has been vulgarized and misinterpreted by his popularizers (*op. cit.*, p. 136).

A long struggle indeed. Teller may have witnessed the result of this battle in Preil's bilingual venture. However, although he hints at his close relationship with Preil ("I have known Preil since his first poem, and even since the eve of his verse-writing"), the latter's bilingualism is mentioned only in the title. In the review itself, Teller merely argues that "In his first book he [Preil] has not yet revealed his whole poetic *geshtalt*, he has not yet touched upon his entire thematic range; he has merely created his poetic instruments...." Apparently, Teller knew what he was talking about. Preil's first decade of writing, summed up by his first book, was indeed his poetic workshop. Being too close to this process, Teller may have been unaware that Preil found his own idiom through a stylistic transfer from Yiddish to Hebrew. The contemporary critic, on the other hand, has the advantage of almost half a century of both historical and aesthetic distance. From this vantage point it is easier to examine closely the tensions underlying Preil's bilingual creativity from its very inception and to determine the effect his bilingualism had on the shaping of his modernistic poetics.

Part Two

The Poetics of Preil's Bilingual Modernism

Chapter VI

Romanticism Revisited: The Early Hebrew Verse

At this time, at this place,
defending a curious romanticism. (1976:51)

Once there was an unfathomed romanticism
experienced by youngsters
at the turn of the century. (1981:46)

Attempts to retrieve a writer's initial creative impulses often encounter psychological and practical obstacles. This problem is particularly acute when the writer in question has gone through considerable changes and may even have taken measures to erase those beginnings that seemed alien to his present self-image. Thus, for instance, Hebrew Nobel laureate S.Y. Agnon, whose fame stems (in part, at least) from his crisp style and ironic distance, has excluded from his authorized canon any trace of his early "struggle against sentimentality," to use G. Shaked's helpful phrase.[1] More recently, the "collected poems" of Hebrew poet laureate H.N. Bialik were found wanting in their chronological accuracy. The new scholarly edition of his work shows that he was, in fact, rewriting the history of his evolution as a creative artist by tampering with the actual order in which his poems had been originally composed (Miron, 1983:66–70).

A similar tendency is at work in Preil's case. It begins with the marked difference between his early work, collected in his first two volumes (1944, 1954), and his mature work, collected in the volumes of 1960 and 1968. As we have shown above (chap. III), Preil's popularity and recognition were firmly established by the 1960s, after the publication of his third book, *Mapat 'Erev* [*Map of Evening*] (1960). From then on, he was acknowledged as an "American Imagist" who had revitalized Hebrew verse by his terse and economic images and by his verbal "painting" of colorful landscapes. That this kind of Imagism/Objectivism constitutes one of the distinctive features of Preil's Hebrew verse is no doubt true. Nevertheless, this "trademark" does not do justice to the full range of his oeuvre, although it is precisely this labeling that was greatly encouraged by the poet himself. When he made the selection for his collected poems, *Mi-toch Zeman ve-Nof* [*Of Time and*

Place] (1972), not only did he present his books in a reversed chronological order, but he also eliminated more than half of the poems in his first two volumes. A close examination of these "rejected" poems reveals that the choice was neither accidental nor arbitrary; rather, it underlined the poet's mature awareness of the sharp difference between his romantic point of departure and his current modernist posture, as well as his unquestioned preference for the latter. If we remember, in addition, that his first volume had been published in New York in a small edition and was soon out of print, we should not be surprised that Preil's "other self," the youthful romantic, was conveniently forgotten by his readers and critics from the 1960s on.[2] Yet these acts of rewriting, underrepresenting the poet's formative years, should not deter us from investigating this very period. On the contrary, because Preil seems to have found his unique voice only in his third volume, it is in his preceding work that we will find the strain and struggle of his creative effort. It is, therefore, the heterogeneous experimentation summed up in the poet's first book, *Nof Shemesh u-Chefor* [*Landscape of Sun and Frost*] (1944), which must now command our attention.

1. *Nof Shemesh u-Chefor: The Romantic Code*

Although this volume is the most heterogeneous of Preil's books, the majority of its poems express such traditional romantic themes and concerns as the painful passage of time, personified nature (the "pathetic fallacy"), the poet's empathy for the world's agony and for the suffering of child and mother. Predictably, the rhetoric is also in the tradition of Hebrew romantic verse: The diction is rather literary, and the imagery is rich and allusive, complete with anaphoras, invocations, rhetorical questions, and other intensifying devices. This elevated style prevails in the first and third parts of the book. In these poems the imagined world still constitutes a whole, despite its flaws and instability, and the poet's role in it remains unmistakably clear, though painful.

Interspersed among these predominantly romantic poems we find the beginning of an impressively new style, quite reminiscent of Preil's earlier Yiddish poems. The most memorable of these experiments in pure imagism is a compact poem, properly entitled "*Rikmat Sin*" [Chinese Embroidery] (see chap. IX for a detailed analysis). The dramatic divergence between these two genres cannot be overemphasized. A string of lucid images, seemingly disconnected, a lowering and thinning of both diction and syntax, and an effacement of the poetic voice—all adumbrate the crisp shape that many of Preil's poems assumed in later years, when spoken rhythms and diction replaced romantic pathos.

This tendency towards the spoken idiom is also noticeable in a third and very different genre—the narrative poem. The descriptive narrative, with its long Whitmanesque lines, takes precedence in Preil's second volume (see the section *Mi-Nof Amerika* [From the American Landscape], particularly "*Volt Vitman ve-ha-'Eglon*" [Walt Whitman and the Coachman], "*Beit Kevarot Amerikani*" [An American Graveyard], "*Shirim le-'Avia*" [Poems for Avia], and "*Tiyulim*" [Walks] [1954:64–82]). Yet, the first indications of this genre can be found in the shorter narratives of "Nancy Lincoln," "Grandpa John," or "Frans Hals" of the first volume (1944:26–29).[3]

Interestingly, this generic diversity is not reflected in the thematic organization of the book, as is indicated by the subtitles of its three divisions: *Demuti ba-Demuyot* [My Image Among Others] (pp. 7–34); *Ga'agu'ei Te'iya* (an unusual Hebrew collocation, probably the translation of the Yiddish *Vanderlust* [Wanderlust], pp. 37–52); and *Lehavot ve-Laila* [Flames and Night] (pp. 53–76). The first part is the least coherent of the three; it has a fair share of personal poems as well as third-person portraits. The second part is devoted mainly to nature poems, while the third focuses on topical verse, dealing with World War II and the Holocaust. More significant, however, is the fact that the book, as a whole, is framed by two poems that together constitute the opening and concluding statements of a poetic credo. In the first poem, "*He'arot 'al Gevil 'Atik-Yomin*" [Notes on an Ancient Parchment], the poet seems to harken back to antiquity, thus presenting himself as a link in a poetic chain that is rooted in the remote Hebrew past. In the closing poem, "*Tzava'a*" [A Will], he links himself with the future by equating his poetic writing with a humanistic last testament in a cataclysmic universe: "If the world is lost and wiped out in roaring fire/While there is time I sing of Man's glory and the sunny open spaces" (p. 76). Both poems are written in the lyrical mode; in each of them, the poetic voice identifies itself as a practicing poet who speaks about his art and its social function.

Judged by a surface reading, these poems hardly represent a departure from the norms of Hebrew verse of the Revival period. Thematically, they perpetuate Bialik's position of the prophet-poet, intent on rescuing a declining world; stylistically, they seem to follow Bialik's norm of elevated diction and rhetorical devices; figuratively, they are organized around a central image or metaphor. They even give the impression, at least at first glance, of traditional stanzaic segmentation.

These first impressions notwithstanding, a closer scrutiny will reveal the buds of prosodic and linguistic strategies aimed at the deautomatization of traditional linguistic and poetic formulae, some of which had been consecrated by Scripture and others by the more recent "canon" of Bialik. Most conspicuous of these is the absence of any of the metrical systems recognized before in Hebrew tradition; the prosodic principle governing these poems is neither biblical parallelism nor syllabo-tonic versification. It would be best defined as free verse or free rhythms (various reservations and qualification of these terms notwithstanding[4]). Free verse entails lines of uneven length, determined by the natural flow of syntax (from eight or nine to twenty or twenty-one syllables per line in our two poems[5]). It also implies the absence of rhyme and the use of colloquial sentence structure.[6] It often means the obliteration of stanzaic organization, which is probably the first graphic change to be caught by the reader's eye. These poems, however, preserve the *semblance* of strophic symmetry—thus veiling their other non-traditional prosodic features. The veil itself is quite transparent, three-line stanzas being rather rare in Hebrew syllabo-tonic versification. In addition, the symmetry breaks down in the last strophe, when a fourth line is added. We could say, then, that the graphic-prosodic structure of the poems functions as a "double sign": It points to a former tradition and deviates from it at the same time.

A similar pattern also exists for the figurative and thematic levels of many of the "romantic" poems of this group. By way of demonstrating the techniques employed by Preil in constructing his version of the romantic poem, we propose a close reading of a typical sample of this genre, "*He'arot 'al Gevil 'Atik-Yomin.*" Selected by the poet as the opening for his first book, this poem readily demonstrates the double message of his poetic credo at this early stage in his career. In its argument, the poem adumbrates the continuity of the romantic stance, typical of both English and Hebrew Romanticism. However, its style and use of language manifest subtle shifts toward strategies of innovation, thereby deautomatizing its own premises. Because these strategies are sometimes lost in translation, the reading herein consists of a close linguistic analysis, which borrows its basic procedures from recent schools of theory and criticism variously known as "literary semiotics" and "reader-response criticism."[7]

These analytic approaches conceive of the poem as "a text," namely as a coherent unit unified by an integral design. It is assumed that the ultimate design or significance of a given text does not necessarily overlap the mimetic or referential meaning of its language; consequently, its significance could not be deciphered by a linear or syntagmatic reading alone. This first sequential reading leaves gaps in our perception, or, in other formulations, creates deviations, ungrammaticalities, or cognitive incongruities, which no referential reading can settle. In order to circumvent these obstacles the reader is expected to reread the text, this time modifying his understanding in accordance with the information gathered in his second reading. By so doing, one should be able to perceive the implicit equivalences existing between the incompatible elements offered by the text and to decode the underlying nucleus generating its significance. In this process, the closure of the poem has a central role; it vouchsafes the perception of the "correct" pattern, because only at the moment of closure is the design revealed in its entirety (Smith, 1968:13) and a re-experiencing of the poem is made possible (*op. cit.*, p. 36).[8] However, the "decoding" of this design or pattern would be inconceivable without some foreknowledge of the general "system" (*langue*) of which the given text constitutes an instance (*parole*). Following their linguistic models, semiotic critics emphasize the reader's competence, both linguistic and literary, as a *sine qua non* of an appropriate reading; hence, the heavy reliance on the identification of all levels of codes or conventional sign-systems—linguistic structures (grammar), idioms and bound phrases (the sociolect), literary conventions (genres, prosodic systems, and period styles), and finally, the broad-range features of cultural systems.

With this approach as a guideline, we will proceed to suggest a rereading of "Notes on an Ancient Parchment" and to outline its implications for Preil's oeuvre in general.

2. *"Notes on an Ancient Parchment": Vision and Revision*

הֶעָרוֹת עַל גְּוִיל עַתִּיק־יוֹמִין

1. הָעוֹלָם פָּרוּשׂ לְפָנַי כִּגְוִיל עַתִּיק־יוֹמִין, —
2. וַאֲנִי סוֹפֵר אוֹתִיּוֹת וְתָגִים כִּמְנוֹת אִישׁ
3. רִגְעֵי־חַיִּים בְּשַׁעַר־מָוֶת.

4. הָעוֹלָם פָּרוּשׂ לְפָנַי כִּגְוִיל עַתִּיק־יוֹמִין, —
5. וַאֲנִי בָּאתִי לְחַדֵּשׁ חֶרְמֵשׁ־הַיָּרֵחַ וּלְמַלֵּא פְּגִימָתוֹ,
6. וּלְהַעֲנִיק מֵאִשִּׁי לִמְדוּרוֹת־שֶׁמֶשׁ גּוֹוְעוֹת.

7. הָעוֹלָם פָּרוּשׂ לְפָנַי כִּגְוִיל עַתִּיק־יוֹמִין, —
8. וַאֲנִי מְעָרֶה לְשַׁד־מֹחַ וַעֲצָמוֹת עַל פָּנָיו,
9. וְחוֹרֶת שְׁמֵי אַרְגָּמָן וְשָׁחוֹר בֶּחָרוּז.

10. הָעוֹלָם פָּרוּשׂ לְפָנַי כִּגְוִיל עַתִּיק־יוֹמִין, —
11. וְיָדַעְתִּי שֶׁפַּיְּטָנִים מִדּוֹר לְדוֹר
12. נָשְׂאוּ לִבָּם הַמְפַרְפֵּר בְּכַף־יָדָם הַפְּתוּחָה,
13. וַיִּצְרְחוּ מַר כִּנְשָׁרִים שַׁכּוּלִים — הַזְּמִירִים.

He'arot 'al Gevil 'Atik Yomin

1. *Ha-'olam parus le-fanai ki-gvil 'atik-yomin,—*
2. *va-'ani sofer 'otiyot ve-tagim ki-mnot 'ish*
3. *rig'ei chayim be-sha'ar mavet.*

4. *Ha-'olam parus le-fanai ki-gvil 'atik-yomin,—*
5. *va-'ani bati le-chadesh chermesh ha-yareach ule-male pegimato,*
6. *ule-ha'anik me-'ishi li-mdurot shemesh gove'ot.*

7. *Ha-'olam parus le-fanai ki-gvil 'atik-yomin,—*
8. *va-'ani me'areh leshad moach va-'atzamot 'al panav,*
9. *ve-choret shemi 'argaman ve-shachor be-charuz.*

10. *Ha-'olam parus le-fanai ki-gvil 'atik-yomin,—*
11. *ve-yada'ti she-paitanim mi-dor le-dor*
12. *nase'u libam ha-mefarper be-chaf yadam ha-petucha*
13. *va-yitzrechu mar ki-nsharim shakulim—ha-zemirim.*

Notes on an Ancient Parchment

1. The world is spread before me like an ancient parchment,
2. [while] I count letters and jots as a man counts
3. moments of life at the gate of death.

4. The world is spread before me like an ancient parchment,
5. [but] I come to renew the sickle moon and fill out its defect
6. and bestow of my fire upon the expiring flames of the sun.

7. The world is spread before me like an ancient parchment,
8. [while] I infuse it with the marrow of [my] mind and bone
9. and engrave my name in crimson and black verse.

10. The world is spread before me like an ancient parchment,
11. [but] I know that poets of all generations
12. bore their fluttering hearts in their open palms,
13. and bitterly, like bereaved eagles—the nightingales screamed.

A cursory reading of the poem yields a misleading impression of a traditional frame of reference, mimetic as well as literary.

The referent of the title, *gevil*, is an object belonging to olden times and is associated with sacred writings; it is the rough, unprocessed parchment, discussed in the Talmud in connection with scribal law (*Soferim* 1:4). In Bialik's poems, its plural form, *gevilim*, often represents the volumes of the Talmud itself, thus connoting antiquity and religious authority.[9] These connotations are here intensified by the epithet *'atik-yomin*. As an independent nominal phrase in biblical Hebrew, it designates one of the names of God, literally meaning "The Ancient of Days" (Daniel 7:9). Modern usage, however, has treated it as an adjective, mostly in collocation with the noun *'am* (a people), meaning simply "an ancient people," and usually referring to the people of Israel. Thus, this referent would be construed today as "an ancient parchment," although it preserves also the older meaning of "the Ancient's parchment."

Other traditional referents are evoked in the first strophe (line 2)—the *sofer* (the scribe of the holy writ) and the *tagim* (the jots or small crowns decorating the letters of the Torah).[10] The second strophe overtly refers to a religious ritual and its own sacred text—the renewal of the moon at the beginning of each lunar month and the prayer recited on this occasion. The *nusach* (formulation) of the prayer, in which God is asked to continue the growth of the newly-born moon, is represented here almost verbatim by the phrase *u-le-male pegimato* (line 5), "and to fill out its defect" (the part in shadow).[11] Less conspicuous are the references of the third strophe: The verb *me'areh* (line 8), meaning both "pour out" and "infuse" (any liquid, but often blood), cannot function as an unambiguous semantic marker because its connotative range includes many possibilities (as will be shown presently).[12] It can, however, serve as a stylistic marker. Despite its semantic multivalence it unequivocally signals elevated, even biblical diction. Similarly, the verb *choret* (inscribe, engrave) (line 9) readily signals a sacred context, the giving of Divine Law;[13] its connotative field includes, however, such modern secular associations as a love poem by Bialik.[14]

With the fourth and last strophe we descend from the divine to the less hallowed, and historically more recent institution of *paitanim* (line 11). This Aramaic version of the Greek *poiētēs* originally pertained to liturgical poets, who allegedly were also the first "cantors" in Jewish synagogues (see Fleischer, 1975:51). The ritual of prayer is suggested, even if obliquely, by some phrases (line 12) reminiscent of the supplicant's gesture of raising his hands. True, the Hebrew phrases *nasa kapav* and/or *nasa yadav* do not appear in their entirety in the text; but they seem to be the sources of the "scrambled"[15] expression *nase'u* [......] *be-chaf yadam*, literally meaning "[they] raised [......] in the palm(s) of their hand(s)" (line 12).

We could therefore conclude that, at first glance, the poem is girded by references to the realm of *religious rituals*. This observation might presuppose an attitude of veneration for tradition and its corollaries, the relationship among God, Nature, and Man. However, the word *God* itself is never mentioned in the text; instead we are presented with a chain of rituals, traditionally aimed at establishing contact with the Divine. Significantly, as the poem unfolds, the references to these rituals grow less and less direct. This decrease in textual representation is paralleled by a similar change in the referents' weight in terms of sanctity and veneration. Thus, we move from the role of the scribe (line 2), in whose hands the wholeness and holiness of the sacred text are entrusted, to the role shared by Every-[Jewish]-Man in assuring the smooth operation of nature (*Kidush ha-Levana* [Sanctification of the New Moon]) (line 5). Similarly, we step down from associations of the Day of Atonement (line 8) and the foundation of Divine Law (line 9) to the human and demotic realm of liturgy and prayer (lines 11–12). This descending scale "echoes" historical chronology, in which the last two activities (liturgy and prayer) had actually replaced the earlier sacrificial rites. In our poem, however, this scale comes to an abrupt halt with the final line. The sentence "The nightingales [which ones?] screamed like bereaved [?] eagles" seems completely out of context. Indeed, this line takes us by surprise, thus functioning as a *closure* on all textual levels. Graphically, it is an added fourth line after three three-line strophes; morphologically, it contains the only verb in the biblical form of the 'narrative perfect' (= the conversive *vav* + the imperfect): *va-yitzrechu*. This causes a sudden breach in the modernized morpho-syntactic norm established by the poem thus far, and endows the last line with a dramatic crescendo.[16] Finally, it is the only sentence whose syntactic order is reversed: Its logical subject, *ha-zemirim* (the nightingales), is placed at the very end, securely isolated from the rest of the line (and the poem) by a dash. Thus, the literal translation of the final line is:

> And [they] screamed bitterly like bereaved eagles—the nightingales.

This unexpected formal reversal is further underlined by uncertainty concerning the syntactic subject of the line: In a sequential reading of a modern text the reader can hardly avoid the conjunctive function of the conversive *vav*; we could therefore construe the verb *va-yitzrechu* (line 13) as a second predicate of the preceding subject, *paitanim* (line 11). Only when we come to the very end do we realize that in this line the order is reversed and the verb actually precedes its subject (*ha-zemirim*). But the momentary hesitation suffices to establish in the mind of the reader an equivalence between *paitanim* and *zemirim*:

paitanim...nase'u... va-yitzrechu...ha-zemirim.[17]

However, syntactic equivalence is not enough to explain a semantic equation. The latter relies, as we shall see, upon a single semantic constituent, which is shared by the otherwise disparate words *zemirim* and *paitanim*.

When translated into English, the image of the singing poet or the nightingale-as-poet may be taken for granted and even seem trite. In Western culture the metaphorization of the nightingale as an emblem of the lyric poet has had a long history. It goes back as far as Greek mythology, to Ovid's Philomela (or her sister Procne in other versions—see Ovid's *Metamorphoses*, book 6, 1965:153–158). In this etiologic story, the moaning nightingale is the embodiment of a bereft woman, telling and retelling her tragic story. Later, the bird became identified with the lyric poet, thus reuniting poetry with singing, its ancient root. The poeticizing of the nightingale reached its peak in the Romantic movement where it actually became a stock metaphor, immortalized in Shelley's well-known definition:

> A poet is a nightingale who sits in the darkness and sings to cheer his own solitude with sweet sounds (Shelley, "A Defence of Poetry," 1951:1031).

Not so in Hebrew. Before reaching an equivalence between the Hebrew words *paitan* and *zamir*, two separate semantic shifts had to take place—one, transposing the word *paitan* from the realm of ritual and liturgy to the realm of secular lyric poetry; the second, metaphorizing the bird *zamir* to connote a lyric poet. The first shift took place in modern times, when Hebrew poets adopted it as a synonym for *meshorer* and usually used it to designate the *lyrical* poet.[18] It took just as long to establish the second shift. A late medieval derivation, the *zamir*, as a poet, did not seem to gain acceptance among Hebrew writers. Possibly, the word could not shed the biblical connotations of its source: The root *z.m.r.* and its derivatives are generally applied to liturgical singing, whether in the Temple of antiquity or in contemporary ritual (*Zemirot-Shabbat*). The slow development of the semantic field of *zamir* may point to an intrinsic historico-cultural grid which emphasized the collective and played down the personal. Thus, as late as the end of the nineteenth century, Mendele criticized the helplessness of his people by juxtaposing them with nature's nightingale: "*Ha-zamir bi-nginot ve-Yisra'el be-kinot*" (The nightingale sings its melodies while Israel chants its litanies) (*Susati*, 1958 [1888]:323). With the romantic poetry of the Revival period, the nightingale finally made its way into Hebrew lyrical verse. Bialik openly identifies the nightingale with the lonely poet. "*Shira Yetoma*" [Orphaned Singing/Poetry] is his earliest treatment of the theme of the poet's tragic fate (1973:108). The poem concludes with a rhetorical question directed at the reader:

כִּי־יִפְגַּע אָזְנֶיךָ שִׁיר זָמִיר הַמְצַפְצֵף וְהוֹמֶה —
הַאֻמְנָם לֹא־תָנוּד לַמְשׁוֹרֵר הַבּוֹדֵד, הַיְּחִידִי,
וְלֹא־תִשְׁמַע שִׁירָתוֹ כְּשִׁמְעַ קוֹל שִׁירָה יְתוֹמָה!

When your ear is struck by the moaning chirping of the nightingale's song,
Would you not bemoan the lonely, lonesome poet?
Would you not hear his song as the voice of orphaned singing (= poetry)?

Whether this suffices to establish a *Hebrew* stock metaphor is rather doubtful. However, noting Preil's familiarity with English Romanticism, we should not hesitate to identify the romantic grounding of his metaphorized bird.[19]

It is clear, then, that despite its surface encoding, this poem progresses toward a statement about a contemporary lyric poet whose world view is probably different from the one reflected in the ritualistic code employed in the construction of the poem. This incompatibility is a signal in itself, sending us back to re-examine the poem and find out how the poet manipulated his materials. And it is the jarring closure, of course, that further prompts a retrospective reading in search of an interpretative hypothesis.

Reading the title again, we may perceive a somewhat startling collocation even there: The word *he'arot*, although meaning "comments" or "(foot)notes," is not the one currently expected in conjunction with "an ancient parchment." (Contemporary usage distinguishes between glosses or commentaries on sacred texts, customarily designated as *be'ur[im]* or *perush[im]*, and *he'arot*, which is largely reserved for footnoting a modern text or for adding [editorial] remarks [although not exclusively so].) Thus, we realize that the title itself may generate two opposing contexts, those of past and present, antiquity and modernity, the sacred and the secular.

Although the first line continues this duality ("the world" and "the ancient parchment"), it also arouses the suspicion that the title is actually a misnomer. The subject of the poem is not the ancient parchment after all. If "the *world* is spread before me like an ancient parchment," sacred antiquity only serves as a vehicle in the description of the world of here and now. This retrospectively endows the tenor (the world) with connotations of sacredness, perfection, and veneration usually reserved for the Torah scroll. At this juncture we might also recall the midrashic tradition that claims that the Torah itself is the blueprint of the created world (a quite venerable source for the present simile).[20]

Because this simile is repeated four times throughout the poem, it is impossible to escape the sense of centrality and importance with which the tenor (the world) is endowed. With the poetic persona's declaration that he "counts letters and jots" (line 2), this value judgment seems to be warranted. By attributing to himself the work of the scribe (*sofer*), the poetic persona seems to undertake a scribe's stance *vis-à-vis* the object of his work, namely, an attitude of obedient veneration and self-effacement.[21] Read as a transcoded description, this image clearly evokes the picture of a *mimetic* writer, the one who holds a mirror up to nature (see Abrams, 1953:30–35, *et passim*), doing his best to copy or preserve the world as he sees it.

However, this image is undercut even as it is fashioned.[22] The wholesomeness and wholeheartedness of the scribe's effort is not possible in a world in which a "gate of death" (line 3) is present in every act. The awareness of this tragic flaw prompts the poetic voice to assume another role, that of an active donor who can *rescue* the world rather than *record* it (cf. Abrams, 1953:131,280–281,331). This change of masks is effected through a clever grafting of two diverse, though related images—the renewal of the moon and the seasonal decline of the sun.[23]

At first sight, the moon imagery (line 5) seems to be a natural expansion of the scribe imagery in line 2. In the ordered world of a scribe it is possible to secure the moon's renewal by a proper ritual. The valorization of the first (line 2) is automatically carried on to the second (line 5), but only to the extent that we momentarily disregard some highly untraditional elements. However, when stumbling upon the following sun imagery (line 6), the reader realizes that he has been taken in: The *dying* flames of the sun reinforce the *negative* pole of the moon image rather than the *positive* one. Of the two phases of the moon, only its waning is recapitulated in the description of the sun (*pegimato//gove'ot* [defect//expiring]). This signals an inversion of our value judgment. A world with expiring solar flames and a waning moon is far from perfect. Because perfection is an illusion, there is no need and no room for a scribe, for preservation or mimesis. Instead, a Promethean figure is called for, someone who can revive a declining universe. Thus, the poetic persona dons the mask of the savior, declaring "*I* came to renew the moon..." Only now do we realize how unorthodox this statement is. It is not a request directed at the Divine, but a human self-assertion in the best Romantic tradition.[24] The traditional prayer "And may it be Thy will, O Lord, my God, and the God of my fathers, to fill out the defects in the moon" is replaced by a heroic declaration that actually subverts not only the text from which it derives, but the whole world view represented by that text.[25] This subversion is marked by slight textual changes: The moon is designated not by the traditional *levana* but by its synonym, *yareach*; furthermore, *yareach* is modified by *chermesh* (sickle), a modern collocation that goes back to Bialik's diction;[26] finally, the ritualistic term *Kidush ha-Levana* (blessing over the [new] moon) is very strongly alluded to, but is actually absent from the surface text. Of the two options available in the sources, "renew" (*le-chadesh*) and "sanctify" (*le-kadesh*), the poet chose the form *le-chadesh* (line 5). By so doing he managed to preserve a semblance of the tradition and to undercut it at the same time. The two verbs are morphologically and phonologically identical except for one consonant (*kof* vs. *chet*). Semantically, however, they represent a meaningful shift from sanctifying an action of God (the renewal of the moon) to the taking of this very act upon oneself.

This transition is signaled by a dense repetition of verbs (to renew, to fill out, to donate, lines 5–6), and by the anaphora *va-'ani* (and I) (in lines 2, 5, 8, and 11), which competes with and counterbalances the parallel anaphora of the world-as-parchment (lines 1, 4, 7, and 10). No wonder, then, that in the third strophe the allusion to the world of tradition grows increasingly vague. The verb *me'areh* (line 8), read in collocation with "the marrow of mind and bones," is interpreted as "*in*fuse" rather than as "pour *out*." Thus, it evokes less the ancient sacrificial rite than the modern medical term *'erui dam* (blood-infusion). Though the word *dam* (blood) is avoided altogether, it is easily surmised. The synonyms *leshad* and *moach* (marrow) belong to a semantic paradigm of life-sustaining elements, in which *dam* is an obvious member. All three nouns are used to denote vitality. *Dam* is the least poetic of the three, but it is the one used most often in conjunction with *me'areh* (infuse). Thus, the line "And I infuse the world with the marrow of [my] mind and bones" brings together two connotations, both relevant to the new image of the heroic poet—the redeemer and the sacrifice. Unlike Keats' famous poet, who "is a sage, / A humanist, *physician* to all men,"[27] Preil's poet redeems the world by infusing his *own* marrow/blood, consequently becoming a sacrifice himself.

Curiously enough, the notion of self-sacrifice can also be expressed by the root *'.r.y* in another formation (the causative, *he'era*). Despite their differences, the phonetic resemblance of the two verbs is strong, and their semantic relevance is quite clear. The idiom *he'era nafsho la-mut* (poured his soul out unto death) (Isaiah 53:13) connotes risking one's life for the benefit of others or a heroic self-giving[28] (and cf. line 6: "And I bestow of my fire...").

Summing up the verbal associations enumerated so far, one realizes that though semantically related, they are too diffuse in their codes. They can partake of either ritual, medical, or heroic encoding. However, what transposes them all into a single unified signifying system is a literary allusion that is suppressed by the text. Line 9, "and inscribe (engrave) my name in crimson and black verse," secures our "correct" understanding of the preceding line. The verse is crimson because it is infused with the poet's blood, and this forces us to choose the heroic code for the whole statement. The same line also signals a specific intertext, a classic in Hebrew lyrical poetry: Bialik's "*Lo Zachiti ba-'Or min ha-Hefker*" [I Did Not Gain My Light Without Travail, 1973:135]. Using a spark of light as a metaphor for poetry, Bialik describes the painful process of artistic creativity, which he compares to the act of quarrying. The poem concludes with a statement about the tragic fate of the poet: Even when his spark succeeds in kindling a fire in his readers' hearts, the poet is the one who pays dearly, with his "own marrow and blood."[29] The similarity between the images cannot be missed, especially in translation. In Hebrew we have two different surface actualizations of the same idea. Preil is very careful to avoid Bialik's vocabulary: Bialik's *Va-'ani be-chelbi ve-dami / 'et ha-be'era 'ashalem* (And I with my marrow and blood / will pay for the fire) is replaced here by *leshad moach* and *'argaman* (marrow and crimson). A closer look reveals still more replacements: Bialik's act of quarrying (*nikartiv va-chatzavtiv*) is represented by the act of engraving (*choret*, line 9); the poetic spark, *nitzotz*, has turned into a fire (*'ishi*, line 6); and the readers' fire (*ha-be'era*) might have evolved into the sun's bonfires (*medurot*, line 6). The last changes indicate that Preil's modifications transcend simple lexical replacement; they point to a situational-ideational displacement. The axis of poet↔readers is elevated and universalized to include the relationship poet↔world. We are on a higher scale here, but the internal relationship is the same. It is the tragic fate of the poet to risk himself heroically for the benefit of his readers or for the world at large. [30] Little wonder, then, that our poem comes to its logical completion by the poet's acceptance of the poetic tradition he is about to join. His predecessors are described as the *paitanim* who "bore their fluttering hearts in their open hands" (line 12). Though the Hebrew sentence is intuitively divined as standing for "risking and sacrificing their innermost life and emotions," it is not immediately clear how this reading takes place.

This sentence contains some of the most idiomatically prolific Hebrew words, the nouns *lev* (heart), *yad* (hand), and *kaf* (palm of the hand) and the verb *nasa* (raised, lifted, carried). Nevertheless, none of the actual idioms materializes in the text. We can only reconstruct some of the most relevant. The latent idiom connoting prayer (*nasa yado* or *nasa kapo*) is cancelled out by our retroactive reading. Once more, there seems to be a second reading based on a suppressed text: Our intuitive comprehension of the line apparently derives from two known idioms: *sam nafsho be-chapo* (put his soul in his hand, i.e., risked himself) and *yad petucha* (an open hand, i.e., generosity, donating). Thus, our second reading follows a familiar paradigm, moving from an ancient passive ritual (prayer) to the "modern" activity of generous self-sacrifice. This metamorphosis ends on a bitter note: One cannot be a Prometheus, cannot attempt to redeem a declining world, without risking one's lyrical "gift." Previous experience has shown that the nightingale cannot remain a lyrical singer for long. The pain and frustration of the poetic process transform him into a bereft eagle, screaming bitterly (line 13).

The image of a bereft eagle is unprecedented in Hebrew. The epithet *shakul* usually designates a person who has lost his child(ren). The prevalent idiom *ke-dov shakul* (like a bereft bear), conveying fearless bitterness, derives from a biblical description of David's warriors (2 Samuel 17:8; cf. Proverbs 17:12). A bereft bear, however, would not fit into the "birds code" borrowed by Preil from the Romantic imagination; it would not do as a figurative opposition of the nightingale. Therefore, "bereavement" was grafted onto the equally fearless eagle, which has a long-standing literary tradition in Hebrew. Of all biblical references, only the following seems particularly relevant: Divine Providence is likened to an eagle hovering and watching over his young (Deuteronomy 32:11). From this simile it is only one step to its mirror image, the bear-like, bereft eagle. Yet, this alone does not transpose the bird into the romantic code we have been tracing so far. This transposition is achieved, again, through an implicit allusion, this time to Tchernichowsky's biographical-poetic credo, "*Ha-'Adam 'Eino 'Ela*" [Man is Nothing But...] (1967:228–231). In this poem, the poet projects his alienation into the image of the "solitary-barren" (*'ariri*) steppe-eagle, whose wild screaming nobody understands.[31] Apparently, the poetic persona speaking in the poem is aware of the tragic literary tradition in which he intends to participate. Nevertheless, he prefers the prospects of becoming an eagle to being a scribe; the romantic mission is more compelling than the mimetic. It would seem that the manifesto obliquely unfolded in our poem stems from an unverbalized statement: In a declining world one can no longer be a scribe, one must become a creative writer despite the risks involved in the role.

The dichotomy generating this statement is the famous Romantic opposition between the mirror and the lamp; yet the textual actualization of this opposition seems intrinsically Hebraic. In addition to all idiomatic and literary sources processed in this poem, the poet seems to play on the semantic shift of *sofer* from "scribe" to "author, writer." Though neither of these words surfaces in the text, the verb *sofer* (count)[32] definitely actualizes the older meaning; the new meaning is periphrased by the metaphors of strophes 2–4.

To sum up, the poetic manifesto expounded in "Notes on an Ancient

Parchment" subverts the very tradition that it pretends to perpetuate. Its claim to continuity[33] only partially materializes in the linguistic, figurative, and thematic aspects of the poem itself. In its diction, imagery, surface encoding and fundamental attitudes, it appears to continue the rhetorical pathos as well as the ethos of Bialik's generation. Still, these familiar features are manipulated in ways that undercut and deautomatize them. Thus, scrambled idioms, grafted metaphors, rarely used words, and contextual shifts—all contribute in transposing the traditional material into a *personal, supra-national*, romantic credo.

A parallel transition is to be perceived on the *prosodic* level.[34] For one thing, the absence of a rhyme scheme and of any clear-cut syllabo-tonic grid prevents an unequivocal determination of the poem's stress system. This poem was written in the 1930s, just when Hebrew was undergoing a change in its stress and pronunciation (see chap. II). It is quite plausible that "free rhythms" were used as a way out of the clash between the two stress systems. At the same time, there is no hint here of any biblical parallelism, so we have no recourse to the intrinsically Hebraic free rhythms of the Bible. Thus, if we scan the poem in accordance with Ashkenazi stress (I), we predictably perceive an amphibrachic grid modified by paeons, trochees, and occasional iambs; while a Sephardi-oriented scanning (II) (which, incidentally, is the one insisted upon by the author himself) yields an anapestic-paeonic grid, disrupted mainly by iambs (see Appendix 3 for prosodic charts). In view of such diversity of metric feet, we would do better to replace the syllabo-tonic system with an accentual (or purely tonic) one (chart III, Appendix 3). When we subordinate the metric stresses to the syntactic ones, we reveal groups of words clustered around a single strong stress.[35] These are often marked by constructs, syndetic members, and other quasi-enclitic or -proclitic combinations.[36] Read in this manner, the heterogeneity of measures (in number and kind) is reduced to mostly three or four accentual stresses per line, thus facilitating our perception of the rhythmo-syntactic principles regulating the poem.[37] The perception of this organization is further reinforced by other rhetorical devices, including the fact that each strophe is a complete periodic unit; that there is a similar clausal structure within each strophe;[38] that, refrain-like, all first lines are repeated (lines 1, 4, 7, and 10); and that all second lines (lines 2, 5, 8, and 11) are anaphoras.[39]

Because the apparent free flow of syntactic units is combined with declamatory rhetoric and heightened diction and tone, this poem could be classified as a variation of the *elevated free rhythms* that were introduced into Hebrew by Frishman and Bialik and had been inspired by the German Classical Ode (see chap. I, section 2). We should not be surprised then that quite a few of Preil's early Hebrew poems bear some resemblance to this genre. Titles such as "To the Grass" (1944:9), "To a Poem" (1944:8), "A

Letter from Man to Time" (1944:11), "On the Loss of Youth" (1944:19), are reminiscent of English odes of the Romantic period.[40] Yet, though in their themes and subject-matter these Hebrew "odes" may echo their English counterparts, they totally differ from them in their prosody. With few exceptions, most of these ode-like rhetorical poems lose the semblance of strophic segmentation still upheld in "Notes on an Ancient Parchment."

In most of the poems, lines as well as strophes grow longer and more irregular (up to thirteen lines per strophe and up to twenty-two syllables per line). Line lengths seem to be determined only by thematic considerations: A sentence may coincide with one or more (up to five) uneven lines. This cancels out the vital contrapuntal tension between metric norms and syntactic structures, thereby creating the impression of "speaking" rhythms.[41] On the other hand, the harmony between line and sentence is retained by the limited use of enjambment. Most lines overlap secondary syntactic units (clauses or phrases), which are demonstrably marked off by punctuation marks (commas, dashes, semi-colons).

It was, no doubt, this prosodic structure that reminded the American Hebrew critic A. Epstein (1952) of the American poets Whitman, Jeffers, and Sandburg. It is possible that Epstein's suggestion was enhanced by Preil's translations from Jeffers and Sandburg.[42] Still, Preil's prosodic freedom was not as daring as the one exercised by these imputed American models. His rhythmo-syntactic units neither overreach nor obliterate line boundaries, his use of enjambment is very limited, and his reiterative devices are much less explicit. Clearly, the checks and balances inherent in Hebrew prosody were still operative in Preil's emancipated rhythms. We would be better off, then, looking for a mediating link within the Hebrew tradition.

Such a link may be suggested by a rather unique poem, one that Preil neglected to include in his "selected poems" of 1972, as well as in any of his earlier volumes. Surprisingly enough, the subject of this forgotten poem is none other than the poet mentioned briefly in chapter V, Zalman Shne'ur (1887–1959). We may now recall that it was precisely Shne'ur's rhetoric that was the object of Teller's scathing critique. In Teller's view, furthermore, Preil's poetics constituted a clear deviation from those established by Shne'ur. Whether this was indeed the case is a question that we will discuss in the next chapter. Moreover, we will soon see that Shne'ur's poetics offer significant insights into two literary codes regulating Preil's transition from romanticism to modernism—the development of free verse and the emergence of his "poetics of despair."

Chapter VII

Toward a Poetics of Despair: The Budding of Hebrew Modernism

אֵין זֶה הָאֵד הַמְרַפְרֵף

אֵין זֶה הָאֵד הַמְרַפְרֵף שֶׁל שְׁנֵיאוּר
בָּא כָּרָגִיל בְּשָׁעָה שֶׁל אִי־רָצוֹן
וּבַקָּשַׁת מִפְלָט וּמוֹצָא
בְּמָקוֹם שֶׁאֵינוֹ בְּנִמְצָא,
אֲבָל נָחוּץ לַטָּמִיר שֶׁבָּנוּ
כִּנְשִׁימָה זוֹ, שֶׁבְּדֶרֶךְ מִקְרֶה
שֶׁלָּנוּ הִיא.

אוּלָם הָאֵד שֶׁעוֹטֵף עָלֵינוּ כַּיּוֹם
הוּא עֵד שֶׁמִּתְרַבּוֹת בְּחַיֵּינוּ
תַּחֲנוֹת לֹא מֻגָּעוֹת.
אוֹקְיָנוֹס הוֹלֵךְ וּפוֹשֵׁט
עַל כָּל הָאִיִּים הִצַּלְנוּ.
וְאָנוּ לֹא נְדַכֵּא מִרְדֵּנוּ
בְּתַנְחוּמֵי שָׁוְא,
גַּם כְּשֶׁהַשָּׁמַיִם מְחַיְּכִים לָנוּ
בִּתְכֶלְתָּם הַיְשָׁנָה:
הֵם רַק מְשַׁקְּפִים הָעֲרָפֶל
בּוֹ תּוֹעֶה דּוֹרֵנוּ לְכוּד הָאֵימוֹת,
הֵם רַק אִלְּמִים מְאַשְּׁרִים
דְּעִיכַת הַכּוֹכָבִים.

הָאֵד הַמְרַפְרֵף שֶׁל שְׁנֵיאוּר
נִרְאֶה כַּיּוֹם קַל וּפְנִינִי,
מְשֻׁבָּץ בְּמִסְגֶּרֶת הָעוֹלָם, שֶׁאֵינֶנּוּ עוֹד.

Not the Hovering Mist

It is not Shne'ur's hovering mist
descending as usual at unwelcome moments
of search for a refuge and exit
in a place not existing;
yet the mystery within us has need of it,
just like breath itself, only accidentally
ours.

The mist that envelops us today
attests to the increasing number
of unreachable stations in our lives.
An ocean continues to cover
all our safeguarded islands.
And we cannot suppress our rebellion
with false comfort
though the sky smiles at us
with its ancient blue:
it but reflects the fog
in which our horror-trapped generation wanders,
it but mutely affirms
the waning of the stars.

Shne'ur's hovering mist
now seems pearl-like, light,
set into the frame of a world that no longer exists.

A careful reading of Preil's poem " *'Ein Zeh ha-'Ed ha-Merafref*" [Not the Hovering Mist][1] reveals two different attitudes to Shne'ur's poetic world. In the past, particularly in times of insoluble conflicts, his "hovering mist" was as indispensable as breathing; but "today" (namely, by the late 1940s), Shne'ur's mist seems merely artistic decor, "set into the frame of a world that no longer exists." Its metaphoric suggestiveness has been eclipsed by the thick fog engulfing the present "horror-trapped" generation. It would seem, then, that two conflicting emotions animate this retrospection: The nostalgic impulse is undermined by a subtle irony. However, irony turns into parody when one realizes that Preil's poem is, in fact, somewhat of a spoof: " *'Ein Zeh 'Ed Merafref*" [Not a Hovering Mist] is the title of one of *Shne'ur's* early poems. Written in 1905 (Shne'ur, 1952, I:79), this poem epitomizes the self-dramatized *ennui* and the cloying clichés of "romantic despair" characteristic of turn-of-the-century "decadent" literature. Predictably, the inauthenticity of these claims to resignation and despair is borne out by the prosody of the poem, which meticulously preserves the closed system of trite rhyming and smooth (Ashkenazi) syllabo-tonic meters.

אֵין זֶה אֵד מְרַפְרֵף...

אֵין זֶה אֵד מְרַפְרֵף וְאֵין זֶה גֶּשֶׁם סוֹחֵף,
אֵין זֶה רוּחַ מָצוּי וְאֵין זֶה רוּחַ סַעַר,
אֵין זֶה שַׁחַר חִוֵּר וְאֵין זֶה בֵּין־הַשְּׁמָשׁוֹת,
אֵין בְּיוֹם זֶה חֶדְוָה וְאֵין בְּיוֹם זֶה צַעַר.

לֹא לְחַבֵּק נַעֲרָה אַף לֹא לְהִמֹּק בָּדָד,
אֵינְךָ חוֹלֵם עָתִיד, אֵינְךָ זוֹכֵר עָבָר:
תֵּשֵׁב אֶל הַמְּלָאכָה — וְאַתָּה כְּבָר מְפַהֵק,
תֹּאמַר שֶׁבֶת בָּטֵל — וְלִבְּךָ שׁוֹקֵק דָּבָר.

Not a Hovering Mist

It is not a hovering mist, nor a torrential rain
It is not a gust of air, nor a mighty gale,
It is not a pale dawn, nor a sunset,
I feel no joy today, nor am I upset.

Not embracing a girl, nor languishing alone,
Not dreaming of tomorrow, nor remembering days gone.
When you set to work, you immediately tire,*
If you want to sit idle, your heart knows desire.

Evidently, it is these prosodic characteristics of the subtext that may explain the presence in Preil's essentially *free* verse of the occasional end rhymes and homonyms (*motza*/*nimtza* [exit/exist] and *'ed*/*'ed* [mist/attest]), which are otherwise rare in his oeuvre. Transplanted as they are into a different prosodic system, they seem to stand out of context, underlining the *ir*relevance of the *Weltanschauung* they had originally represented. Consequently, "romantic despair" itself is subject to criticism in Preil's

* The literal translation, "yawn," was replaced by the semantically related "tire" in the attempt to give a semblance of the "closed" rhyme scheme (*badad* / *'avar* / *mefahek* / *davar*) in which assonantal and alliterative devices join together the "free" /a/ rhymes and the pair of /b/ rhymes.

"mist" poem. As we shall soon see, this rejection of Shne'ur's earlier romantic stance was no doubt motivated by extra-literary realities. Without specifically saying "war" or "holocaust," the text periphrastically conjures up their presence. Nevertheless, this poem can also be read as Preil's farewell to the idol of his youth, whom he had greeted most enthusiastically a dozen years earlier as "the symbol of the potential for the revitalization of Hebrew poetry." Celebrating Shne'ur's fiftieth birthday, young Preil hailed his elder's "superb reflective lyricism" as well as his demand to remove all masks and gaze on Man in his insignificance:

> "Take off the mask so we can see God"—says the great old man [Rabbi Shne'ur Zalman mi-Ladi]. "Take off the masks so we can see Man in his nothingness"—says the great-grandson [Zalman Shne'ur]. Yet [Zalman] Shne'ur (public opinion notwithstanding) does not say this in provocation or in teasing. The Black Gardener put a scare into him. Helpless and in pain he [Shne'ur] cries out in rebellion, wishing to extricate himself from Fate's jaws. But no voice echoes in the desert; in a moment the lid will close on him forever. To whom in the world can a lonely man turn? (Preil, 1937)

According to Preil, Shne'ur finds solace in Beauty. Since life, despicable as it is, cannot be relinquished, poems are written which are

> astounding in their exotic descriptiveness and in their primeval effervescence. Poetic landscapes of profound color and sound, which no one has yet discovered, were revealed to this Columbus-poet [explorer] who has listened to the rhythm of the Earth and the stars [planets] (*ibid.*).

Three issues are worth noting here: Thematically, the preoccupation with the abstractions of death, fate, and Everyman; figuratively, the personifications in which these themes are couched; prosodically, the incidental remark concerning what is labeled in scholarly jargon "organic rhythms" (Hrushovski, 1954:257–264; Allen, 1975:225–230). To be sure, Shne'ur was the only one of Bialik's disciples to indulge in unrhymed free rhythms, although he did not let this practice outweigh his predominantly syllabo-tonic versification. The astuteness of Preil's prosodic observation is particularly intriguing because it was formulated in 1937, several years *before* Shne'ur published his last major work, *Luchot Genuzim* [The Concealed Tablets] (*Sefer ha-Shana li-Yehudei Amerika*, New York: 1940–1942, 1947).

It was precisely this epic that Shne'ur considered his major contribution to Hebrew prosody, "the renewal of the ancient biblical rhythm."[2] Yet, the truth is that his earlier work included several attempts at freeing himself from his syllabo-tonic tendencies. Curiously enough, some of these occasional slips into free rhythms exhibit the peculiar blend of reflective and descriptive elements that Preil pointed out. In "*Mastema*" [Hatred] (1912, in 1952:142), Time (*Zeman*) is personified and is equipped with "ancient scissors" to cut the poet's "thread of life." In "*Necha'im*" [Dejection] (1917, in 1952: 217), the poet resignedly bows down to another personification of Time, '*Et*. A cursory reading of Preil's first book reveals similar elements. In many of the ode-like poems, he is preoccupied with time, aging, man in general, and "the human condition." The proportions between conceptual reflections and vivid imagery vary significantly in different poems. But even in the more descriptive poems of the lot, the images are still subordinate to the poetic voice that comments upon and interprets the picturesque tapestry it has created. Nevertheless, it is in these very poems that Preil has slowly abandoned the romantic pathos and made the transition to reflective free verse. The descriptiveness of the latter enabled him, in turn, finally to leave behind conceptual reflections and emerge as an "Imagist," speaking through images rather than about them. It is not our intention to offer here detailed analyses of these poems. Rather, we will briefly delineate some of their salient thematic or stylistic features, which are most relevant to the poet's artistic development.

1. *The Shne'urian Model: Reflective Free Verse*

"*La-'Esev*" [To the (Blade of) Grass] (1944:9)

The title of this poem may be readily associated with a romantic context. Like so many odes to nature, it opens with a ceremonial invocation that clearly partakes of the pathetic fallacy:

עֵשֶׂב רַחֲמָן, רָז יָרוֹק וְחוֹזֵר,
עָלֶיךָ אֶצְנַח, לְךָ דָּבָר אֲגַל:

'Esev rachaman, raz yarok ve-chozer,
'Aleicha 'etznach, lecha davar 'agal:

Merciful grass, a perennial green mystery,
Upon you I will fall, to you I will whisper [divulge]:

The association with Whitman's *Leaves of Grass* is perhaps unavoidable, as was indeed observed by Silberschlag (1962). However, the differences between the two are more intriguing. In "Song of Myself" the grass is not the addressee of an apostrophe, but rather the object of observation; nor are the lines so symmetrically organized: "I loaf and invite my soul; / I lean and loaf at my ease, observing a blade of summer grass." In fact, Preil's opening lines lack entirely Whitman's undulating rhythm which properly expresses the poet's identification with nature; Preil's formal apostrophe gives the impression of the traditional, neoclassical rigidity, which only points to the distance between the poetic voice and his addressee. Furthermore, the apostrophic rhetoric and the declamatory tone are reinforced by several heightening devices. The first impression is that of parallelism, caused by the internal symmetry of the lines: The hemistichs of each line complement each other semantically. This is underscored by syntactic (additive) parallelism in the first line and by morphological symmetry in the second line. Thus we have:

1	n + adj	/ n + adj + adj
2	pron + v (dative) (future) (2nd per) (1st per)	/ pron + o + v (dative) (future) (2nd per) (1st per)

In addition, the elevated tone is created by the choice of diction—literary vocabulary (*raz* and *'etznach* [mystery and fall]), biblical morphology (*'agal* [disclose, reveal] in place of the normative form *'agaleh*), and rhetorical word order (pronouns preceding verbs). Equally poeticizing is the effect of alliteration (*r* in the first colon, *ch* in both cola) and the assonance ($\bar{a}$) observable in both cola. Indeed, despite the absence of a rhyme scheme, these opening lines look like a classical couplet because of their relative brevity and their even length (eleven syllables, as opposed to the following lines). Their typographical symmetry is supported by the rhythmic structure, with each line evenly divided by a caesura:[3]

1	2		3	4
'E – sev	ra – cha – man	,	raz ⋮ ya – rok	ve – cho – zer

1	2		3	4	5
'A – lei – cha	'etz – nach	,	le – cha	da – var	'a – gal

Figure A

Such a formally controlled invocation naturally arouses certain expectations, but the unfolding of the poem frustrates these expectations. The "secret" of the poetic persona is disclosed in two long strophes of uneven lines (eleven and thirteen lines of six to twenty syllables), which have no observable formal symmetry. The theme is clearly an expansion of one of

Bialik's central motifs: the poet's tear. However, its unavoidable pathos (How can I, the poet, contain all mankind's tears, while my single [orphan] tear cannot exhaust my own sources?) is mitigated by a fusion of the literary and the spoken, in both lexicon and syntax.[4] Scriptural allusions are largely eliminated, while the tone and syntax simulate speaking rhythms. Nevertheless, the latter are occasionally interrupted by unusual morphological and syntactical deviations. Thus the verb *she-shak'á* (that set or expired) is rendered in the archaic (longer) form *she-shaká'a*; this forms an endline assonantal and rhythmic (paeonic) symmetry with *she-kaháta* (that darkened) of the former line.[5] Similarly, in an adjectival phrase meaning "his heavy ennui" (line 7), the obligatory definite article is missing—*shimemono (ha-)kaved.* This slight change is enough to turn the adjective into an adverb. The resulting effect is one of a heightened diction, which works against the general conversational tone of the strophe. The formal unity of these free-flowing strophes is subtly retained only by a few reiterative devices (corresponding rhetorical questions and contrapuntal statements), but nowhere is it as tightly organized as in the opening poem ("Notes on an Ancient Parchment"). Instead, thematic principles are distinctly employed in shaping the design of the poem (cf. Smith, 1968:78–79; Riffaterre, 1978:115–124). The motif of the tear is counterpointed by a motif of laughter. Two types of laughter are contrasted with each other and are viewed from two different perspectives; the poetic persona is juxtaposed against the blade of grass, and his pain and grief are compared to the ennui of man in general. This net of relationships is finally resolved by the closure: "Until I, too, become a blade [of grass]". (עַד אֶהְיֶה אַף אֲנִי לְגִבְעוֹל)

This final statement ties in nicely with the verb *chozer* (return, repeat) of the first line, thus revealing the matrix of the poem, its generating nucleus, i.e., the poet's preoccupation with time and its corollaries, the lot of human life vs. the perennial cycle of nature.

"*Lelo Temura ha-'Adam*" [Man Never Changes] (1944:12)

This poem represents a group of poems in which the concerns of "*La-'Esev*" are directly verbalized; cf. "*Perek Tuga la-'Alamot*" [On the Grief of Young Girls] (1944:17); " *'Al 'Ovdan ha-'Alumim*" [On the Loss of Youth] (1944:19); "*Mizmor ha-Chayalim ha-Metim*" [Hymn of the Dead Soldiers] (1944:21). Here the poetic voice does not address nature (nor any other entity); consequently, the heightened rhetorical effect of "*La-'Esev*" is missing. In three strophes (consisting of seven, five, and seven lines, respectively) of very irregular lines and syntactic units, the human condition is described and lamented. The immutability of man's fate is contrasted with nature's versatility ("Only the seasons take on four shapes and seven charms"); death is personified in a way that is very reminiscent of Shne'ur's poetry ("The Giant Harvester"). There is also an attempt at a colorful description of both mankind (youth contrasted with old age) and nature (the seven charms of four seasons). Still, the "dissociation of sensibility" (to borrow Eliot's long-disputed term)[6] is not overcome. Here, frequent statements of cognitive nature ("But I don't know," "Only this I know"), characteristic also of other poems in this group, stand between the reader and the imagery, which is still felt as decorative and subsidiary.

"*Mi-Yomano shel Malach*" [From a Sailor's Diary] (1944:14)

This is one of the few poems in which Preil employs a distinct mask or separate persona. Still, the sailor's voice does not differ greatly from the poetic voice of other poems. His specific milieu is used metaphorically to comment on life in general: "Sometimes I imagine that man's life is not a vague writing on the waters." An analogy between himself and the sailors of antiquity triggers a colorful, exotic description of far-away lands and days gone by, which again echoes one of Shne'ur's famous sensual depictions in "*'Im Tzelilei ha-Mandolina*" [To the Sounds of the Mandolin] (1912, in 1951:176). This descriptive digression is sealed, however, by another interpretive conclusion:

אַךְ מַלָּחִים בִּתְקוּפַת־אַגָּדָה זוֹ בִּקְשׁוּ מַתַּת־אֹשֶׁר לַשָּׁוְא —
כָּמוֹנִי הַיּוֹם.

But sailors in this legendary age searched in vain for the gift of happiness–
like me today.

"*Ha-'Adam ba-Shevi*" [Man in Captivity] (1944:16)

Although clearly propelled by the same concern as other reflective poems, this short poem leans more in the direction of imagistic expression. True, the subject is still "Everyman," and "death" is still personified (The Ruler of Rulers), but lines and strophes become shorter (seven plus four lines), and conceptual vocabulary is partially replaced by figurative language: Days are "sands lingering between fingers," an obvious transferral from English ("the sands of time"), and deceptive nights are "smoked velvet." Cognitive expressions still take part in shaping the closure ("Man does not know that," "And he forgets that"), but an imagistic tendency is definitely felt. This is accompanied by a more regulated line length and rhythm: Most lines contain two or three phrase-groups; most sentences are periodic and create rhythmic (though rhymeless) bi-cola, thus anticipating the rhythmo-syntactic nature of Preil's later imagistic free verse.

Only a few of these reflective poems were incorporated by Preil into his collected poems (1972). Faithful to his intention "to comprehend the essence and motivation of his verse," he stressed his early imagistic experiments at the expense of his rhetorical-reflective beginnings. This tendency is doubly felt in his screening of the topical poems grouped in Part III of the first book. Again, we cannot let the poet's retrospective selection stand in the way of our attempt to trace the development of his poetics. For it is in these poems, associated with World War II, that the turning point had taken place and a new modernist idiom emerged. It is therefore to this chapter in the evolution of Preil's poetics that the next section is devoted.

2. *The Holocaust Crisis: "Words Are Gone"*

This group of poems, written mostly between 1938 and 1941, is what some critics have labeled Preil's Holocaust poems. Preil himself, however, entitled this segment "*Lehavot ve-Laila*" [Flames and Night]—a generalization that does *not* point to the concrete historical or national context of the poems.[7] Nor is this accidental. The rhetoric of most of these poems does not differ significantly from that of the reflective poems described above. Their pathos is at times intensified, as called for by the theme, but a specific national color is only rarely encountered, despite concrete references that are scattered here and there.

Only a small number of these poems survived the author's severe process of selection. Unpredictably, this selection ends with the most rhetorical and, as we show below, the most Hebraically marked of all the poems in this group, the poem "*'Azelu Milim*" [Words Are Gone]. This choice is indeed intriguing. Because the poem "*Tzava'a*" [A Will], which had originally constituted the concluding statement of the book, was left out, we have a new ending here and consequently a change in artistic view. This calls for an investigation of the relationship between the romantic aspirations of 1944 and the new twist they were given in 1972. Let us recall, then, the poet's "last testament" that seals the volume *Landscape of Sun and Frost* (1944).[8]

צַוָּאָה

אִם תֹּאבַד תֵּבֵל וְתִכְלֶה בָּאֵשׁ הַשּׁוֹאֶגֶת,
בְּעוֹד מוֹעֵד אָשִׁיר עַל כְּבוֹד־הָאָדָם וּמֶרְחֲבֵי־שֶׁמֶשׁ.
תִּהְיֶינָה מִלַּי גֵּאוֹת כְּנוֹצוֹת־טַוָּס וְתוֹכָן רָצוּף רַחֲמִים.

בְּטֶרֶם יְעֻקַּר מַסַּד־בַּיִת, תֵּעָצֵר נְקִיפַת־לֵב,
בְּטֶרֶם יְבַקְשׁוּ כּוֹכָבִים דּוֹקְרִים עֵינֵי־הַזְּכוּכִית לָאָדָם, —
אֵלֶּה נִיבִים חוֹתְכִים כָּל שְׁחוֹר־אַכְזְרִיּוּת יַחֲוִירוּ,
אֵלֶּה נִיבִים כַּיּוֹנִים הַהוֹגוֹת כָּל חֶסֶד יָאִירוּ.

A Will

If the world is lost and ends in the roaring fire,
While yet there is time I sing of man's glory and sunny open spaces.
Let my words be peacock-proud but inherently imbued with mercy.

Before homes are uprooted, before heartbeats stop,
before piercing stars seek out man's glassy eyes,
these cutting utterances will whiten all dark cruelty,
these utterances like cooing doves will illuminate all kindness.

Placed as it is at the very end of the book, "A Will" clearly complements, in message as well as in tone and expression, the heroic manifesto of the opening poem.[9] Although the world is on the verge of a catastrophe, words can still function and have a lasting effect on the real world outside them. This faith in the power of language is precisely what the poem "Words Are Gone" negates. Inasmuch as the poems in the third section of the book are arranged more or less chronologically, the fact that "A Will" *follows* "Words Are Gone" (although it had been published one year before) must be meaningful. Apparently, the utter despair expressed in "Words Are Gone" was not deemed suitable for an artistic framing of the book as a whole; it would have undermined the romantic aspirations and promises conveyed by the structure of the book. It is also possible that the strong Hebraic color of this poem was felt as an appropriate final crescendo only for a section dealing with the Holocaust. Indeed, the opening strophe is so highly traditional in its rhythm, diction, and intertextual connotations, that translation can hardly do it justice:

אָזְלוּ מִלִּים...

I. אֶת הַמִּלָּה כַּחַלָּמִישׁ תְּבַקְשׁוּ מֶנִּי, אֶת הַמִּלָּה־הַגַּחֶלֶת,
זוֹ שֶׁתִּסְפֹּג דַּם־עַמִּי, זוֹ תַּחֲלִימֵהוּ כַּצֳּרִי.
אַךְ אַלְלַי כִּי בִּימֵי־שֹׁד הָיָה הַנִּיב כְּצִפּוֹר שְׁבוּרַת־גַּף,
כְּסֻכָּה צָרַת־קִיר־וָגַג,
הָכִיל לֹא תֵּדַע מַשָּׂא־נֶהִי.

II. אֵין שָׁמִיר יְפַלַּח הַיַּתְמוּת הַמְּרוּדָה לְלֵילוֹתֵינוּ:
וְהַדָּם — אֵי סֶכֶר יִסְתֹּם נַהֲרוֹתָיו בְּגֵאוּתָם,
אֵי צִנּוֹר יְנַהֲלֵהוּ לְוְרִידֵי־יְלָדִים נִטְבָּחוּ?
וְהַצְּרִי — אֵי מַרְפֵּא לְאָדָם חַי וְאֵינוֹ נִטְרָף,
עַל אֵיזֶה מַזָּל מְדֻמֶּה — שִׁלּוּמִים לַקָּרְבָּן?

III. גַּם מִלִּים אָזָלוּ.
שְׁמָשׁוֹת חֲדָשׁוֹת, יֵינוֹת עַתִּיקִים
שׁוּב לֹא יָנוּבוּ בָּהֶן.

'Azelu Milim...

I. 1. *'Et ha-milá ka-chalamísh tevakshu ménni, 'et ha-milá ha-gachélet,*
2. *zo she-tispóg dam-'amí, zo tachliméhu ka-tzóri.*
3. *'Ach 'alelái ki bi-yemei shod haya hanív ke-tzipór shvurat-gáf,*
4. *ke-suká tzarat-kir-vagág,*
5. *hachil ló teda' masa-néhi.*

Words Are Gone

I. 1. A flint-like word you ask of me, a coal-word,
2. to absorb my people's blood, to heal them as with balm.
3. But alas that in these violent days any utterance is but a broken-winged bird,
4. a shelter [hut] of narrow-walls-and-roof,
5. unable to hold an oracular lament.

The genre as well as the rhetorical situation are quite transparent. The poetic seer is asked to be a comforting prophet, but all he can produce is an elegy. In fact, he is asked to fulfill what he has formerly promised in "A Will." Both poems treat the same referent—"the word," *ha-mila* or *milai* (my words) and "the utterance," *ha-niv* or *nivim* (plural). Nevertheless, they significantly diverge in their respective similes. The proud peacock and the cooing dove are replaced by a broken-winged bird—a far cry from the bereaved eagle we encountered in the opening manifesto.[10] Paradoxically, the helplessness of language triggers a heavier reliance on bound expressions. Thus, the poem evokes not only Bialik's prophetic/elegiac stance, but specific biblical utterances of diatribes, of lamentations, and of promised redemption. While the title is reminiscent of "*'Al ha-Shechita*" [On the Slaughter], Bialik's famous lament/diatribe, the poem itself is permeated with clear echoes of the elegiac moods of Jeremiah, Isaiah, and Job.[11] These sources reveal a peculiar fusion of wrath and consolation, of vengeance and lamentation—the very ambiguity that underlies the figurative structure of this poem.

At first glance it is not clear, for instance, how a rock or coal (ember) can absorb blood or heal like balm; but *chalamish*, a synonym for the words *sela'* or *tzor* (rock, flint), is not only associated with strength and power, but also signals the benevolence of Divine providence (Deuteronomy 32:13, 8:15 and Psalms 114:8); and *gachelet*, despite its copious negative connotations (in Proverbs and Psalms), can also stand for survival (2 Samuel 14:7), and was canonized precisely as such by Bialik.[12]

Yet neither strength nor healing can now be provided by verbal expression. Reversing the sheltering associations of *suka* (cf. Psalms 27:5, Isaiah 4:6), the poet-prophet denies the potential of language to deliver even *masa-nehi* (an oracle of lament). This oxymoronic collocation sums it all up: Words are powerless to utter either oracles or wrath or words of mourning.

It is evident by now that the opening strophe is structured as a self-contained elegy, with its own rhetorical and closural effects. The second strophe is anticlimactic; representational rather than figurative, and more contemporary in diction and syntax, it inadvertently confirms the assertion made by the title:

II. 6. *'Ein shamir yefalach ha-yatmut ha-meruda le-leilotenu;*
7. *ve-ha-dam—'ei secher yistom naharotav be-ge'utam,*
8. *'ei tzinor yenahalenu li-vridei-yeladim nitbachu?*
9. *Ve-ha-tzeri—'ei marpeh le-'adam chai ve'eino nitraf,*
10. *'al 'eize mazal medumeh — shilumim la-korban?*

II. 6. No sharp blade could pierce our wretched orphaned nights;
7. And our blood—where is the dam to block its rivers when rising?
8. Where is the channel to carry it into the veins of slaughtered children?

9. And the balm—where is the cure for a man alive and not yet torn apart,
10. on what imaginary planet—retribution for the victim [sacrifice]?

However, a more successful verification is attained in the third strophe:

III. 11. *Gam milim 'azalu.*
12. *Shemashot chadashot, yeinot 'atikim*
13. *shuv lo yanuvu ba-hen.*

III. 11. Even words are gone.
12. New suns, ancient wines
13. will never flourish [speak] in them again.

Since words cannot effect any change, not even express emotions, this elegy ends on a different note. Rhetorical devices and high diction unexpectedly disappear, lines are shortened, and ideas are conveyed in a purely imagistic technique, with no intervention of the poetic voice. The immediacy of expression is quite striking; potential Scriptural connotations do not detract from the basically universal appeal of such images as "new suns" and "old wine." Their significance is further enriched when we place them in the wider context of Preil's own verse. The possibility, which is negated here, of poetically recreating "new suns" calls to mind the initial promise to renew the moon and revive the expiring sun (see "Notes on an Ancient Parchment"). "Ancient wines," on the other hand, can be conceived as an updated and more universally accepted antithesis of new suns/moons, thus replacing the ancient parchment itself. The traditional (crimson and black) "rhymes" of the opening statement (line 9) are here superseded by the less formally determined "word" or "utterance." But even on this level, the power of verbal expression is denied. This is successfully conveyed by the final image: The verb *yanuvu* is commonly construed as "thrive" or "flourish," and as such, should be read figuratively in connection with suns and wines. With a slight phonetic change (*u* to *i*), it also contains the noun *niv* (utterance),[13] thus activating the less familiar meaning of the verb—to utter or speak (based on Proverbs 10:11). It is this secondary meaning or reading that actually integrates the final image with the rest of the poem. It enables us to perceive the semantic equivalences of the poem, despite and beyond its formal divergences. This double perception can readily motivate the syntagmatic structure of the poem. Its changing technique is the logical conclusion as well as the artistic realization of its pessimistic message.

It should be clear by now that "Words Are Gone" demonstrates three experimental phases in Preil's early period—the elevated rhetoric of the prophetic stance, the speaking rhythms simulating colloquial speech (though still disrupted by heightening devices), and the seemingly voiceless and imagistic miniature, which will later usurp the center of Preil's mature verse.

Obviously, the order of appearance of these stages is not arbitrary. It prefigures the direction of Preil's evolution from prophetic pathos and romantic rhetoric to the imagistic understatement. In the framework of the poem itself, this progression is motivated by the experiences of World War II. Because the emergence of Anglo-American Imagism is historically associated with feelings of doom and despair, which were prevalent on the eve of World War I (see Smith, 1968:238–240), we may conclude that *in his generic/stylistic evolution, Preil personally recapitulated a central chapter in the history of Western literary Modernism.*[14] A similar three-stage progression also underlies the prosodic structure of this poem, thus further supporting our contention. The first strophe exhibits a degree of organization that we have not hitherto encountered in Preil's poems. Three rhythmic systems seem to overlap here: (a) the biblical, (b) the purely accentual, and (c) the syllabo-tonic.

Biblical parallelism is the first perceived organizing principle of the opening two lines. They constitute a biblical verse (a bi-colon), complete with its paratactic hemistichs, anaphoric repetitions (*'et...'et / zo...zo*), and internal semantic synonymity. A more complex design marks lines 3 through 5; if line 5 is moved back to line 4 (where it rhythmically belongs, as we shall presently see), we will get a bi-colon with a chiastic symmetry. The second hemistich of line 3 corresponds to the first hemistich of lines 4–5.

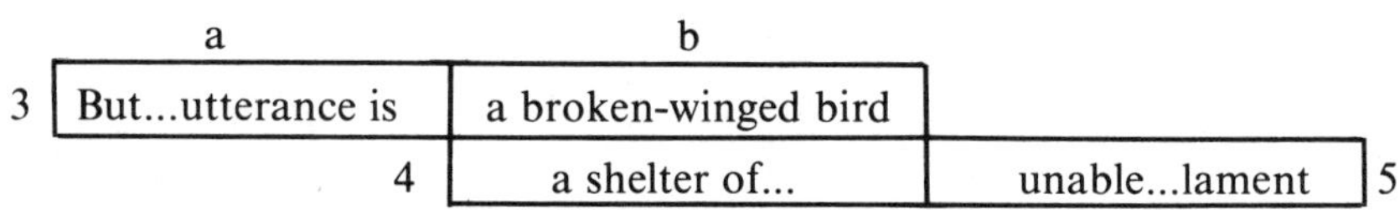

Figure B

Conditioned by the internal parallelism of the former bi-colon, we tend to read hemistich 3:b and 4 as an independent colon, consequently rearranging the order of lines 3 through 5:

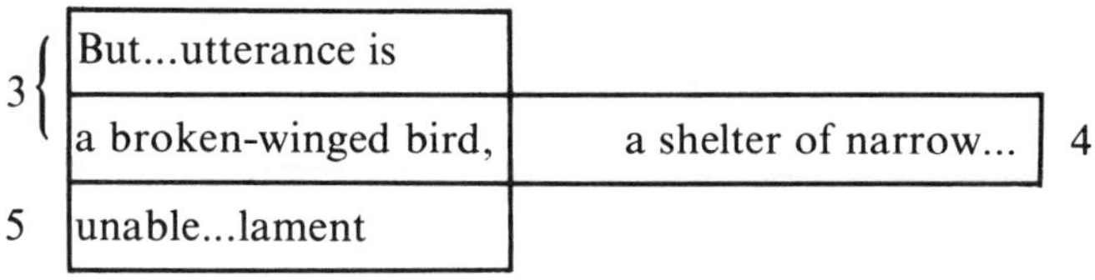

Figure C

The effect of this semantic-figurative chiasm somewhat resembles that of syntactic enjambment: This chiasm runs against line-boundaries, thus avoiding the danger of monotony inherent in symmetrical parallelism.

The same tension revitalizes the accentual scheme of the strophe. The wide range of line lengths (between eight and twenty syllables) is considerably reduced if we merge lines 4 and 5; this yields syllable counts of twenty, sixteen, eighteen, and seventeen. If we use the bi-colon (rather than the line) as a rhythmic unit, the symmetry is even greater: thirty-six and thirty-five. The same holds true for the number of accents: The variety in beat count (5, 4, 5, 2 or 3, 2 or 3) can be rearranged as a regular alternation of 5 + 4, 5 + 4 (the weaker beats being canceled out in a longer unit).

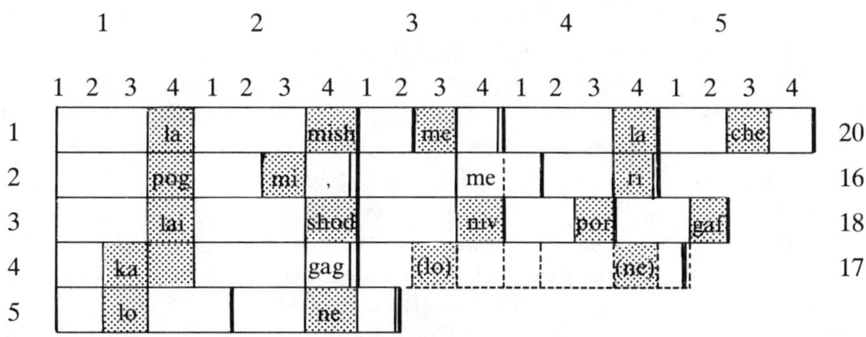

Figure D

Rubrics represent phrase-groups, *not* syllables or words.

Again, this balanced rhythm is violated by the typographical arrangement of the lines. It is further upset by the chiastic parallelism of lines 3 and 4. Even though there is no overt caesura in line 3, we do tend to pause after the third beat, conditioned by the inertia of line 1. This releases 3b to be read together with 4 as a four-beat colon divided evenly by a caesura, analogous to line 2.

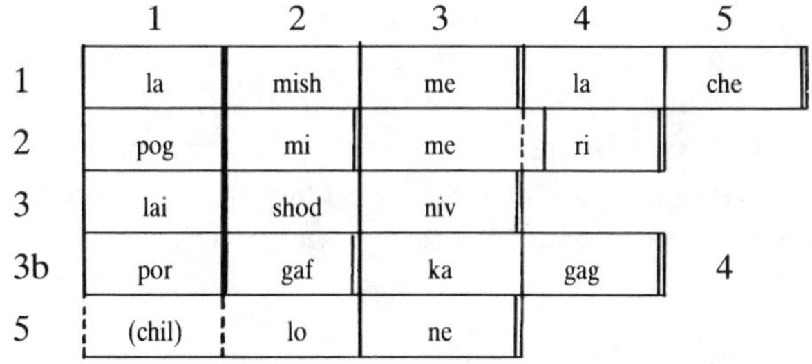

Figure E

These two schemes are not mutually exclusive. On the contrary, it is precisely their existence side by side that lends to this strophe its vital rhythmic and syntactic counterpoint. It seems that Preil found a viable means of compensation for the disadvantage of free-rhythms (cf. Hough, 1960:104): Line rhythms are juxtaposed against chiastic parallelism rather than against an abstract metric grid. It is not as if a metric net did not exist here; in fact, the syllabo-tonic regularity exhibited by these lines is greater than any we have so far encountered. The first bi-colon is perfectly paeonic; in lines 3 through 5 the paeonic mesh is disrupted precisely where a caesura is activated and the chiasm is at work (3b and 4). Still, syllabo-tonic meter is not the dominant system of this poem, and its regularity is only a corollary of the other two systems.[15]

Curiously enough, this kind of rhythmic variety, achieved by a juxtaposition of synonymic and chiastic parallelism, is characteristic of one of the longest disputed biblical prosodic systems, i.e., the prototypal book of threnodic literature, the book of Lamentations (*'Eicha*).[16] This should not come as a surprise; consciously or unconsciously the structure of this book has been the formalistic model of many elegies and laments throughout post-biblical times. What seems unusual is the fact that in its lexicon and rhetorical devices our first strophe does not rely at all on Lamentations. These are somehow relegated to the second strophe, whose rhythm, by contrast, shows no affinity to Lamentations.

The organizing principle of the second strophe is that of the catalogue—the dominant feature of "speaking" rhythms as in Walt Whitman.[17] There are four rhetorical questions here, all beginning with *'ei*, (where?) or *'eizeh* (which?). Reinforced by two occurrences of *'ein*/*'eino* (is not), they clearly echo the Hebrew name of Lamentations, *'Eicha* (how). Except for this device, this strophe lacks any distinct formal properties; it has no internal parallelism, no enjambment, and no interplay between different prosodic systems. Even the typically elegiac tension between short and long lines is missing. The syllable count is from thirteen to seventeen and the beat is a dull 5,5,4,4,4.

A third prosodic type is encountered in the last strophe. It is not the tightly organized system of the first nor the loose monotony of the second. This imagistic miniature features a variety of line lengths and beat counts—six, ten, and seven syllables and two, four, and three beats. Predictably, the second line is divided evenly by a caesura (2:2) and exhibits an antithetic parallelism. The disappearance of the paeonic scheme is a meaning change; metric scanning shows a variety of bi- and tri-syllabic feet:

	1	2	3	4	5	6	7	8	9	10
1			gam	mi	lim	'a	za	lu		
2	shma	shot	cha	da	shot	yei	not	‘a	ti	kim
3	shuv	lo	ya	nu	vu	ba	hen			

Figure F

Rubrics represent syllables; double lines indicate a caesura.

As on other levels of expression, this rhythmic structure suggests Preil's future development. In his more interesting poems, this narrower range of beats and meters will later be combined with an interplay of line and phrase similar to the one evidenced in our first strophe, but without the strong biblical features that accompany it here.

As mentioned before, this kind of imagist miniature was quite rare in the Hebrew verse of Preil's first decade of writing. Although the first Hebrew representatives of this genre had been written as early as 1937 (see below, chap. IX), most of the Hebrew poems written from 1938 on belong to the rhetorical genre. In his Yiddish poetry, on the other hand, there was never any trace of the rhetoric or pathos of the romantic impulse, even in its Shne'urian guise. Here the dominant posture was that of the modernist understatement. It is, therefore, in this early realm of the poet's creativity that we should look for the initial impulse for his imagism.

Chapter VIII

Yiddish Beginnings: Études in Imagism (1935-1936)

A poem should not mean
But be.

Archibald MacLeish, "Ars Poetica" (1926)

In 1935, when Preil made his début in the *Nyu Yorker Vokhnblat* (February 8), Yiddish was a poetic milieu in which "modernism" had been a catchword for two decades. Thus, a year later (February 1936), the modernist periodical *In Zikh* became a natural home for Preil's *Dray Lider*.[1] His contribution may be readily perceived as another link in a recently established poetic tradition.[2]

Typical of Preil's Yiddish début is the publication of small groups of imagistic miniatures that give the impression of études, not unlike the way young painters practice by drawing still lifes. Indeed, these miniatures reveal different degrees of compliance with the tenets of the Imagists, who were quite openly trying to "paint in words," and for this reason sought their inspiration in the Far-Eastern tradition (China and Japan), which has always combined poetry and painting (Gombrich, 1957:99–106; Kenner, 1971: 192–222; Yip, 1974).

In contradistinction to his reflective Hebrew verse, Preil's Yiddish beginnings avoid conceptual or generalized topics. They hardly lend themselves to cognitive paraphrasing. From "*Frost*" (1935) to "*Shpet Zumer*" [Late Summer] (1936), there is a growing attempt to render a slice of reality, be it internal or external, without the intervention of the poetic voice or any other kind of rhetoric. This is also felt on the figurative level, where the simile, so common in Preil's early Hebrew verse, is displaced by the metaphor. Particularly prevalent is the metaphor of the kind <a> is <b>, which is classified by Christine Brook-Rose as the copula-metaphor (1965: chapter V, especially 112–113), "the most direct way of linking a metaphor to its proper term or terms" (*op. cit.*, p. 105).[3] This directness seems to play an important role in Preil's poetics, and it is later transferred to his mature Hebrew verse.[4]

Another characteristic of Preil's oeuvre which has its roots in these

Yiddish études is his use of colors. The author of these poems seems to compete not with music, as French symbolists strived to do, but with painting. His fascination with colors and with the effects of light attests to a visual interest typical of French Impressionism (cf. Pratt, 1963:24–25). This will later surface in his Hebrew verse, where the names of Monet and Van Gogh constitute a large part of his figurative repertory, and where the poetic enterprise is often compared to the fine arts.[5] Furthermore, as is shown below, Preil clearly employs colors not only descriptively or ornamentally, but as an encoding of thematic oppositions (cf. Schwartz, 1972). Nevertheless, visual dimensions do not overshadow the audible ones. The euphony created by some of these poems is unmatched by any of Preil's Hebrew poems; it is perhaps unique in all his works. This should be attributed to the influence of Glatstein's early verse, which abounded in language experimentations and phonic orchestrations (Hadda, 1976), in accordance with the *In Zikh* platform to put to use "such elements as alliteration," which had hitherto been neglected in Yiddish verse (*In Zikh*, 1920:16).

What should be stressed, however, is that the aesthetic problem faced by young Preil was that of a transfer from sense impressions to verbal expression (cf. Schwartz, 1979). Among these sense impressions, sight—although by no means the only one—occupied a central position. This explains such "painterly" titles as "*Peyzazh*" [Landscape], "*In April Ram*" [In April's Frame], or "*Vunder Shpigl*" [Wonder Mirror]. Predictably, the need to recreate verbally concrete sensory perception affected choices of the poetic diction. No wonder, then, that in solving this problem Preil relied less on traditional literary allusions, collocations, and associations (as he did in his early Hebrew verse), and more on *ad-hoc* correlations between different scales of sensory data, mainly sight and sensation but also sound, taste, and scent. These sensory details, generally expressed in the most common idiom, are tightly organized so as to guide the reader in "making sense" out of the supposedly objective description, without the aid of the poetic voice. As we shall see, this self-effacement was not immediately achieved. The author of the heroic Hebrew "I" (see chap. VI) must have found it difficult to relegate his own voice to the background. What helped him to overcome this hurdle was the discovery of the encoding potential of even the most colloquial vocabulary. In the following discussion, we demonstrate the development of this mechanism by a detailed analysis of his first poem, "*Frost*," and by briefly elucidating the rest of his early poems.*

*For the convenience of readers with Yiddish comprehension but with no reading facility, all Yiddish poems are transcribed.

Frost (1966:53)	פֿראָסט
1. *Shney-shvalbn in geflister*	שניי־שוואַלבן אין געפֿליסטער
2. *Zaynen fregtseykhns*	זײַנען פֿרעגצייכנס
3. *Oyf shtare shoybn,*	אויף שטאַרע שויבן,
4. *Hoykhn vaysn retenish*	הויכן ווײַסן רעטעניש
5. *Oyf shvartser nakht;*	אויף שוואַרצער נאַכט;
6. *Shney geflister iz blanker sod*	שניי־געפֿליסטער איז בלאַנקער סוד
7. *Oyf groye flakhn.*	אויף גרויע פֿלאַכן.
8. *Ver sheptshet vaysn goyrl*	ווער שעפּטשעט ווײַסן גורל
9. *Unter vognrod?*	אונטער וואָגן־ראָד?
10. *Shney shvalbn in geflister*	שניי־שוואַלבן אין געפֿליסטער
11. *Zaynen vayse kameyes*	זײַנען ווײַסע קמיעות
12. *Oyf shvere tirn fun shrek,*	אויף שווערע טירן פֿון שרעק, —
13. *Shimern vi hel gezang*	שימערן ווי העל געזאַנג
14. *In tunkl blut.*	אין טונקל בלוט.

1. Snow-swallows in a whisper
2. are question marks
3. on stiff [congealed] panes,
4. breathing white riddles
5. on black night;
6. snow-whisper is a glittering secret
7. on grey plains.
8. Who whispers white fate [destiny]
9. under a wagon-wheel?
10. Snow-swallows in a whisper
11. are white charms [amulets]
12. on heavy doors of dread,
13. shimmering like a bright chant [singing]
14. [in] through dark blood.

Although reprinted in *Lider* as one unit, "*Frost*" had been originally published in three strophes of seven, two, and five lines. Such a segmentation makes sense because it singles out the rhetorical question (line 8–9) which subverts the objectivity that lines 1–7 strive to achieve. Indeed, a strong impression of pictorial descriptiveness is attained by minimizing the number of verb predicates and by restricting them to the present tense (lines 4,8,13). In fact, we have here a series of "still life" presentations (technically speaking they are copula-metaphors), which are constructed along parallel lines:

1.	snow-swallows	tenor: concrete / metaphoric
2.	question marks	vehicle a: metaphoric
3.	(on) panes	complement: concrete
4.	riddles	vehicle b: metaphoric
5.	(on) night	complement: concrete (?)
6.	snow / secret	tenor & vehicle c: concrete / metaphoric
7.	(on) plains	complement c: concrete (?)

The result is a verbally constructed static nature picture whose concrete details are quite minimal:[6] snow (flakes?) on window panes, through which, presumably, a pair of eyes watch the night and some undefined plains outside. Paradoxically, most of these concrete materials are derived from the vehicles, while the tenor itself is presented through a construct-metaphor (snow-swallows) which altogether blurs the demarcation lines between the concrete and the imagined. A further fusion is caused by attributing visual dimensions to abstract notions ("white riddles" and "glittering secret"). Clearly, a syntagmatic reading of the poem does not help too much in sorting out the described reality from the impressions associated with it. However, when we read the metaphoric chain paradigmatically and separate the vehicles from their complements, we get two series of equivalents, only one of which seems to make sense:

A.	question marks	(2)	B.	panes	(3)
	riddles	(4)		night	(5)
	secret	(6)		plains	(7)

Group A forms a clearly defined semantic field, one we can entitle "the unknown"—a category that introduces a process of human cognition.[7] The members of group B, on the other hand, do not seem to enter into any kind of relationship. Moreover, in their own right, the two groups do not show any organizational properties either. Only when the attributes defining each of these members are added, does an interesting net of relationships surface:

A.	_____	(2)	B.	stiff	(3)
	white	(4)		black	(5)
	glittering	(6)		grey	(7)

If we replace the unmarked member (line 2) with the softness implied by the falling snow (line 1), two sets of equivalences emerge which enter into an oppositional relationship. What strikes the reader first are the color contrasts (white vs. black, glitter vs. grey); but there is more here than meets the eye (quite literally). First, the opposition white and glitter vs. black and grey is intuitively understood as positive vs. negative. This forces the reader to perceive the "unknown" as valorized, perhaps even against his better judgment. Secondly, the mere participation in each group imposes relations of inter-sensory equivalence among its members. Thus, *shtare* which conveys freezing and stiffness is automatically identified with the negativized black and grey; whereas the surmised "soft" (inferred from the snow-swallows but also reconstructable as the polar opposite of *shtare*) is intuitively positivized.

This inter-sensory transfer leads us to an issue that has been extensively dealt with in art criticism: What relationships can be established between moods or emotional attitudes and sounds, colors, or shapes? E.H. Gombrich's reply, based on the ideas of both semanticists and information theorists, is unambiguous: "There is some inborn disposition in all of us to equate certain sensations with certain feeling tones" ("Expression and Communication," 1962, in Gombrich, 1978:58). In order to help us establish these relational equations he supplies the following chart.[8]

Feeling		Sensation		Sight	
					red
				bright	
			light		
		warm			
friendly	gay				
hostile	sad				
		cold			
			heavy		
				dark	
					blue

Figure G

If Gombrich's friendly/hostile terms are replaced by +/− markings, Preil's "objective" depiction may be conceived as being divided into a hostile (concrete?) world (panes, night, plains) and a friendly metaphoric world of snow-swallows, mystery, and enigma. In this connection it may also be suggested that the choice of *shvalbn* (swallows) was probably phonetically and not only semantically determined. It helps to establish the initial alliteration which is repeated throughout the poem: ***sh**ney* ***sh**valbn* ... ***sh**tare* ***sh**oybn* ... *(reteni**sh**)* ... ***sh**vartser* ... ***sh**ney* ... ***sh**ept**sh**et* ... ***sh**ney* ... ***sh**valbn* ... ***sh**vere* ... ***sh**rek* ... ***sh**imern*. This alliteration onomatopoeically recreates the whispered mystery that appears to be valorized by the poem. It is reinforced, of course, by the sibilants of *geflister* (whisper) and *sod* (secret), which are echoed in the thrice-repeated *vayse/n* (white).

In view of this strongly marked distribution we should perhaps pause for a moment to realize how far off we are from the objective nature description promised by the title ("*Frost*"). The extent to which this poem deviates from the expected could best be gauged by comparing it to Y. L. Teller's "First Frost" or "Snow Shovelers" (translated in Appendix 2). With the exception of a few similes or synesthetic statements, Teller's poems are basically chains of descriptive details, whose objectivity is warranted by both the effacement of the poetic voice and the avoidance of any other encoding organization or markedness.[9] Obviously, Preil's "*Frost*" takes another turn. It does not focus on external realities, but rather interprets them; the interpretation is subtle, because it is implicit. It inheres in the imagery rather than explicating it. Still, the poet seems unable to trust this indirect instruction for his readers. His poem cannot just be; it has to mean. Therefore, a rhetorical question is interjected, and with it the grand issues of fate and destiny. The sound of the crushed snow on the road is taken as an intimation of human concerns and fears which hitherto could have only been surmised.

This rhetorical question adds another dimension to the color white. In collocation with "fate" and "wagon-wheel" (and outside the opposition black vs. white), white is liable to take on a negative markedness and to ominously evoke death ("shrouds").[10] Consequently, an ambiguity is created between the opposing connotations of "white" in lines 1–7 and lines 8–9. Similarly, the verb *sheptshet* (whisper) seems to contradict the positivized semantic field of *geflister* (whispering) and its paradigmatic equivalents. This seeming paradox is neutralized in the third part (lines 10–14). The new copula-metaphor, the "charms" or "amulets," contains in it both negative and positive connotations: It has magical powers to defend *against* unknown destinies. These charms are needed because the concrete foundations of the world created by this poem turn out to be the "heavy doors of dread." Such a sudden metaphoric twist (this time using a "genitive link metaphor," according to Brook-Rose's classification [1965:146]), in which the concrete (windows, night, plains, doors) suddenly dissolves into the abstract (dread), leaves the reader with nothing visual to hold onto. Finally, with the only simile of the poem ("shimmering like a bright chant"), the whole description is internalized and humanized. The struggle between white and black represents the internal battle between verbal charms (*gezang* [chanting]), and dread (in "dark blood").[11] Interestingly, the last adjectives used in the poem fit smoothly into the scheme offered by Gombrich — "heavy" and "dark" join "cold" and "black" on the negative pole, while "bright" and "shimmering" reinforce the positive pole of "white," "glitter," and "soft." Curiously enough, what is achieved within the boundaries of each pole is an indirect synesthesis (i.e., a fusion of sense modalities) without the actual use of synesthetic expressions. This retroactively sharpens our perception of the sensations depicted by the text. It also brings us full circle to the question of the relation between this perception and the title of the poem: Have we experienced the "frost" promised by the title?[12] Yes and no. We have definitely had a full share of the sights, sounds, and sensations effected by frost (the crisp glitter, the soft whisper, and the freezing cold). Yet, we have experienced more than that. These multi-dimensional images were transported or translated (*meta-pherein*) into the realms of feelings and attitudes. The cold we were meant to feel and the glitter we were shown were more than literal—they were made to lead toward a belief in the power of song, as an incantation against "white fate."[13] It is not the grand stance of the heroic "I" of "Notes on an Ancient Parchment," but there is still a "human message" here (cf. Pratt, 1963:30; Juhasz, 1974), helped along by the rhetorical question of the poetic voice.

Let us see, then, what happens when this kind of interjection is totally suppressed.

Vunder Shpigl (1966:42)

Meydl-gang in levone
murmlt hele reyd
in tunkeln samet.
Zi blitst oyf shpiglen
shnaydt siluetn
in farankerte ogyn.
Zi trogt heysn vint
iber kile shtern,
ayzikn otem
un zun.

ווּנדער־שפּיגל

מיידל־גאַנג אין לבֿנה
מורמלט העלע רייד
אין טונקעלן סאַמעט.
זי בליצט אויף שפּיגלען,
שנײַדט סילועטן
אין פֿאַראַנקערטע אויגן.
זי טראָגט הייסן ווינט
איבער קילע שטערן,
אײַזיקן אָטעם
און זון.

Wonder Mirror

Girl's walk in moon [light]
murmurs bright words
in dark velvet.
She flashes off mirrors,
cuts silhouettes
in anchored eyes.
She carries a hot wind
over cool stars,
an icy breath
and sun.

Unlike "*Frost*" or "*Peyzazh*" (see p. 53), the title "*Vunder Shpigl*" is less predictable. True, the painterly element is clearly represented by the mirror, which promises a visual reflection of some kind,[14] but because it is a wonder mirror, we should not be surprised at its ability to transcend visual dimensions and capture other sensory perceptions as well (sound and sensation). These different perceptions are again organized in paired oppositions, but this time without the covert markedness imposed on them in "*Frost.*" Paradoxically, the mirror reflection is not static; its dynamic nature derives from the verb-metaphor (murmurs) which replaces the copula-metaphors of the earlier poem. In fact, the opening tenor of the poem is itself an action-noun (*gang* [walk, step]), which is personified through another (human) activity (murmuring bright words). As such, it seems to begin from the point at which "*Frost*" leaves off: The synesthetic perception, *hele reyd* (bright speech) replaces *hel gezang* (bright chant), and *tunkeln samet* (dark velvet) substitutes for *tunkl blut* (dark blood). What is missing here, however, is the subjective element, introduced into "*Frost*" by the connotations of fate, dread, and blood. "*Vunder Shpigl*" is, indeed, an external reflection, aspiring to the state of "absolutely accurate presentation and no verbiage."[15] In place of the question that implies a poetic voice ("*Frost,*" lines 8–9), all we have here is the human source of visual perception, the pair of "anchored eyes," connoting, no doubt, subjective fascination with and attraction to the object perceived.

Predictably, it is just after the introduction of this subjective source of perception that the visual oppositions (bright vs. dark, flashes, vs. silhouettes) are extended to include the opposition of hot vs. cool. If we make use of Gombrich's scheme once more, we can group the bright/hot elements under the "friendly" pole, and thus get a positive valorization of the girl (walk), her speech, her reflection, and whatever she "carries." The "hostile" pole is less homogeneous, including the night, the stars, and plausibly the staring eyes. We can perhaps read into this organization an opposition of human vs. inanimate; but this option is negated by the last lines, which neatly reverse the preceding image (hot → icy; stars → sun), thus subverting the pattern developed by lines 1 through 8. This bars the way to any meaningful interpretation of the mirrored image. It rather underlines the mere existence of a pair of "anchored eyes" fascinated by a set of contrasts for their own sake. It is instructive, however, that even when immersed in the direct presentation of images, Preil could not avoid some kind of oppositional organization (at least at that early stage of his writing).[16] It was only when he learned to manipulate his fascination with polarities that his verse reached its highest level. This he did by avoiding a straightforward presentation either of sense perceptions or of their contrastive framework. The beginnings of these strategies were clearly manifested in the next group of études published in the *Nyu Yorker Vokhnblat* a year later (March 6, 1936).

Oktober

Farpaynigte nakht on shtern
iz a briender shteyn
fun opgrunt gehakt, -
a shvarts shrayendike kro
oyf hayzer farvorlozt
vi nekhtens,
oyf hertser besalmens
in harbst.

אָקטאָבער

פֿארפּײַניגטע נאַכט אָן שטערן
איז אַ בריענדער שטיין
פֿון אָפּגרונט געהאַקט, —
אַ שוואַרץ שרײַענדע קראָ
איף הײַזער פֿאַרוואָרלאָזט
ווי נעכטנס,
איף הערצער בית־עלמינס
אין האַרבסט.

October

An anguished night without stars
is a burning stone
from the abyss hewn, —
a black screaming crow
over houses abandoned
like yesterdays,
on hearts—graveyards
in autumn.

This is the only Yiddish poem not incorporated into *Lider*, and it is not difficult to guess the reason. The pessimism it evokes is unmatched by any of Preil's poems, particularly of the imagist kind. The impact of the purely imagistic expression is undeniably more direct than that of analogous rhetorical verse (cf. "Words Are Gone" in chap. VII, section 2). As in all imagist poems, the immediacy of presentation is unmitigated by verbal adornment or interpretation. But unlike other poems, this poem seems to lack Preil's central compositional device, the polar oppositions which balance his imagistic poems both structurally and thematically. "October" contains only the hostile pole of Gombrich's chart, with nothing of the friendly one. Furthermore, this bleak picture is particularly shocking against the background of former "autumnal" verse (cf. Teller's "*Harbst*" and an untitled poem, Appendix 2). Not unlike "*Frost*," "*Oktober*" unfolds a series of extended copula-metaphors, which are meant to evoke a mood rather than to present an external reality. It differs from "*Frost*" in that there is no tension here between the different parts of the metaphor: *a briender shteyn* (a burning stone) is not contrasted with an abyss, nor a black crow with abandoned houses or graveyards. Only one opposition is hinted at, the one condensed in the tenor itself — night vs. stars. True, syntagmatically it is only the first line that puts into relief the negative model ("without"), which is expanded by the rest of the poem; but lexically the word *stars* is a clue to the potential opposition suppressed or denied by the text. If the word *on* (without) points to the process of negativization which takes place *in* the poem,[17] the word *shtern* (stars) points *outside* the poem—not so much to the real world as to other texts and to known repertories of nature descriptions[18]—stars, moonlight, sky, singing birds, houses in the sun, and . . . heart's joy. It is plausible, then, that the author excluded "*Oktober*" from his collection not only because of its bleak mood, but because of its unusual "negative" manipulation of the models customary in this genre. Characteristically, none of Preil's later autumnal poems (and he wrote many) constitutes such an extreme deviation from the norm as does this abandoned poem.

In April Ram (1966:12)

Ven tsarter friling iz ir ponem
vern oygn taykhn in zunikn dorsht
un s'poykt mayn harts shlyakhn
far ire trit;
Shtern vi toybn vorken
oyf ir brust,
a tseblite levone
shloft in ire hor
un s'shpiglen shkies
ire lipn.

אין אַפּריל־ראַם

ווען צאַרטער פֿרילינג איז איר פּנים
ווערן אויגן טײַכן אין זוניקן דורשט
און ס׳פּויקט מײַן האַרץ שליאַכן
פֿאַר אירע טריט;
שטערן ווי טויבן וואָרקען
אויף איר ברוסט,
אַ צעבליטע לבֿנה
שלאָפֿט אין אירע האָר
און ס׳שפּיגלען שקיעות
אירע ליפּן.

In April's Frame

When gentle spring is her face
eyes become rivers in sunny thirst
and my heart drums out roads
for her step;
stars coo like doves
on her breast,
a blooming moon
sleeps in her hair
and sunsets mirror
her lips.

"In April's Frame" is another portrait of a female figure, a variation on the motif of "Wonder Mirror." However, the emphasis here is less on the visual reflection than on the scrambling of two pictorial codes—the portrait and the nature description. Thus we have rivers and roads, moon and stars, doves and sunsets, all obvious motifs of paintings of spring (April) which are used here to describe a female portrait—hair, face, breast, eyes, and lips. Although the device itself is not new (it is at least as old as the Song of Songs), it is endowed here with a special vitality. Rather unexpectedly this portrait brims over with verbs, and verbs of quite unusual nature. In addition, this is the first poem in which syntactic order is manipulated so as to deautomatize the old tradition: "spring is her face" rather than the customary "her face is...." More importantly, the simplistic use of colors disappears. They can be inferred, however, from the imagery: The eyes must be river-blue; the breast, dove-white; the hair, moon-shine; and the lips, sunset-red. When this technique of inferred attributes is cleverly grafted onto an implicit grid of contrasts, Preil attains one of the most economical of his early nature descriptions, the crisp poem "Late Summer."

Shpet-Zumer (1966:29)	שפּעט־זומער
1. Teg fun hele shoybn	טעג פֿון העלע שויבן
2. un frishn onheyb	און פֿרישן אָנהייב
3. ven farb glantst veykh	ווען פֿאַרב גלאַנצט ווייך
4. oyf pendzlen,	אויף פּענדזלען,
5. un likht zingt	און ליכט זינגט
6. in di hor.	אין די האָר.
7. Nikht fun bloyen roykh	נעכט פֿון בלויען רויך
8. un kalte sofn,	און קאַלטע סופֿן,
9. ven levone iz tsitrin	ווען לבֿנה איז ציטרין
10. oyf di lipn	אויף די ליפּן
11. un shtern-shvalbn	און שטערן־שוואַלבן
12. shimern in tol.	שימערן אין טאָל.

Late Summer

1. Days of bright panes
2. and fresh beginnings
3. when paint [color] shines softly
4. on brushes,
5. and light sings
6. in the hair.
7. Nights of blue smoke
8. and cool endings,
9. when [the] moon is lemon
10. on the lips
11. and star-swallows
12. shimmer in the valley.

This succinct poem, one of "Three Poems" published in *In Zikh* (February 1936), finally reaches a state of being, instead of meaning, or rather it achieves meaning through being. Without sacrificing its pictorial clarity, it manages to create an atmosphere and convey an emotional attitude. This is done by the reduction and manipulation of the figurative and compositional devices we have followed thus far.

The extended copula-metaphor is replaced by a compound-metaphor in which the concrete material outweighs the metaphorical. Bright panes and colorful paint brushes readily conjure up the light effects of a summer day. The personification involved in "light sings in the hair" may be taken for the shining of hair in the sun. Thus, the only abstract notion metaphorized in the description of the day is the concept of "beginning" (line 2). Its attribute, "fresh," is semantically redundant (fresh = new = has just begun), but it functions figuratively as a synesthesis, describing the abstract in terms of the concrete. This concretization facilitates the transition from the abstract, *onheyb*, to its concrete metonymies—paint, morning light, and clear panes. In other words, Preil found here an appropriate "objective correlative," to use Eliot's much-debated term,[19] for the feeling of a new start. A mirror image of this objective correlative is provided by the second half of the poem. Repeating the same syntactic structure, line 7–12 replace each element of the Day depiction by its "antonym" from the Night inventory. Thus we can make the following list:

	Day		*Night*
	bright pane	blue smoke	[blurred, dark]
[hot]	fresh *beginnings*	cool *endings*	[old, stale]
[colorful]	paint	moon	[pale]
	shines softly	lemon	[sour]
[sweet]	(on) brushes	(on) lips	
[sun]	light	stars	[dark]
	sings	shimmer	[discontinuous?]
[human]	(in) hair	(in) valley	[inanimate]

The two central columns demonstrate the internal symmetry of the poetic world created by this poem. It also vividly shows how minimal is the conceptual element actually verbalized in the text, the single opposition of beginnings vs. endings. But this central polarity is dramatized and actualized through a series of metonymic correspondences taken from the inventories of Day and Night, respectively. Although their +/− markedness is clear enough, the number of adjectives (and colors) is surprisingly low. This economy is achieved (a) by the juxtaposition of attributes or objects that belong to *different* sensory domains, e.g., fresh vs. cool, paint vs. lemon (moon); and (b) by leaving out one pole of the opposition (light without dark; sour without sweet). This forces the reader to fill in the gaps and complete the missing information by inferring their unnamed contrasts. Thus, although the text opposes "bright" (panes) to "blue" (smoke) and not to "dark," our sensory experience tells us that smoke can be dark, or at least blurred, and this readily fits in with our semantic intuition that bright should be contrasted/complemented by these added sensory perceptions.[20] The next pair illustrates a more deviant coupling by crossing the boundaries between sense modalities. "Fresh" and "cold" belong to two different categories of sensation; the reader may bring back to the text the proper antonyms, consonant with experience, which the poem has left unused. Such semantic completion concretizes the abstractions defined by them in the most multiple sensory way: Beginnings are viewed not only as fresh, but also as hot or warm, and endings are also old or stale.

This synesthetic principle does not work merely horizontally. Checking the different potential sensations of each pole (added in brackets), we realize that the vertical lines combine the dimensions of sight, sensation, and even taste (fresh, sour [lemon]). *Sound*, however, appears only on one side of the scale; predictably it is the sound of *song*, and it belongs to the positivized pole of Day. Again, we could perhaps read into the description an antithesis of human vs. inanimate (cf. the poem "*Frost*"), but this would do an injustice to the syntagmatic unfolding of the text. In the poem itself, the oppositions are not arranged horizontally (i.e., paradigmatically); they are presented in an asyndetic sequence. Not even the slightest hint of contrast or juxtaposition between the two parts of the poem is expressed by its syntax or lexicon.

This brings us full circle to the "poetics of discontinuity" imported from the Far East (see note 9, above) and to the anti-closural tendency of modern verse (Smith, 1968:234–260). "*Shpet Zumer*" definitely does not "click like a box," since "closure in the 'pure' imagist poem was usually weak" (*op. cit.*, pp. 237, 255). This was, of course, part of the intended effect, "the object of objectivity" (*ibid.*); but such effects, acceptable as they were in Yiddish (and, needless to say, in English) verse, were not acceptable in Hebrew. It was not yet possible to write Hebrew poems that "did not assert the speaker's motives or personality" (*ibid.*) or that threw "a group of elements together without predication" (Frye, 1957:123). Little wonder that the first imagistic étude translated by Preil into Hebrew was of a rather different nature and actually violated the Imagists' principle "not to deal in vague generalities, however magnificent and sonorous" (Pratt, 1963:22). But before turning to this poem and to Preil's practice of autotranslation, a word on his Yiddish imagist prosody and diction is in order.

In his early Yiddish poems Preil observed the imagist aspect of the Inzikhists' tenets quite faithfully (see his 1957 article, discussed on p. 59 above). These poems present not only "the union between the poet's soul and the phenomenon about which he sings, as well as the specific image or images which he sees *within himself* while so doing" (*In Zikh*, 1920:6); they also use the language of common speech and prefer the musical, free cadence to the conventional "sequence of the metronome" (*op. cit.*, p. 25). This fusion of conversational idiom and rhythm is likely to create its own problems by running the risk of crossing the boundaries between prose and poetry. However, this danger does not seem imminent in Preil's case. The strongly metaphorical (even synesthetic) flavor of his presentation renders it poetic despite the colloquial vocabulary. Indeed, during this early period it was mainly imagery that attracted Preil's creative imagination. His use of rhythmo-syntactic figures, on the other hand, seems quite predictable and unimaginative. On the whole, there is a complete overlapping of syntactic and rhythmic units. This is underlined by the regular use of syntactic anaphoras. Conjunctions (*un*) or prepositions (*oyf, in*) are found more often than not at the beginning of lines, usually those in even positions (line 2, 4, 6, etc.).

The lines themselves are short. The range of most of them is from three to six syllables; few reach seven, eight, or nine syllables. The greatest variety of line length is in the poem "*In April Ram*" (3–9), which is the most dynamic in its imagery as well. Two-syllable lines occur occasionally, but only in conjunction with (modest) enjambments, when syntactic complements are isolated from the rest of the expression (see the endings of "*Oktober*" and "*Vunder Shpigl*").

The number of accents is less varied: It does not exceed three per line. This holds true even for the longer lines because of the prevalence of polysyllabic words as well as proclitic and enclitic combinations, as, for example, *in geflíster, vi hel gezáng, farpáynigte, shráyendike*. This prosodic feature of Yiddish was described in detail by Hrushovski, who argued that, rhythmically, Yiddish was influenced by Slavic patterns and not by German ones, despite its Germanic origin (1954:241–245). What is of interest for us, however, is that this natural paeonic distribution is apparently also responsible for the nature of Preil's early *Hebrew* free verse, as described in chapter VII, section 2 (pp. 104–105). However, when the long reflective strophes are superseded by the short imagistic lines, this paeonicity tends to disappear; and it is not surprising that this trend, too, begins in the Yiddish études. The polysyllabics are often counterbalanced by one-syllable words, thus considerably modulating the intervals between stresses. It seems, then, that the greatest prosodic variety is achieved by Preil in the ratio between line length and accent count, which can range from one accent per line of two to four syllables, to three accents per line of seven to nine syllables. His natural syntactic building-block, however, is a line of two or three accents; the latter shows a tendency to divide into two and one, usually at the end of a poem (or a phrase). This sometimes has a closural effect, particularly when combined with a lapse into tonic meters (cf. Hrushovski, 1954:256–257; Smith, 1968:93–95). The end of "*Oktober*," for instance, sounds like a catalectic trimeter of amphibrachs:

Oyf hértser besálmens
in hárbst.

The closure of "*Vunder Shpigl*", on the other hand, is a trimeter of binary feet—two trochees and an iamb: *aýzikn ótem / in zún.*

As on other levels, "*Shpet Zumer*" evidences a somewhat more sophisticated prosodic awareness than the other early poems. It is composed of only two sentences, spread over twelve short lines. As we have shown, the imagery of these two long sentences is organized in an oppositional relationship. Interestingly, this semantic polarity is contradicted by a syntactic and rhythmic symmetry:

1				–	∪	∪	∪	–
2		∪	∪	–	∪			
3			∪	–			∪	–
4			∪	–				
5			∪	–				–
6		∪	∪	–				
7				–	∪	∪	∪	–
8	∪	∪	∪	–				
9		∪	∪	–	∪	∪	∪	–
10		∪	∪	–				
11			∪	–				–
12				–		∪	∪	–

Although not identical in their details, the two halves of the poem echo each other in their relational makeup. The two opening lines (1 and 7) are identical and, except for the last two lines, each consecutive pair (1–2, 3–4, etc.) forms a unit with a constant ratio of 2:1 accents. The change in lines 11–12 (2:2) obviously functions as a rhythmic closure. This, in turn, runs against the thematic "open" closure of the poem and perhaps encourages a paradigmatic rereading of the type we suggested above. It is evident, in any case, that the interplay between line and sentence (or rhythm and theme), which surfaces later in Preil's mature Hebrew verse, developed from the modest experiments we have described here.

But what made this development possible? How did the transition from one language to another, or from one literary system to another, take place? Answers to these questions may be found in the poet's own "bilingual system," in the specific strategies of literary transfer utilized in his autotranslations.

Chapter IX

Autotranslation as Literary Transfer

שִׁעוּר בְּתִרְגּוּם

הַמְתַרְגֶּמֶת נִסְּתָה לַחֲשֹׂף
דְּבָרִים שֶׁלֹּא נֶאֶמְרוּ
אֶת אָפְנוּת הַמְכֻוָּן וְהַהַסְוָאָה
אֶת כֹּרַח הַגִּשּׁוּשׁ וְהַהַגָּעָה
(פַּעַם קָרְאָה מָה בְּפָנַי).

יוֹתֵר מִכֹּל חָשְׁבָה לַחֲרֹשׁ
בַּתַּשְׁתִּית הַמְיַחֶדֶת, לְזַהוֹת
זִיפֵי שָׁרָשִׁים, כְּוִיַּת הָעִצּוּב.
הָיוּ רְגָעִים שֶׁנִּמְשְׁכָה לְדִמּוּי כְּמוֹ
עֲצֵי בֹּקֶר שָׁרִים צִפֳּרִים
לַמִּקְרִי הַמִּתְזַמֵּר כְּמֵאֵלָיו
אִירוֹנְיָה דַּקָּה, כִּסּוּפִים.

הַמָּקוֹר, אֶפְשָׁר לְהַנִּיחַ, עוֹדֶנּוּ מָקוֹר
הִיא לֹא הָפְכָה אוֹתוֹ לַאֲחֻזָּתָהּ
אוֹ לִכְלִי שֵׁנִי, אַחֵר, שֶׁלִּי.
כָּל בַּיִת שֶׁבַּשִּׁיר, נִדְמֶה, מוּגָן — כָּרָגִיל
בֵּין סְתָו לִסְתָו מִסַּכָּה אֲמִינוּתוֹ.

עִם זֹאת אֲנִי שׁוֹאֵל אֵיךְ טֶקְסְט קָרִיר־זָהִיר
גַּם הוּא נַעֲשָׂה עָצוּב, מֵבִיס אֶת הַשַּׁלְוָה.
לָמַדְתִּי שִׁעוּר בְּתִרְגּוּם?

A Lesson in Translation

The translator attempted to bare
things unsaid:
Modes of intent and disguise,
the compulsion of trial and arrival
(once she read something in my face).

More than anything she thought of ploughing
its unique foundations, of identifying
the bristle of roots, the burn of shaping.
At times she was attracted to an image like
"trees-of-morning sing birds," or
to the incidental, orchestrating
a subtle irony, longings.

The source, one may assume, is still the source.
She did not make it her own estate,
nor [an]other, secondary version of mine.
Every stanza seems guarded,
its credence flowing as always
from autumn to autumn.

With this, I still question how a cool-careful text
can also turn sad, can defeat tranquility.
Have I learnt a lesson in translation?

'Adiv le-'Atzmi [Courteous to Myself: Poems 1976–79] (1980:29)

The persona speaking in this "Lesson in Translation" is that of the mature poet, who for the past two decades has often experienced both the joys and pangs of being translated (into English). As this poem amply demonstrates, he is fully aware not only of the complex relationship between an original text and its translated version, but also of the uneasy co-existence of the two "progenitors," the author and his translator.

Clearly, the poet is relieved to learn that the new version did not slow down the immutable flow of the authentic source nor did it undermine his own authorial hold on it. Appropriately, the overt praise for the translator's effort to penetrate beneath the surface of the finished product and to get at the secret of the creative process is couched in figurative language that unwittingly uncovers the ambivalence plaguing any author involved in an act of translation. Thus, the third strophe of this poem alludes to the author's fear of losing his possession to the translator, as well as to his worry lest the outcome be an inferior version of the original. In Hebrew, there is a conflict between the connotations of the word *makor* (a source, a fount, or an original) and those of the idiom *keli sheni* (a secondary source, and by implication something of less authority and reliability). The term *'achuza*, on the other hand, means *estate, property* or *possession*, but is in fact a derivation of the verb *'achaz* (hold, grasp, possess). In a way, the original poem, the source text, is portrayed here as a (legal) possession providing some sense of security and shelter. The latter connotation is particularly reinforced by the polysemy of the Hebrew word for stanza, *bayit*, which means also house, home, or family. It is not difficult to hear the author's sigh of relief, so to speak, upon realizing that his stanza/home remains well guarded even when translated, and furthermore, that the translation has achieved the almost impossible fusion of remaining "his" ("she did not make it her estate"), while regaining the stature of a primary source, an original.

That such an ideal translation is hardly attainable is only too obvious. Perhaps this is what is implied by the resigned questioning of the closing lines of "A Lesson in Translation." Despite the effort and the formal achievements, some *affective* transformation has taken place. A "cool-careful" text has lost its "tranquillity," implying perhaps the emotional detachment and ironic distance characteristic of so much of Preil's mature verse. Unlike the original, the translated version is emotionally committed, it is touched by "sadness." What is, then, the lesson learnt by the translated poet of our poem? Possibly, that the textual element least controllable in translation is that of tone and emotional register. In his economical-enigmatic way, Preil points here to one of the perennial pitfalls plaguing the process of translation, what recent translation theory has termed *the shift of expression* (Popovič, 1977).

That Preil should be well aware of this problem is only natural. After all, his poetic career has been intimately bound up with his translating activity.[1] As early as 1936, he began to publish Hebrew versions of his own Yiddish poems. Of course, we cannot rely on publication dates alone as sufficient evidence for chronology of composition. This uncertainty, moreover, may cast some doubts on the direction of the translation (Yiddish to Hebrew or vice versa?). Nevertheless, considerations of style and genre allow us to argue that Preil's earliest autotranslations were indeed made from Yiddish to Hebrew. It is only from the late 1940s on that poems were published in both languages concurrently, and it is possible to assume that these had also been simultaneously composed. The fact nevertheless remains that in both cases (be it autotranslation or dual composition) some patterns of modification consistently recur. These patterns are much more involved than the affective shifts pondered in "A Lesson in Translation." In fact, they sometimes result in two different modal or generic variations on the same theme. These variations could be categorized as "romantic" vs. "imagist," each consistently correlating with the language employed, Hebrew or Yiddish respectively. This correlation, in turn, assumes specific significance when it is placed in two broader contexts—the historical poetics of Hebrew modernism (see chaps. I and II above) and the theory of literary translation as it has been recently developed by Czech Structuralists and their European and Israeli colleagues. According to this theory, literary translation is part and parcel of the larger phenomenon of cultural communication and literary contacts (Holmes, 1971; Popovič, 1977; Toury, 1977; Even-Zohar, 1978:45–53; Ivir, 1981; Lefevere, 1981). As such, the process of translation is bound to be affected not only by the structural (linguistic) features of the target language, but also, and to no less extent, by the literary norms dominant in that culture. In other words, the question of literary translation may be conceived today as a particular case of the general process of "literary transfer" (Even-Zohar, 1981), and perhaps even of the very basic processes of signification and comprehension (Steiner, 1975:47). The practical outcome of this new approach is a shift in the focus of investigation: At the center of attention now are the nature and function of those *constraints* that determine and control the position of a translated text between its source language and its target language. Consequently, linguistic "adequacy" (i.e., faithfulness to the source language) is not the main criterion against which a translation is measured. Rather, it is the manner in which it is adjusted to the target literary system (its "equivalency") that is now under examination. This mode of adjustment is the result of both linguistic (Jakobson, 1959; Levenston, 1965; Dagut, 1976; Van den Broeck, 1981) and cultural constraints. However, it is particularly the latter that broadens the scope of our investigation. Insights into the mode of existence of a literary system and its norms enable us to deal with such phenomena as literary "reworkings" and even with the selective process operative in the decision of what gets translated and what does not (see Even-Zohar, 1975, 1980; Toury, 1981; Perry, 1981).

That such norms were of utmost significance in the literary transfer from Yiddish to Hebrew we have already witnessed in the monumental autotranslation of Mendele Mokher-Seforim and his contemporaries (chap. I, above). On a smaller scale, we saw them when we traced the (Yiddish) *intra*literary transfer between Teller's "hard" imagist miniatures and Preil's "softer" treatment of the same genre (chap. V, above). We explained this divergence by Preil's dual literary allegiance and alluded to a more severe interference of this duality in the *inter*literary transfer resulting from his autotranslation. It is now time for us to prove this assertion and embark on a closer look at Preil's autotranslations (or dual compositions). The following textual analyses aim, therefore, at gleaning the specific strategies operative in these autotranslations, and through them, at understanding the inner workings of this (possibly last) case of literary transfer from Yiddish to Hebrew.[2]

Velt in Mir (In Zikh, Feb. 1936; *Lider*, 1966:60)	וועלט אין מיר
Ikh veys az velt iz parmet	איך ווייס אַז וועלט איז פּאַרמעט
vos flakert durkhn vald fun yorn	וואָס פֿלאַקערט דורכן וואַלד פֿון יאָרן
vi uralter vayn in geshrey	ווי אוראַלטער וויין אין געשריי
fun a toyznt zunen.	פֿון אַ טויזנט זונען.
Kh'veys, az ire fentster un tirn	כ׳ווייס, אַז אירע פֿענצטער און טירן
hengen ibern mentshn	הענגען איבערן מענטשן
vi tlies geshotnte,	ווי תּליות געשאָטנטע,
az zi iz groyzam vi	אַז זי איז גרויזאַם ווי
a trakht vos otemt	אַ טראַכט וואָס אָטעמט
mit trukene lipn.	מיט טרוקענע ליפּן.
Kh'veys, az in kaluzhes	כ׳ווייס, אַז אין קאַלוזשעס
fun shvartsn vanzin	פֿון שווארצן וואַנזין
tsaplt zikh di velt,	צאַפּלט זיך די וועלט,
un az ire henker	און אַז אירע הענקער
farbn mit sharlekh	פֿאַרבן מיט שאַרלעך
di hofenung.	די האָפֿענונג.
Un kh'veys –	און כ׳ווייס —
az ire shteynerdike vent	אַז אירע שטיינערדיקע ווענט
veln amol tsepralt vern,	וועלן אַמאָל צעפּראַלט ווערן,
un oyf ir farshmakhtn ponem	און אויף איר פֿאַרשמאַכטן פּנים
vet friling shteyn	וועט פֿרילינג שטיין
in tseblitn zig.	אין צעבליטן זיג.

The World in Me

1. I know that [the] world is a parchment
2. which blazes through a forest of years
3. like ancient wine in the outcry
4. of a thousand suns.
5. I know that its windows and doors
6. hang over people
7. like shadowy gallows
8. and that it is as gruesome as
9. a womb panting
10. with parched lips.
11. I know that in swamps
12. of black insanity
13. the world is trembling,
14. and that its hangmen
15. paint hope
16. in scarlet.
17. And I know –
18. that its stone walls
19. will be thrown open one day
20. and on its languid face
21. spring will rise
22. in blooming triumph.

Judging by this poem, it is not difficult to imagine why young Preil had decided *not* to translate his earlier imagist miniatures. Although this poem is no less imagistic, it is not an attempt to capture the experience of a momentary reality, be it internal or external; here, the long list of colorful images is subordinate to a generalized concept, "the world" (or even "history"). The resemblance of this abstraction to "man" in general in Preil's early *Hebrew* verse cannot be overlooked. Furthermore, this pictorial portrayal of the world is not presented as an independent reality but rather as a figment of the poet's cognition. The opening *ikh veys* (I know) has many analogues in Preil's Hebrew reflective poems (see chap. VII, section 1). It seems that it was this personal involvement, coupled with the concern with universal issues (exactly the two items objected to by the Imagists[3]) that made this poem fit for rendition into Hebrew.

In fact, the rhetorical structure of "The World in Me" antedates that of "Notes on an Ancient Parchment" (the opening poem of his first Hebrew volume, see chap. VI above). Although graphically presented as one long strophe, the poem's syntactic make-up points to a fourfold division, marked by the anaphora "I know that" (lines 1,5,11,17), which corresponds to the anaphoras that open each of the four strophes of "Notes on an Ancient Parchment." Just as similar is the use of the basic image (the world as parchment) even though it is employed in a totally different manner in each case. Typically, the Yiddish poem does not take advantage of the cultural-historical connotations of a Torah parchment; rather, the concrete physical attributes of the object (its dryness, its inflammability) participate in the image of the blazing world. Thus, it is not sacredness and antiquity that are brought to the fore, but the strife and self-destruction demonstrated throughout history (the "forest of years," the "thousand suns"). Similarly, there is a clear tendency here to concretize even such abstract concepts as time or insanity by using an age-old device, the "concretizing construct" ("forest of years" [line 2], "swamps of insanity" [lines 11–12]).[4] A similar effect is achieved by synesthetic combinations through which abstract concepts are "colored" ("blooming triumph" [line 22] and "scarlet hope" [lines 15–16]).

This brings us to another characteristic of the poem—the change in the artist's palette. A new color is introduced here, or rather a new shade (or connotation) of the color red. The implicit connection between fire, blood, and scarlet and their collocation with "shadowy gallows," "hangmen," and "black insanity" point to a use of colors akin to the expressionistic palette. In the context of the general topic of the poem, it is possible that these colors connote political movements (communism and fascism, respectively), as they did in Jacob Glatstein's famous political satire, "Shpigl Ksav."[5]

Personification is also used here, though the associations are much more startling than in the Hebrew reflective poems: Suns clamor, a womb pants, the world has a face, and spring rises. A special effect is caused by a grammatical feature of Yiddish: The feminine gender of *di velt* may have given rise to the womb-metaphor or to such predicates as "trembles" and "languid." As we shall see, this was one of the difficulties the poet confronted when translating this poem into Hebrew (*'olam* being masculine).

The Hebrew rendition, entitled simply "*'Olam*" [World], was published at the end of the same year (December 1936) in *Niv*, the journal of young Hebrew writers in New York.

World (from the Hebrew)

I know that the world is like a parchment
set ablaze in the forest of years,
catching fire like wild and ancient wine
in the outcry of a thousand suns.
I know that the world's windows
and doors
hang over man['s back]
like shadowy gallows
and [that] it is as cruel as a dried-out womb.
In swamps of black madness
the world is trembling-shaking
and its hangmen paint
the hope crimson.

עוֹלָם

יוֹדֵעַ אֲנִי שֶׁהָעוֹלָם כִּקְלָף
מִשְׁתַּלְהֵב בְּיַעַר הַשָּׁנִים,
מִתְלַקֵּחַ כְּיַיִן פֶּרֶא וְנוֹשָׁן
בְּזַעֲקַת אֶלֶף שְׁמָשׁוֹת.
יוֹדֵעַ אֲנִי שֶׁחַלּוֹנוֹת הָעוֹלָם
וְדַלְתוֹתָיו
תְּלוּיִים עַל גַּב הָאָדָם
כִּתְלִיּוֹת מְצִלּוֹת,
וְאַכְזָרִי הוּא כְּרֶחֶם מְצֻמָּק.
בְּבִצּוֹת שִׁגָּעוֹן שָׁחוֹר
רוֹעֵד־רוֹטֵט עוֹלָם
וְתַלְיָנָיו צוֹבְעִים אַרְגָּמָן
אֶת הַתִּקְוָה.

Surprisingly, the original closure (17–22) was completely omitted, thereby undermining the oppositional structure characteristic of the Yiddish miniatures. (Did the poet feel that the optimism was artistically unmotivated?) Another major change is the reduction of the womb-metaphor: lines 8–10 are rendered as one line, stating "it is as cruel as a dried-out womb." Possibly the original image sounded too daring in Hebrew and out of context with the masculine gender of *rechem* (womb) and *'olam.*[6] Other modifications point in another direction, one which becomes the norm in Preil's autotranslations. The rendering of *Ikh veys* as *Yodea' 'ani* (literally, "Know I") is a symptom of the need to preserve a heightened poetic diction in Hebrew (the syntactic order VS is the classical literary one, as compared to the colloquial SV; and cf. chap. VI, p. 80 ff.). The choice of lexical equivalents attests to a similar attempt—*flakert* is rendered as both *mishtalhev* (line 2) and *mitlakeach* (line 3), *uralte* becomes *pere ve-noshan* (wild and ancient), and *tsaplt zikh* turns into *ro'ed-rotet* (trembling-shaking). In all of these cases the lexical doubling is redundant (from the semantic point of view); this is, however, in the tradition of Hebrew literary style, which favors parallelism and synonymic expressions (cf. Toury, 1977a [162–171, 265–267]) and 1982; Perry, 1981).

These modifications notwithstanding, "*'Olam*" did not find its place in any of Preil's Hebrew books. It seems that the imagist impulse evident in Preil's Yiddish beginnings could not have been transferred immediately to Hebrew. Thus, what befell the first "*Dray Lider*," which appeared in the *In Zikh* issue of February 1936, illustrates the three options. "*Shpet Zumer*" was not translated; however, a year later Preil started to publish Hebrew nature poems which clearly bear the mark of his first Yiddish études on this subject.

"*Velt in Mir*" was translated, but never made the Hebrew "corpus"; it nevertheless signaled the direction of later autotranslations, both in its lofty subject and in the modifications of the Hebrew rendition. The third poem, "*Kontrast Motiv*" (*Lider*:22), was not translated until the 1960s. It is one of Preil's few poems that could be classified as erotic, though only in a very subtle way. Its central image is a variation on the classical figure of the *hortus conclusus* (Frye, 1957:152), which derives, of course, from Song of Songs (4:12): "My beloved is a locked garden, a sealed fountain." In "*Kontrast Motiv*," the beloved is first identified with "night" (*nakht biztu*), which, in turn, "is a sealed fountain / is a locked womb / is death." The second strophe reverses this virginal image ("night is a fresh-mouthed river / is an open book / is light") and the polarities are finally neutralized by "pale satisfaction." Even though the poem is far from audacious by any poetic standards, it looks as if Preil could not quite conceive of subjecting Hebrew to this kind of "erotic openness." Only when license was given (by the appearance of erotic poems by Yehuda Amichai, for instance), dared he render this miniature into Hebrew; still, the closure has been changed: Satisfaction is only "hinting" (hinted?), and "all thirst is forgotten" (*Mashehu 'al Nigudim*, 1968:22; 1972:30).

Observing this development in retrospect, one could say that if in its topic "*Kontrast Motiv*" does not belong to the mainstream of Preil's oeuvre,[7] in its title it does. This concept of polarities, which upon closer scrutiny may turn into similarities (or vice versa—see the in-depth analysis of this feature in Perry, 1972, 1979; cf. Feldman, 1979, 1980), became one of the central concerns of Preil's mature poetry, both thematically and structurally. This is clearly demonstrated by the titles of his volumes, as well as by his use of oxymorons, such as "frosty fire," "the motion of repose," or "an icy fire" (more about this in chap. X). However, what distinguishes his later verse from the earlier is the introduction of the element of time into this structural paradigm. In his best poems he exploits the polar options of the visual dimension in order to delineate the otherwise uncapturable passage of time. The recollected sights of a Lithuanian autumn are juxtaposed against the present vistas of an American spring (1968:28; 1972:35); "mother's snowy valley" is contrasted with the poet's past "autumn path" or "hint of spring" (1980:47). It seems that the poet is disturbed by the contradictory oppositions of here and there, now and then, youth and old age, spring and autumn—in short, by all the gradual changes effected by time: "...time, color-blind and tone-deaf, is the thief and the theft..." (1976:33). If we remember the personifications of time and death used by him in his early reflective Hebrew verse (see "A Letter from Man to Time," 1944:11), we can conclude that his mature poetry is a successful fusion of his romantic concern with Time, man's arch-enemy, and his imagistic fascination with both contrasts and nature descriptions. The early attempts at such a fusion, although not always so felicitous, are the subject of our next analysis.[8]

טאַטעס יאָרצײַט

איך וואָגל היינט בײַנאַכט.
אויף יענער זײַט ים זוכט מיך אַ בערגל,
פֿון אונטער וועלכן עס גייט אויף רײַך און גרין
אַ טאַטע.
זײַנע גלידער רעדן פּלאַנץ־לשון
אונטער אַראָפּגעבויגענע ליטווישע הימלען.
זײַנע גלידער פֿאַרשטייען זומער־לויף, ווינטער־גאַנג,
און פֿאַרנעמען צײַטן.
זיי פֿאַרמאָגן קיינמאָל־ניט־געמינערטן פֿרילינג,
זיי זײַנען גלאַנציק־פֿרישער כּתבֿ נאָכן רעגן
און ווערן פֿון שטערן געלייענט.

און איך, זײַן זון אין אַמעריקע,
טראָג אומגליק ווי אַ צווייטע הויט.

לְזִכְרוֹ שֶׁל הָאָב הַמְאֻשָּׁר

אֲנִי נוֹדֵד הַלַּיְלָה וּבְדָמִי כְּמִיהָה לְמוֹלִידִי.
וּמֵעֵבֶר לָאוֹקְיָנוֹס תֵּל־עָפָר מְבַקְשֵׁנִי וּמְצַפֶּה לְבוֹאִי:
זֶה אַבָּא חוֹתֵר וְעוֹלֶה מִפְלָג בְּעָשְׁרוֹ הַיָּרֹק.
אֲבָרָיו מְדַבְּרִים בִּלְשׁוֹן־צְמָחִים וְרוֹאִים אֶת הָאֱלֹהִים
בִּשְׁמֵי־לִיטָא הַשַּׁחִים.
אֲבָרָיו מְבִינִים מַהֲלַךְ־חֲרָפִים וּמֵרוֹץ־קֵיצִים
וּמַקְשִׁיבִים לַזְּמַנִּים בְּזָרְמָם.
אוֹצַר־אֲבִיבָם לֹא יִגָּרַע לְעוֹלָם,
אַחַר גֶּשֶׁם כְּתָבָם מַזְהִיר וְרַעֲנָן,
וְהַכּוֹכָבִים קוֹרְאִים בָּהֶם.

וְעָלַי, עַל בְּנוֹ בַּאֲמֶרִיקָה, קָרַם עוֹר שֵׁנִי —
הַצַּעַר הַמְשַׁכֵּל.

In Memory of Father [from the Yiddish][9]

I wander tonight.
Across the sea a small hill looks for me,
from which rises, rich and green,
a father.
His limbs speak plants-language
under the bent Lithuanian skies.
His limbs comprehend summer's race, winter's pace,
and sense Time.
They own a never-changing spring,
they are fresh-shining [hand-]writings after rain,
[always] read by the stars.

And I, his son in America,
wear misery like a second skin.

In Memory of the Happy Father [from the Hebrew][9]

1. I wander tonight and in my blood there is yearning for my begetter.
2. And across the ocean a knoll seeks me and awaits my arrival:
3. This is father breaking through and rising, excessively [endowed] in his green wealth.
4. His limbs speak plants' language and see God
5. in the low skies of Lithuania.
6. His limbs comprehend the pace of winters and summer's race
7. and listen to the times as they flow.
8. The treasures of their spring will never diminish,
9. after rain their [hand-] writing is shiny and fresh,
10. and the stars read in them.

11. And on me, on his son in America, a second skin was overlaid —
12. the bereaving grief.

The two versions seem to speak for themselves. The heightening tendencies that are signaled by the Hebrew title (from the familial *tate* to the formal *ha-'av* [the father]) are actualized throughout the poem. The Hebrew version seems to revert precisely to those additional words that "do not contribute to the [direct] presentation," and which the Imagists vowed to avoid (Flint, 1913; cf. *In Zikh*: 25). A closer look, however, reveals that the modifications are not just a redundant embellishment; they disclose a consistent pattern of creating a higher *reality*, one that is altogether alien to the original. Consequently, we can divide the modifications into two groups:

I. *Semantic Redundancy:*

1) synonymic doubling:	Y: looks for	H: seeks and awaits
	Y: rises	H: breaking through and rising
2) added complements:	Y: misery	H: bereaving grief
	Y: rich and green	H: excessively [endowed] in green wealth
	Y: Time	H: the times as they flow

3) syntactic extensions: lines 1,2,4, (6), all add a whole sentence to the original.

II. *Thematic Heightening:*

1) realemes[10] substitution:	sea → ocean
	hill → knoll[11]
2) stylistic substitution:	*tate* → father, begetter
	look for → seek, await
	never changing → will never diminish
	wear → overlay
3) added realemes:	(line 1) yearning (in my blood...)
	(line 4) God
	(line 7) treasures

The latter three types of modification have one feature in common : They all indicate a replacement of the smaller, lower, simpler, and daily by the larger, more sublime, and more ceremonial, whether in style or in reality. Together with the unexpected additions, most of all of "God" (which is hardly ever used in Preil's mature verse), these changes dramatize the Hebrew version and endow it with "grand" style and atmosphere, which are out of tune with the original. Consequently, the same images that in Yiddish convey a direct, refreshing treatment of a personal and emotional topic, appear in their Hebrew guise as lofty, flowery tropes (*melitzot*). Such stylistic shifts also characterize the next group of autotranslations, which were originally published in *In Zikh* in 1938.

In the Hebrew version of "I See in 1938" (*Lider*:24), the Hebrew date (תרצ"ח)[12] replaces the original, and the globe is described as "terrible" instead of just "round." The culturally laden term *shenot 'alpayim* (two thousand years)—of diaspora—is added, as is a whole phrase based on biblical allusions pertaining to issues of reward and punishment. The elevated pathos of the Hebrew translation (published in *Gilyonot*: 1939) should not surprise us. It was appropriately included in the third part of *Landscape of Sun and Frost*, the one devoted to the Holocaust (1944:60; 1972:230).

However, even the more personal poems do not escape this "shift of expression." Thus, the poem "*Mame*" opens with the image "Mercy walks in wooden shoes" (*Rachmones geyt in hiltserne shikh*), whereas its Hebrew version, entitled "Mercy" (!), loftily states "Mercy is hollow in a blood-sated world..." (1944:70; 1972:233). But most "disappointing" is the treatment of the very first imagistic étude, "*Frost.*" In fact, we can hardly recognize it. Three years after its Yiddish publication, the Hebrew poem "Sparrows and Man with Snow[s]" (*Ankorim ve-'Adam 'et Shelagim*) was published in *Sefer ha-Shana li-Yehudei Amerika* (1938; see 1944:50). It took a good deal of detective work to trace it back to its Yiddish antecedent. But once the two poems are juxtaposed, their common themes surface and the *imagist* / *rhetorical* opposition becomes clear as well.

אַנְקוֹרִים וְאָדָם אֶת שְׁלָגִים

אַנְקוֹרִים יוֹצְקִים לַחַשׁ בֵּין שְׁלָגִים:
בָּא הַקֶּטֶב מִמֶּרְחַקִּים מִתְקָרְבִים,
וְעַל זְגוּגִיּוֹת עָלוּ פִּרְחֵי־אֲבַדּוֹן.

אֵימָה כְּבֵדָה עוֹטֶפֶת פִּתְחֵי־עוֹלָם.
פְּתוֹתֵי־שֶׁלֶג נִתְלִים עֲלֵיהֶם, כִּקְמֵיעוֹת זְעִירִים,
וּנְמוֹגִים חֶרֶשׁ:
טֶרֶם הֵאִיר הַבִּטָּחוֹן לְבָבוֹת.

רַחַשׁ שֶׁלֶג — סוֹד מַבְהִיק בְּמִישׁוֹרִים אֲפוֹרִים.
מַה יְמַלֵּל גּוֹרָל לָבָן בְּהִתְחַדֵּשׁ חֹרֶף עַתִּיק?
מַה פֵּשֶׁר חִידוֹת לְבָנוֹת בְּאִישׁוֹנֵי־לֵילוֹת?

Sparrows and Man with Snows

Sparrows pray [pour whisper] in the snow:
Disaster [plague] approaches from far away,
and on glass [panes] blossoms of doom grow.

Heavy dread envelops doorways everywhere.
Snowflakes hang there like tiny amulets
and melt softly:
Faith [trust] has not yet lit up [Man's] heart.

A rustle of snow—a glittering secret on grey plains.
What does white fate utter when an ancient winter comes again?
What is the meaning [interpretation] of white riddles in the black of
nights?

The "shifts of expression" between this version and its Yiddish antecedent (see chap. VIII above) are more than stylistic. They actually amount to a generic (or modal) divergence, whose general lines may be discerned even in translation. Apparently, the young poet did not trust the power of Hebrew to speak in images. The original tenor, snow-swallows, is split into sparrows *and* snow, thus losing the direct metaphor;[13] man, although not mentioned explicitly in the poem itself, is introduced into the title; "question marks" are superseded by "blossoms of doom," and the economical image of a "wagon-wheel" is replaced by a host of explicit statements about the approaching plague or disaster and the lack of faith. In short, the concrete description drowns in conceptual formulations; all that was hinted and implied is now spelled out; the reader is left with very little to do, inasmuch as the poem interprets itself by itself. Last, but far from least, the poem almost loses its euphonic charm as well as the immediacy of the common idiom. In its overt concern with Shne'urian abstractions (Man, Time and its corollaries) this poem resembles the rest of Preil's early *Hebrew* verse more than it reflects its Yiddish antecedent. We can conclude, then, that like every other speech-act, the act of autotranslation is overdetermined not only by the linguistic properties of the languages involved, but also by the *literary norms* upheld by the respective communities (cf. Popovič, 1968; Holmes, 1971; Ivir, 1981; Toury, 1981).

All this being said, we should revert to the appropriate historical perspective. The above poems and others like them (cf., for instance, "*Libe Tsu Teg*," *Lider*:75, and "*Le-Yamim 'Ahava*," 1944:37; 1972:280) should be judged not from the point of view of Hebrew poetry (and language) today, nor from a comparatist perspective. In other words, aesthetic genesis should not be confused with literary acceptance, nor with evaluative judgment. Against the background of the Hebrew poetry of his time, Preil's autotranslations, modified as they were, were still accepted as a deviation from the norm. His ability to treat New England landscapes (and later, New York urban scenes) directly and in the most conversational idiom (without the constraints of rhyme or meter), was a refreshing change in Hebrew poetry. This directness, however, was not attained right away, nor by immediate translational transfer. Curiously enough, very few poems of Preil's first Hebrew book (1944) came close to his Yiddish imagistic poems in either theme or technique. Furthermore, none of these can be traced back to any Yiddish original. Only when writing outside of the confining bilingual system of Yiddish/Hebrew could the poet free himself from the stylistic norms operative in translations from Yiddish to Hebrew. Thus, although his modernist breakthrough was no doubt facilitated by his apprenticeship in Yiddish verse, it was nevertheless achieved not through direct translation, but rather by circumventing those very strategies that had been traditionally used in preserving the heightened rhetoric of the target language. We will therefore conclude our discussion of Preil's literary transfer by taking a close look at two samples of his earliest *Hebrew* experiments in imagist verse.

In 1937, Preil published two variations on his Yiddish imagistic motifs—a girl's portrait and a description of nature. A sense of novelty was immediately conveyed by the title of one of them—"Chinese Embroidery." The choice could not have been accidental. The title signals that emphasis has shifted from vision to craftsmanship (Frye, 1957:60) and that a new kind of poetics was to be expected of this genre:

> Chinese poetry shows salient differences from that of the Occident. Thematically it is little concerned with some of the major subjects of Western verse—idealized love, heroic adventures, religious devotion... The epic is unknown, and long narrative poems of any kind are rare.... Chinese poets achieve their effects by reticence not rhetoric; draw their images from nature,... imply their emotions instead of anatomizing them" (Preminger, 1974:123).

Chinese Embroidery (1944:43; 1972:224)	רִקְמַת־סִין
a. Night sleeps in the girl's hair. She carries a slim and gentle dawn – a gift for the sea.	לַיְלָה לָן בְּשַׂעֲרוֹת הָעַלְמָה. הִיא נוֹשֵׂאת שַׁחַר זָקוּף וְעָנֹג — שַׁי לַיָּם.
b. Stars bloom in her face. She brings a basket of suns: Day is born.	כּוֹכָבִים פּוֹרְחִים בְּפָנֶיהָ. מְבִיאָה הִיא סַל־שְׁמָשׁוֹת: יוֹם נוֹלָד.
c. Seas and days—ladders. Upon them step the feet of gods.	יַמִּים וְיָמִים — סֻלָּמוֹת. עֲלֵיהֶם תִּדְרֹכְנָה רַגְלֵי־הָאֵלִים.

On first reading, this poem gives the impression of actualizing the characteristics implied by its title; it seems to be Preil's first Hebrew poem that does not mean "to mean," but simply "to be." Its descriptive repertory is reminiscent of "*In April Ram*" and other Yiddish predecessors (see chap. VIII). Details of a girl's portrait are described in terms of natural phenomena. A closer look nevertheless reveals that the resemblance is only partial; in fact, it is difficult to differentiate between the tenor and the vehicle of the imagery. True, the girl's hair and face are described in familiar terms (night and stars), but no other attributes pertain to her. The only two adjectives used in the poem refer to a natural phenomenon, the dawn, which slowly emerges as the center of the image—"a day is born." Most surprising is the absence of any explicit colors (except for the inferred darkness of the hair and brightness of the face). This entails the avoidance of thematic encoding. Indeed, two poles are juxtaposed here (night vs. day, stars vs. suns), but without any +/− markedness. Instead, they are simply placed one after another (the same order is repeated in strophes a and b) "without predication," to use Frye's term (1957:123). This symmetrical poetics of "discontinuity" (*ibid.*) or of "reticence" (Preminger) is upset, however, by the insertion of a third party—the sea. The latter tinges the imagery with shades of mythology: The newly born day is perceived as a (ritual?) gift to the sea. Finally, the three-way net of relationships is resolved hierarchically, and mythology steps in, full scale: Both days and seas are subordinate to the feet of gods.

When we reach this "clicking" closure (B.H. Smith, cited above, p. 119), we are surprised to realize that by now the concrete girl herself has been forgotten; we somehow feel a sense of incompatibility between the mythological aspect that was suddenly sprung upon us and the promises conveyed by the title. Still, the effect of "oriental" or "imagist" poetics is sustained throughout the poem, despite its subversive elements. This is achieved not so much by the imagery or the subject matter, as it is by simple syntactic manipulations. The poetics of discontinuity is manifested here in the avoidance of any linking device. In contradistinction to most Yiddish études of this period, here there are no syntactic connectives, no prepositional anaphoras and even the copulas are suppressed (cf. note 3, chap. VIII). This paratactic structure is most evident in the ratio of line and sentence. These nine brief lines contain seven (!) sentences, in contrast to the two sentences of "*Shpet Zumer*", for example, which are spread over twelve lines. Each of these sentences constitutes an independent image, which appears to be unrelated to the rest. When the "click" of the closure finally occurs, we hardly notice it, because the "disconnected" style camouflages the thematic-mythic relatedness. We may conclude, then, that in "Chinese Embroidery" the poet managed to thin out and lower Hebrew syntax, diction, and style, despite a certain loftiness of the subject matter which he has not managed to avoid.[14] Most of the devices used for this were not copied from Yiddish, but rather grew out of the linguistic nature of Hebrew; only one feature was imitated, and not very convincingly. The alliterations of this poem (*__laila lan__, '__al__ma, no__la__d, su__la__mot; __sh__achar, __sh__ai*) and the quasi-homonym *yamim* (the plural of both *yam* [sea] and *yom* [day] with a slight [unpronounced] difference in vowels), is a phonetic orchestration independent of its meaning, unlike "*Frost*," for instance (cf. Hrushovski, 1968). However, Preil found a better solution in the following poem:

Shir Mayim (1944:38)

Pirperu ha-mayim ke-tzamot mavrikot
'al gagei chefar ba-geshem;
sharu pizmon shovav u-mitholel
'al ketalim charuchim ba-kerach,
ve-hivhavu be-'einayim zakot
'al penei 'arava mishtokeket.
Peta'—ve-tziltzul kesef
mehaded 'al shulchano ha-yarok
shel ha-'elohim:
Kasam shikui mi-marom
la-'aretz ha-tzeme'a,
veha-'olam—ra'anan tzeva'
u-metzuchtzach ka-yeled.

שִׁיר־מַיִם

פִּרְפְּרוּ הַמַּיִם כְּצַמּוֹת מַבְרִיקוֹת
עַל גַּגֵּי־כְפָר בַּגֶּשֶׁם,
שָׁרוּ פִּזְמוֹן שׁוֹבָב וּמִתְהוֹלֵל
עַל כְּתָלִים חֲרוּכִים בַּכְּרָךְ,
וְהִבְהֲבוּ בְּעֵינַיִם זַכּוֹת
עַל פְּנֵי עֲרָבָה מִשְׁתּוֹקֶקֶת.
פֶּתַע — וְצִלְצוּל־כֶּסֶף
מְהַדֵּד עַל שֻׁלְחָנוֹ הַיָּרֹק
שֶׁל הָאֱלֹהִים:
קָסַם שִׁקּוּי מִמָּרוֹם
לָאָרֶץ הַצְּמֵאָה,
וְהָעוֹלָם — רַעֲנַן־צֶבַע
וּמְצֻחְצָח כַּיֶּלֶד.

Song of Water

Water fluttered like glistening braids
upon village roofs in rain;
[they] sang a naughty, wild refrain
on charred city walls,
and flickered with bright [innocent] eyes
upon an eager prairie.
Suddenly—[and] a ringing of silver
reverberates on the green table [desk]
of God:
A potion from above charmed
the thirsty earth [soil],
and the world [is] freshly painted
and shining-clean, like a child.

In many respects this crisp, charming poem is the opposite of "Chinese Embroidery": Its title denotes a concrete natural phenomenon rather than artistic craftsmanship; it quite openly tells a continuous story, consequently avoiding paratactic structures and economical metaphors;[15] concomitantly, it bursts with movement and joyfulness, in contrast to the restrained (and static) grandeur of the Chinese embroidery; finally, the matrix of its figurative language is the image of the child, with which the poem also concludes—a far cry from the "sublime" attained by the former poem.

This mood of childish playfulness, which begins with the rain-song and engulfs the whole world, is created by several devices. Most conspicuous is the abundance of verbs: This poem not only predicates; it activates all its nouns, even by means of their attributes.[16] A second energizing element is the constant topographical change. The first three images perform two concurrent movements—from top to bottom (roofs, walls, the prairie) and from enclosed areas to the wide-open spaces (village, city, prairie). This movement is further dramatized when the prairie is metaphorized ("God's table") and is finally replaced by all-embracing terms—earth, world. However, these last generalizations do not undermine the concreteness of the picture. The detailed realistic depiction is fully grounded before it is metaphorized. The fullness of the description is achieved here, as in some of the Yiddish études, by a combination of sensory impressions, which are sometimes only implied (as in the title itself). The opening picture, for instance, is designed as a visual portrayal: the brightness of the water on [red] roof tops which look like glistening braids. The braids, however, must be generated from another scene—children frolicking in the rain, and probably *voicing* their joy. Similarly, the second image overtly introduces the song of the rain, but at the same time we cannot eliminate the color connoted by the *charred* walls.

It is not surprising that these sensory transferrals culminate in a clear-cut case of synesthesis. The ringing of silver is a perfect fusion of the silvery glitter and coin-like sound of rain drops on flat surfaces, or of coins on a green table (or perhaps we should translate *shulchan* as "desk," the association being the old-fashioned desks covered with green felt).

This consistent alternation of sight and sound adds to the effect of movement created thematically. Precisely the same effect is also evoked by the phonetic level of the poem. Surprisingly, each line contains at least one word with a phonetic doubling (this high percentage of double-letter roots is definitely not representative of Hebrew vocabulary). Thus, we begin with *pirperu* (which connotes both the colors and motions of *parpar* [butterfly]), move through *gag*, *shovav*, *mitholel*, *hivhavu*, and *mishtokeket*, only to reach an onomatopoeic high point that coincides with the "silvery" synesthesis we have already observed: *tziltzul kesef mehaded...*

The energy gathered both thematically and phonetically[17] is finally exploded. It is resolved (once more) in a half-mythologized scene: A monetary exchange takes place between earth (grammatically feminine) and God (masculine). But this interjection is not a serious threat to the rain song.

It is introduced obliquely, via a genitive-metaphor (the prairie is only the desk of ...), and is clearly played down by the humor involved. Thus, the anticlimactic closure completes the circle. The child-like atmosphere has engulfed the whole earth, but this time it is not the mood of "children at play"; rather, it is the relaxation of the nursed and cared-for child, whose "color" is refreshed but whose noise and activity have been toned down. Concomitantly, the closure includes the only nominal predicate of this poem, and the phonetic doubling, although maintained, is considerably subdued.

Needless to say, both of these poems found their place in the middle section of Preil's first book, the one devoted mainly to nature descriptions. Here we find also "Rain Poems" (*Shirei Geshem* [39]), "A Praise to the Stone" (*Shevach la-'Even* [41]), "A Sunset in Fort Tryon" (*Sheki'a be-Fort Trion* [44]), "Poems from Vermont" (*Shirim mi-Vermont* [46]), "Winter Night" (*Leil Choref* [49]), and "Spring Sights" (*Mar'ot 'Aviv* [51]). Most of these poems, however, are more reminiscent of the Hebrew variation on "*Frost*" than of their two succinct predecessors discussed here. It is only in the next collection of poems (1954) that we find a whole section, entitled "*Mi-Nof Amerika*" [American Landscapes], which openly celebrates a direct confrontation with, and description of, nature. The change in titles is also instructive; the implied romanticism of "*Wanderlust*" is replaced by the straightforward "American Landscapes." Moreover, a similar immediacy is conspicuously felt in many other poems of this book, both in their topics ("Painting a Desk" [*Tzibua' Shulchan*, 25] or "A Mailbox" [*Teivat Do'ar*, 32]) and in their treatment. But more than a decade separated these poems (published between 1945 and 1953) from the early experiments of 1937. We can conjecture that Preil sensed the divergence between his own two styles—the romanticism dictated by the mainstream of Hebrew tradition and the imagism he imported from the sister-language. No wonder, then, that this clash sent him off to look for Hebraic kinsmen. We have already heard (chap. III, p. 41) that he was happy to discover a kindred spirit in the Hebrew free verse of his Polish contemporary, Ber Pomerantz (1901–1942). It is intriguing, therefore, to see that his review of Pomerantz's second book *Chalon ba-Ya'ar* [*A Window in the Forest*, 1939] is tainted by the conflict he himself was undergoing at that time (1940):

> Pomerantz is a modernist poet, namely, he acknowledges "good" modernism, which means speaking directly [honestly], expressing ideas in precise visual images, and denigrating cheap artificiality and stylistic embellishment. In his poems there is more colorful picturesqueness than generalized phraseology, and poeticalness outweighs routine.

The imagist principles underlining this evaluative description come through quite clearly. Nevertheless, the romantic impulse does not lag behind:

> In every line of his, one can perceive... individualism bounded by romanticism. But his romanticism is *not* sentimental... it is sober and elated at the same time, tingled by half-expressed irony (Preil, 1940).

This sounds very much like a possible autodefinition of Preil's own oeuvre. It seems that, while writing alone in one geographical periphery of the Hebrew polysystem, Preil was aware of the existence of analogous innovative activities in other peripheries as well.[18] It did not take him long, however, to align himself with other Hebrew precursors who had been relegated to the literary periphery by the canonized norms of their time. Thus, a decade later, while reviewing Halkin's new book *Modern Hebrew Literature—Trends and Values* (New York, 1950), he stated:

> It is a pity that Halkin, who is so close to modernistic literature and treats it so lovingly, does not mention several other poets, who have introduced a refreshing breeze into our literature, while walking softly and silently. I refer here not only to Yaakov Lerner... but also to David Fogel... and Ber Pomerantz. These literary saplings, who grew up as if by accident on the fringes of our diaspora, were swept away by a merciless current. Their place in the framework of pre-World-War-II Jewish society should be re-appraised.[19] Possibly, the critic who would have considered them would have found a direct line leading from the prose of U.N. Gnessin and Devora Baron, not only to our contemporary novelist S. Yizhar, but also to the desperate and disconnected verse... of the 1920s and 1930s, which has been neglected until the present (Preil, 1951).

Although this is never verbalized, Preil obviously considered himself an additional link in this marginal individualistic line of Hebrew literature.[20] Without any subversive declarations, he identified with those poets who were slighted by critics and scholars and demanded their right to be heard:

> It is not impossible to guess what caused our critics to be silent. In those days, modernists like Shlonsky and Greenberg made their appearance; they brought to the scene excellent lyricism, but of the percussive kind.... The voices which sang on the side paths did not reach our critics... (Preil, 1951).

So we have come full circle. In this review Preil anticipated the change of heart of young Israeli poets and critics in the 1950s and 1960s, which, in turn, changed *his* position in the network of modern Hebrew poetry. This enabled him to give full expression to his imagist predilection; but it also helped him in realizing the drawbacks of pure Imagism just in time to emerge as a "romantic imagist." Since this realization has become a central issue in Preil's later verse, we will conclude our tracing of his modernist poetics with a group of his poems in which "poetics" as such is not only the means but the end as well.

Chapter X

Metapoetics: To Imagism and Back

מַה מִּנּוֹף

אֵינִי רוֹצֶה לַחֲזֹר וְלִכְתֹּב
עַל עֲנָנִים, שְׁמָשׁוֹת —
גַּם הֵם בְּוַדַּאי הִתְעַיְּפוּ מִמֶּנִּי
(כְּבָר הִגִּיעַ הַזְּמַן)
אוֹ אוּלַי הֵם הִתְחִילוּ לְנַחֵשׁ
שֶׁאֲנִי עַצְמִי
רוֹצֶה לְהִכָּתֵב
אֲפִלּוּ לִהְיוֹת סַרְסוּר בֵּינֵיהֶם
לִמְכֹּר וְלִקְנוֹת מִזְגֵי־אֲוִיר, גְּוָנִים
לֹא מַעֲשֵׂה־אֶתְגָּר אֶלָּא מִשְׂחָק
שֶׁל שָׁוֶה בֵּין שָׁוִים.
לִהְיוֹת אַחֲרַאי, לַעֲבֹר מִבְחָן
כְּמוֹ אִי־אֶפְשָׁרִי שֶׁל וִכּוּחִים.

אֲנִי כּוֹתֵב כָּל זֹאת מְעֻנָּן כָּרָגִיל
לֹא תַּחַת שֶׁמֶשׁ
נִמְשָׁךְ לְיָרֵחַ צָבֶה
שָׁקֵט וּמְשַׁגֵּעַ.

יֵשׁ מִקְצָת אִירוֹנְיָה בְּעִנְיָן זֶה
שֶׁל עִסּוּקִי בְּמַה־מִּנּוֹף
עֵת מַרְבִּית הַשִּׁירָה נִכְבֶּשֶׁת
בִּידֵי פְּרוֹזָאִיּוּת עַפְרוּרִית
כָּעֲנָנִים הָאֵלֶּה, שֶׁאֵינֶנִּי רוֹצֶה
לִנְגֹּעַ בָּהֶם יוֹתֵר.

Matters of Landscape

I do not want to keep writing
about clouds, suns—
they, too, have surely tired of me
(it is time they did)
or may have begun to guess
that I myself
want to be written about
even to be a middleman among them,
buying and selling weathers, shades,
not as a matter of challenge, but as a game
of equal among equals,
to be in charge, pass an almost impossible
test of argumentation.

I write all this cloudy as usual
not under any sun
drawn to a bloated moon
calm and maddening.

There is a bit of irony here, in
my preoccupation with matters of landscape
when poetry in general has been taken over
by dust-like, grey prosaicness
like these clouds, which I would prefer
to touch upon no longer.

That the persona speaking in this late poem (*Igra* 1, 1984:97) is artistically self-conscious is only too obvious. His is the voice of a spectator, one who is capable of observing himself from without, weighing the ways in which his own poetic activity diverges from the contemporary mainstream. Yet it is not this divergence alone that triggers the sense of *irony* expressed by the poet; rather, it is the metapoetic realization of the gaping distance between the "now" and "then" within his own artistic career. However, for the reader who is familiar with the critical reception of Preil's verse, a third irony is inescapable. The "dust-like, grey prosaicness" by which "poetry in general has been taken over," as the poet observes, was precisely the feature which had been earlier identified as one of Preil's "modernist" characteristics (see chap. III). Paradoxically, the poet himself does not see his work as part of this trend (at least not in this poem). In fact, he "double-crosses" his reader, moving from an opening that may be read as an anti-romantic declaration proper to totally different grounds. This shift in focus is effected by a clever manipulation of the image "clouds."

The first collocation of "clouds, suns" functions as a synecdoche of a romantic code (the association with poetic sunsets is only natural), of which the poet seems to have grown tired. Accordingly, the first strophe builds up an opposition between the overused romantic repertory and another option. This option may seem (at least at first) to be an *Inzikhist* call for poetic individualism: "I myself / want to be written about." But soon enough this option takes on another shape: It is not a certain *kind* of poetry that seems overdone; rather, it is the poetic function itself that is perhaps too "romantic" (in the sense of being impractical, not part of the real world). Being "a middleman," "being in charge," "passing a test"—all these activities may point to a poet's wish to act *in* the world rather than write *about* it.

That this is an impossible dream becomes clear in the second strophe. The poet yearns to leave behind his romantic *topoi*, but may never be able to act out this wish. In a sense, there is nothing new under the sun for this poetic persona, because he does not really live under any sun. His sign is that of the moon, where "clouds" function *in opposition to* rather than as an apposition of "suns." In other words, the verbal sign "clouds" is not perceived here as a hyponym of "nature," the typically romantic code. On the contrary, it is capable of signifying the extreme opposite, as is made surprisingly clear in the last strophe, where contemporary poetry is likened to clouds, precisely because it is taken over by *proza'iyut 'afrurit*. Although *'afrurit* literally means dusty [or earthy, from *'afar* (dust, earth, soil) as in Genesis 3:19], it strongly implies the more common adjective *'afruri(t)* (greyish), from *'afor* (grey). (In modern Hebrew the two words have practically become homonyms, because the difference between the pronunciation of the consonants *'alef* and *'ayin* is often non-existent.) *'Afrurit* functions then as a double signifier or as a quasi-pun. And if the punning quality is not prominent, it is because there is no contradiction between certain connotations of the two signifieds. Though pointing to two referents, this sign creates a single semantic field, one that supports and intensifies the claim for "prosaicness" attributed (here as elsewhere) to contemporary poetry. As we shall soon see, the use of the color grey is not accidental here. It is used by Preil (among others) to contrast the understated poetics of Modernism to earlier Romantic colorfulness. It is therefore precisely this marker that removes the sign "clouds" from a romantic descriptive system and transplants it in a modernist one. Thus, it is finally the modernist rather than romantic connotations of "clouds" that have tired the poet and made him declare "I would prefer to touch upon [them] no longer." This is an ironic reversal of our initial reading of the first strophe of "*Ma mi-Nof*"; it is doubly ironic for a poet who has been recognized as a pioneer of modernism in Hebrew verse.

Such retrospective (and often ironic) self-examination is not unique in Preil's writing. Admittedly, it is not unexpected in a poet who started out hoping to redeem "Man's glory," "whiten all dark cruelty," and "illuminate all kindness" ("A Will," 1944; see chap. VII), but who has recently come to the conclusion that the only beneficiaries of his poetic labor are "the wandering words" ("*Sheyar ha-Shirim*", 1982; more about this below). The chasm between these two positions and the bridge from one to the other is one of the dominant topics in Preil's verse. Each and every one of his books opens with one version or another of "*metapoetics*"—poems in which poetry as such (as well as in its relations to the world, the poet himself, or its poetic tradition) is the subject.[1] We have already seen the romantic manifesto framing the first volume (1944: "Notes on an Ancient Parchment" and "A Will," see chaps. VI, VII). We have also noticed, however, that by the early 1940s, the poet had begun to transfer some seeds of his "other" system, his Yiddish imagism, to his Hebrew work. By the end of the decade, he had clearly rejected the rhetorical poetics symbolized by his former model, Zalman Shne'ur, and openly identified with the minor, marginal line of Hebrew poets (see chap. IX above). Thus, it should come as no surprise that in the following volumes the romantic promise is not made good. The heroic pathos and the rhetorical experiments of the early years do not resurface. The poet's fascination with the social function of the poetic word dwindles considerably. In subsequent collections he withdraws from the great concerns of the world into the poetic medium which is experienced as an independent, closed system. These volumes open, not with declarations about the writer and the world, but with metapoetic statements about the poet and his art in which the past confidence of the poetic voice is replaced by self-doubt. Thus, the 1954 collection, *Ner mul Kochavim* [*Candle Against Stars*] opens with the poem "*Be-Ya'arei Shir*" [In the Forests of Poetry], which metaphorizes the romantic-symbolic tradition, thereby putting its relevance in question.

בְּיַעֲרֵי שִׁיר

כְּכָל אֲשֶׁר תַּחְשֹׁב רַגְלִי לְהַבְקִיעַ יַעֲרֵי שִׁיר,
כֵּן יִרְבּוּ לְהִפָּתַח לְפָנַי אֲפָרִים בֵּין אִילָנוֹת,
כֵּן יִרְבּוּ לִנְהֹר חַלּוֹנוֹת זְעִירִים, תּוֹפְסִים מֶרְחַבְיָה,
עִם בְּרֵכוֹת מַקְצִיפוֹת זָהֳרָן.

לֹא אֵדַע אִם אֲפָר, בְּרֵכָה אוֹ חַלּוֹן
מְעִידִים עַל יְדִיעָה בְּהִירָה שֶׁל דְּבָרִים.
אוּלָם אֵדַע שֶׁלְּיַעַר אֶחָד עָבֹת, עֲתִיר־רָזִים,
יֵשׁ מִשְׁעוֹלִים מְאִירִים, בְּגְדֵי עֲבִיבִים כְּחֻלִּים;
אוּלָם אֵדַע כִּי שָׁעָה יֶשְׁנָהּ, בָּהּ כָּל צֵל
הוֹפֵךְ לְפֶלַח־שֶׁמֶשׁ.

In the Forests of Poetry

The more my foot means to penetrate the forests of poetry,
the more meadows keep opening for me among trees,
the more tiny windows keep sparkling [flowing], embracing [God's] open spaces,
and ponds keep foaming with splendour.

I don't know whether meadow, pond or window
attest to clear knowledge of things.
Yet I know that a certain dense forest, rich with secrets,
has shining paths, clad in light blue clouds.
Yet I know that there is an hour in which every shade
turns into a slice of sun.

If not for the single reference to the title metaphor ("to penetrate the forests of poetry"), this poem might have been placed comfortably within a romantic context. For the Hebrew reader, echoes of Bialik's archetypal poem, "*Ha-Berecha*" [The Pond] (Bialik, [8]1973:361) are inescapable. It is not just the elements of nature (forest, pond, paths) that this poem shares with its intertext. Much more significant is the repeated use of the lexical units denoting *knowledge*—that poetic-mystic insight which the true poet is said to be able to draw from nature (represented by its synecdoche, the secretive pond, in Bialik's poem).[2] The English reader of our translation may have another intertext in mind. The second strophe, and especially the enumeration of "meadow, pond or window," reads like a deautomatized version of Wordsworth's well-known "Intimations of Immortality," in which the poet remembers days gone by, when "meadow, grove and stream/... to me did seem/ apparelled in celestial light" (1920:587). The replacement of Wordsworth's Neoplatonic myth by an anthropocentric "knowledge," as much as the violation of his nature-code (by the mixing of "window" with "pond" and "meadow") only serve to underline the poem's major deviation-from-context. In opposition to both Bialik and Wordsworth, the modern poet is *not* sure "whether meadow, pond or window / attest to clear knowledge of things." If we remember, furthermore, that "nature" is subjected here to the central metaphor of the title, this doubt may be read as directed against poetry as such. This does not mean, however, that nature itself is exempt from all doubt. The metaphoric framework (the poem-as-nature) is relegated to the background soon after being introduced; when we come to the second strophe we actually have to remind ourselves of its existence. Thus, the poet keeps the two options alive simultaneously, foreshadowing the next stage in his metapoetics, where the distinction between the world outside and the world within seems to dissipate, and the poetic voice itself is almost phased out. For the meantime, however, the two elements (nature vs. poetry) are still experienced as distinct ontological entities. And the poetic voice, while struggling to affirm past assurances, still hopes to find an hour "in which every shade / turns into a slice of sun."

The opposition between "shade" and "sun" clearly anticipates the pair "cloud/sun" (or "moon/sun") in the last poem we discussed, as well as many other contrasts and polarities, which are abundant in Preil's verse (cf. Perry, 1972, 1979; Feldman, 1979; 1980:137–139). The roots of this fascination with oppositions go further back in Preil's verse. As mentioned earlier (chaps. VIII, IX), Preil's first published poems (in Yiddish) used thematic and descriptive polarities as their major structuring device. That this was not an arbitrary or unconscious choice can be attested by the title of his early poem "*Kontrast Motiv*" (1936, see *Lider* 1966:22). The source of this preoccupation, as we have claimed in chapter IX, is the poet's need to overcome the devastating effects Time brings about. We may now attribute another poetic feature to the same psychological motive—the striving toward a harmonious co-existence, or even better, toward the blurring of opposites. Out of the contrasts and polarities of human existence the poet is trying to shape "a reconciliation of discordants," or "a fusion of contradictions," to use Coleridge's familiar definition.

Paradoxically, this "esemplastic" drive gains impetus in Preil's verse just when he is on the verge of renouncing romanticism and fully anchoring himself (at least for a while) in the imagists' camp. The difficulties involved in this transition and the pangs of adjustment to the imagist ethos are succinctly demonstrated in the opening poem of Preil's third volume, *Mapat 'Erev* [*Map of Evening*, 1960]. This book, we should remember, was the one that established its author as a Hebrew Imagist, one of the modernizers of

Israeli "young" poetry in the 1950s and 1960s (see chap. III above). It includes some of Preil's most "imagistic" Hebrew poems, in which "he directly faces the colors, shapes, and material qualities of the objective and concrete world... without using this subject matter metonymically, but rather giving it an autonomous existence of its own" (Miron, 1977:168).[3]

אִי וְיַמּוֹ הַנָּסוֹג

הַשִּׁיר בָּא עִם כָּל מֶזֶג־אֲוִיר, —
וְאַחַר יוֹצֵר אֲקְלִים מִשֶּׁלּוֹ,
נוֹטֵעַ גַּנִּים לֹא הֶעֱלוּ זָהָב קֹדֶם,
אוֹ נַעֲשָׂה עָרֵב לְמִדְבַּר חוֹל חָדָשׁ.

לְאַחַר שֶׁהוּשַׁר הַשִּׁיר עַל שִׁלְגּוֹ וְשִׁמְשׁוֹ,
וְכָל הַמַּעֲבָרִים הַפּוֹעֲמִים לְבֵינֵיהֶם,
הוּא נוֹשֵׁם כְּנוֹף עַצְמָאִי,
כִּנְקֻדָּה מוּחֶשֶׁת־מוּשֶׂגֶת
עַל מַפָּה גֵּאוֹגְרָפִית.

רַק מְחוֹלֵל הַשִּׁיר
פְּצוּעַ אַהֲבָה נִשְׁאַר מִבַּחוּץ:
אִי שֶׁיַּמּוֹ נָסוֹג מִמֶּנּוּ.

An Island and Its Retreating Sea

A poem comes in any weather—
then creates its own climate,
planting gardens never touched by gold
or warranting a new desert of dunes.

Once the poem is sung with its snow and sun
and the transitions pulsating between them,
it breathes like its own landscape,
tangible and concrete
on the map.

Only the poem's begetter,
love-wounded, remains outside:
An island whose sea has retreated.

This is the first of Preil's metapoetic poems in which the speaking "I" is not identified as such. The contrast with former poems is stark. Unlike its predecessors, this is a typically modernist text in that it constitutes its own subject. For the artistic worldview informing this poem, the text is an "objective" reality, one that does not "reflect" the world out there, nor act "upon" it, but simply replaces it. This poem knows neither Promethean sacrifices (in the style of "Notes on an Ancient Parchment," see chap. VI), nor Aristotelian mirrors (remember the shiny surfaces in "In the Forests of Poetry"—the glowing windows, foaming ponds, and shining paths). Faithful to New-Critical concepts, it also avoids the infamous "intentional fallacy": It is not the poet but rather the poem that "comes," "creates," "plants," "warrants," and "breathes." The poet's role is only obliquely implied by the passive voice in the second strophe ("is sung"). On the other hand, the text's self-sufficiency is doubly stressed by the activities attributed to it, as well as by the simile that endows it with the existence of a geographic or natural phenomenon.[4] Curiously, this poem within a poem gains its "right for autonomy," so to speak, by working through pairs of oppositions (e.g., fertility vs. aridity; sun vs. snow) in a manner characteristic of Preil's own creative procedures. Its autonomous climate, its independence of "any weather" is created by singing "the transitions" between contrasts and polarities, thereby reaching, it would seem, the state of utopian harmony typical of Preil's poetic vision. Paradoxically, only the poet is excluded from the harmonious reality he (in the final analysis) has created:

> Only the poem's begetter,
> love-wounded, remains outside:
> An island whose sea has retreated.

An ironic self-awareness permeates this poem, that for all other purposes seems to accept the Imagist/New-Critical dream. It is easier, it seems, to phase out the poet's voice when the subject is anything but the creative process itself (e.g., the slices of reality described in the poems listed in note 3). The attempt to write metapoetic poems in the Imagist mode is therefore doomed to fail. In fact, it brings to the foreground precisely those drawbacks that had brought on the demise of Imagism. Thus, the more Preil's verse becomes technically imagistic, the more ironic become the metapoetic poems. This irony is actually a remote echo of the romantic voice of the poet in his youth. Though in a muted way, it voices a resentment of the gradual withdrawal of the human involvement from the poetic function. This is the very process of constriction which underlies certain tendencies in the poetics of modernist verse, as well as in contemporary literary criticism. And it is this movement toward limitation and self-referentiality that may explain the opening poem of Preil's fourth book, *Ha-'Esh ve-ha-Demama* [*Fire and Silence*, 1968], "*Hesberah shel Shura Rishona*":

הֶסְבֵּרָהּ שֶׁל שׁוּרָה רִאשׁוֹנָה

שׁוּרָה רִאשׁוֹנָה שֶׁל שִׁיר
הִיא נֵץ לֹא יַרְפֶּה מִבַּזּוֹ
אוֹ יַעַר דְּלוּק בְּרָקִים
מִכָּל עֲבָרָיו הַסּוּמִים.

אַחַר אוּלַי יְאַוֵּשׁ פַּס־אֲפָר,
תַּפְצִיעַ קֶרֶן דַּקָּה שֶׁל יָרֵחַ, —
עַד בְּשַׁעַר נִצָּחוֹן מְשֹׁעָר
יַעֲלוּ כָּל שִׁבְחֵי הַקִּיָּם
וְשֶׁמֶשׁ כִּבְגִבְעוֹן תַּעֲמֹד.

Explaining a First Line

A first line of a poem
is a hawk holding on to its prey
or a forest struck by lightning
from all its blind sides.

Later, a strip of meadow may rustle,
a slim horn of moon may shine
until at an imagined arch of victory
all praises of Existence will rise
and a sun will stand still as in Gibeon.

Here, as in other poems in this book (cf. "*Nofah shel Shura*" [The Landscape of a Line], 1968:12; 1972:26), the antiromantic bias has been followed to its logical conclusion: Even a single line of verse may be endowed with an autonomous existence. This existence is characterized by a set of traumatic experiences (birds of prey, a forest on fire), which seem to originate the creative impulse. The purpose of creativity, furthermore, is to work through these traumas and to reach the calmer moods of acceptance, even of metaphysical cooperation (as in Joshua 6:12). In the framework of this poem, all these activities and achievements are attributed to the poem's "line," *not* to its initiator. In contrast to earlier poems, the "begetter" is not even mentioned here. The human element seems to have been completely obliterated.[5]

But not quite; for just as Preil's imagist or objectivist bent reaches its limits, it is dialectically counterbalanced by a covert return of a romantic impulse. Interestingly, Preil places the most imagistic of his metapoetic poems at the beginning of a volume in which the human interest is brought back to the poetic stage in many poems of introspection and self-awareness. From observation of the poem as an independent artifact we move to a study of the poetic process. This in turn renews a fascination with the poet's social function in a modern world. Unfortunately, the truth of experience does not allow a full resurgence of the heroic-romantic poetic voice of youth. The romantic option is now viewed from the perspective of an ironic consciousness which often undercuts its own premises. A good example of this new consciousness is the poem "*Shalosh Tziporim ve-'Achat*" [Three Birds and (Another) One] (1968:60; 1972:50), which is of special interest for the issue under consideration here.

שָׁלשׁ צִפֳּרִים וְאַחַת

שָׁלשׁ צִפֳּרִים
הָיוּ שְׁלשָׁה תָּוֵי זִמְרָה,
הָיוּ שְׁלשָׁה נִטְפֵי צֶבַע
עַל חוּט טֶלֶפוֹנִי
אֲפַרְפַּר מוֹלִיךְ קוֹל מִמָּבוֹךְ לְמָבוֹךְ,
מִנּוֹף מֻפְשָׁט אֶל אֶרֶץ הַסְּתָם.

וַדָּאִיּוֹת הֵן רַק אֵלּוּ הַשָּׁלשׁ, אַגָּדִיּוֹת
פָּחוֹת אוּלַי מִמֶּנִּי —
תַּו זִמְרָה עַרְאִי, הֻשְׁלַךְ עַל אֲדָמָה קֵיצִית,
נֵטֶף־צֶבַע מַחְדִּיר כָּל מַלְבִּין וּמַשְׁחִיר.

אֵי־שָׁם תִּרְאֵנִי עַיִן גְּדוֹלָה אַחַת:
אֵיזוֹ צִפּוֹר רְבִיעִית מְנַתֶּרֶת
עַל חוּט אֲפַרְפַּר.

Three Birds and [Another] One

Three birds
were three notes of music
were three drops of paint [color]
on a greyish telephone wire
conducting voice from maze to maze,
from an abstract view to the land of the inane.

Certain are only these three, legendary
maybe less *than me*;
a transient note, cast upon the summer earth,
a drop of paint penetrating all white and black.

Somewhere a great eye will observe me:
Just a *fourth* bird, hopping
on a greyish wire [thread].

This poem differs from most of the poems discussed in this chapter in that it is not overtly metapoetic (nor was it placed at the opening of the book). Reading the first strophe, one is inclined to see it as a schematically structured imagistic miniature,[6] one that describes a "slice of nature," but has no bearing on the poet or the poetic process. Although the three birds on the telephone wire are metaphorized (by the typically imagistic copula-metaphor; see its Yiddish antecedents in chap. VIII above), their concrete existence is nevertheless evoked. Birds on a wire may indeed *look* like notes on a musical staff, and even like stains of color (= paint; in Hebrew there is no lexical distinction). These physical qualities may, of course, have metaphoric (or metonymic) implications as well; but these are not overtly stated by the text. They come to the fore, however, in the second strophe, where the central opposition of the poem is presented: "they" vs. "I."

Certain are only these three, legendary
maybe, less *than me*—

In a move reminiscent of the poem "An Island and Its Retreating Sea," the poetic voice is introduced into the supposedly "objective" description, only to come out of the comparison in an "inferior" position. But unlike its antecedent, this poem seems to juxtapose the poet not with his created world (the text), but rather with the real world—that tangible and concrete slice of nature that triggers the poetic response. This juxtaposition is an answer to a tacit question, one that is not verbalized by the text, but nevertheless constitutes its covert metapoetic matrix: Whose existence (and perhaps values as well) is more real ("certain" in the poem's idiolect)—that of the concrete birds or that of the speaking "I," the one recording the external world as much as creating its metaphoric meaning?

This is an age-old question, reflecting the perennial struggle for priority between art and life, or fiction and reality. For its most known formulation in Hebrew literature we have to turn once more to Bialik's "*Ha-Berecha*" [The Pond], the ur-text of Hebrew romanticism (and symbolism). In Bialik's poem the pond is personified to be read as a metaphor of the artistic (and the artist's) ability to *reflect* the outside world (the forest), while "secretly dreaming" that the forest is not only reflected in it (him), but is actually growing within it. By creating the pond as a metaphoric alter-ego, Bialik was able to distance himself from the issue at hand and to leave it open, watching "the riddle of the two worlds, the twin worlds, / not knowing which of them has precedence" (p. 377). Preil's answer, on the other hand, appears (at least on first reading) quite unambiguous: Only the birds are "certain," while the artist, the poetic voice, is nothing but "a transient note, cast upon the summer earth."[7]

In view of this verdict, the synthesis of the third strophe comes as a surprise. Here the speaker becomes an equal member in the group, "a *fourth* bird." Yet, the basis for this upgrading (if this is indeed the case) is not clear. Furthermore, the *language* of the closure is far from able to accommodate such an optimistic reading—"*just* a fourth bird" is not an expression of value. The Hebrew pronoun *'eizo* (translated here as "just," for lack of a better equivalent) connotes something indefinite, vague, insignificant (colloquially it expresses sheer disrespect). By putting the speaking "I" on equal footing with the three birds, the poet has therefore degraded the three rather than elevating the lyric "I." In other words, if a reconciliation of discordants has taken place here, it has moved in the direction of the negative rather than the positive pole. But why? What made this reversal possible? What happened to the "certainty" previously accorded to the birds?

Searching for clues to this riddle we may discern (on rereading the poem) several "ungrammaticalities" (see chap. VI, section 2) that may offer some pointers. Two of these involve the manipulation of syntactic features of Hebrew which are too complex to be explained in detail here.[8] It suffices to say that in two cases (the enjambments between lines 4–5 in strophe 1 and between lines 1–2 in strophe 2), the sentence is broken in a way that calls special attention to the isolated member ("greyish" appears at the beginning of line 5 in Hebrew), or creates a syntactic/semantic ambiguity ("legendary" may be read as a "syntactic synonym" of "certain," that is, a second predicate of the subject, "three"). Another "incongruity" involves the imbalance between the concrete attributes of the three birds and the strongly metaphoric description of the telephone wire on which they sit. Furthermore, the negative markedness of the wire in this description cannot be missed. Its function is to "discommunicate" rather than to connect. It metonymically stands for an urban world, whose mechanized communication lacks meaning or value. The language describing the wire is heavily laden with derogatory connotations, of the same semantic field as the word *'eizo* in the last strophe: *stam* (inane), *mufshat* (abstract, negatively read, particularly in collocation with landscape) and finally, the adjective *'afarpar* (greyi*s*h).

As mentioned above (see the poem "*Ma mi-Nof*" at the opening of this chapter), the color grey holds a special position in Preil's poetic idiolect, particularly in the volume under discussion, i.e., in poems written during the 1960s.[9] As the connotation of *'afor* is "commonplace," "monotonous," even "worn out," it often describes prosaic, unadorned, even negative reality. Accordingly, the adjective "greyish" is separated from its noun and placed at the beginning of the next line. This is Preil's way of activating a metonymic transfer that paints the whole strophe grey, including the three birds. Under the pressure of this transfer, the metaphoric meaning of the three birds is evoked as well. After all, could they not be construed as symbolic representations of music and painting, poetry's sister-arts? And is this not a more sensible basis for the comparison between them and the poet?

The questions are aroused by the text, but no answers are provided. Thus, the second strophe is quite ambiguous: Who indeed is more "certain" than the poet—the concrete birds or the arts for which they may metaphorically stand? What is juxtaposed here—the transience of the artist as a human being vis-à-vis the certainty of art itself, or the artist's ephemerality vis-à-vis the concreteness of nature? Finally, is the contrast between greyness and colorfulness an illusion or truth? The concluding statement provides only a partial answer. From the vantage point of a future observing authority (an implied metaphysical presence), the poet, with all his doubts and conflicts, is nothing more than "just" a (probably *grey*) bird; he is neither a lyrical nightingale nor a heroic eagle (as he set out to be at the beginning of his career, see chap. VI). All it can perform is "hopping on a grey wire"; here even the "telephone" (that is, the communicative function) has totally disappeared from the surface text. Its disappearance turns the wire into a simple, non-functional thread (in Hebrew there is no lexical distinction), thereby giving full rein to the connotations of the color grey. The conclusion is rather grim then: In a world of mechanized communication there is hardly any room for the elevation of art, as believed by the Romantics and Symbolists. All that is left for the modern artist is to chart the ironic contrast between colorful aspirations and "grey" reality.[10]

It is the above realization that may explain Preil's poetic strategies at that stage of his career. In no other collection is the drive to invite contraries "to the green valley of equilibrium" or "to celebrate the blurring of boundaries" so strongly operative.[11] In some of these poems the happy medium is symbolized by the color silver or grey (!), the middle point on the emotional continuum of the color spectrum; in others, explicit reference is made to "the appeasement," the "moderate square," or "the balanced season."[12] Very rarely, though, is there mention of the term *shalva* (peace, calm, tranquillity) which used to be Preil's ideal in the earlier volumes (and see in particular "*Ha-Shalva ha-Meyuchedet*" [Unusual Calm] and "*Divrei Shikachon ve-Shalva*" [Words of Oblivion and Peace], 1960:42,49; 1972:95,96). It would seem, then, that not only the youthful challenge to the harassment of time (see 1944:11), but even the more mature yearning for personal tranquillity had to be given up. Coming to grips with the realization that oppositions are often too real to be mediated, the poet slowly explores another option. In the poems written throughout the 1970s, metapoetics proper is replaced by the effort to create a personal poetic tradition and endow it with the power of a self-sufficient existence. As we have seen above (chaps. IV, V), the poet attempted to establish a bilingual literary line, be it familial (grandfather) or national (Mapu, Glatstein, Teller). Such an endeavor naturally involved a violation of the Imagistic worldview (though not its techniques necessarily). Thus, in the poems collected in the 1976 and 1981 books, the dominant perceptual dimension is that of *time* rather than *space* (see the poems "*Zeman 'Acher*" [Another Time], "*Pirkei Zeman*" [Chapters of Time] 1976:10, 11, "*Bar Harbor: Lifnei 'Elef Shanim,*" [Bar Harbor: A Thousand Years Ago], and "*Zemani Ka'et*" [My Time Now] 1980:9,47).[13] Unlike the abstract Time of youth, this is a very "personal" time. It involves referential biographical data (poems about his mother, his uncles, and so on) in contrast to the metaphoric "autobiographies" of earlier poems (see chap. IV).

Curiously enough, this new direction is accompanied by the return of a romantic framework—not in practice, but in "theory." More accurately, the term *romanticism* itself surfaces (paradoxically, often in texts of the technically most imagistic and colloquial poems), although never without some reservation or qualification. This term is always joined by an epithet that debunks its validity. It is either *romantika temuha* (a curious romanticism) (1976:51) or *setuma* (unfathomed) (1980:45,46), or *Baironiyut ketu'a* (dislocated Byronism) (1980:9). These references, along with poems whose titles demonstrate generic or modal awareness ("*Shir Romanti Katan*" [A Short Romantic Poem] and "*'Efsharuyot Sheki'a*" [Sunset Possibilities] 1976:26,24),[14] introduce the artistic self-consciousness characteristic of Preil's latest metapoetic verse. Indeed, it would seem that only at this recent stage of his career has Preil actually adopted the "introspective" poetics recommended half a century earlier by the Yiddish *Inzikhists* (cf. chap. III, note 20).

The emergence of this consciousness is no doubt related to the poet's relatively new ability "to dive into deep water" ("Another Time," 1976:10). Reading the "water" of this metaphor as representing internal rather than external depths, we could indeed point to aspects of introspection and self-analysis unprecedented in Preil's verse. Thus, alongside the return of his suppressed Yiddish roots (see chap. V), he squarely faces his present existential predicaments—his exilic Hebraism (chap. IV), his personal loneliness ("No one telephones me, / Communication wires fade. / Perhaps this is how death / begins to announce its existence"[1976:17]), his imminent aging ("Gabriel has turned into Mr. Preil. / Overnight the pampering began / helping him in taking off a coat, in opening a door /...[1976:13]), and his failing eyesight ("Neither Joyce nor Fichman / are limits of blindness. / After the operation a small window opened / within [my] clouded eye. / The colors almost begin to sort themselves out. / I am long sorted out, / a man of hesitations, blessing / the small certainty / of a bright seagull on a wave" [1980:35]). Furthermore, in a move so *un*characteristic of his earlier verse, he comes closer than ever to the psychological roots of his romantic predilection, locating it in his close relationship with his mother (with whom he lived until her death in 1977). It is probably the novelty of this introspection, as well as the directness of the self-image of a frustrated romantic, that underlie the suggestiveness of the poem "*Ba-Zeman ha-Zeh, ba-Makom ha-Zeh*" [At This Time, At This Place] (1976:51):

בַּזְּמַן הַזֶּה, בַּמָּקוֹם הַזֶּה

הָאֵם וּמְחוּשֶׁיהָ. כְּאֵב־הָרֹאשׁ שֶׁלִּי, הַקָּפֶה הָרָגִיל.
הֲצָצָה אוּלַי בְּסֵפֶר וְאַחַר טִיּוּל קָצָר וּמְסֻפָּק.
אֶלָּא שֶׁהַזָּהָב אֵינוֹ נוֹגֵעַ בַּנָּהָר.
אֲנִי מְכַתֵּף עֲנָנִים בִּלְבַד
בַּזְּמַן הַזֶּה, בַּמָּקוֹם הַזֶּה.

הַאִם זֶה הַכֹּל שֶׁאוּכַל לוֹמַר? וַאֲנִי
כָּל־כָּךְ רָצִיתִי לְהַחֲזִיר לְאִמָּא
אֶת כָּל אַגָּדוֹתֶיהָ,
לְהַבְחִין בִּכְאֵב מֵעֵין פִּנּוּק מְעֻצְבָּן
כְּשֶׁאֲנִי קוֹלֵט טַעַם אֶקְזוֹטִי מְסֻפָּל וּמְעֻיָּן
בַּסְּפָרִים שֶׁמְּנַבְּאִים גַּנִּים וִירֵחִים:

בַּזְּמַן הַזֶּה, בַּמָּקוֹם הַזֶּה
לְהָגֵן עַל רוֹמַנְטִיקָה תְּמוּהָה.

At This Time, At This Place

Mother and her pains. My headache, the usual coffee.
A glance in a book, perhaps, then a dubious brief walk.
Yet gold does not touch the river.
I shoulder clouds only
at this time, at this place.

Is this all I can say? But I
wished so hard to give mother back
all her fairytales,
to see in the pain a nervous malaise
while absorbing exotic aroma from a cup,
and to study books
predicting gardens and moons.

At this time, at this place
defending a curious romanticism.

The relative openness of this poem (among others[15]) may finally explain the emergence of a totally new metapoetic sensitivity, of the kind best demonstrated by the whimsical poem "*Mirsham: 'Iyun ba-Milon. Tzeid Shir*" [Prescription: Studying a Dictionary, Hunting a Poem] (1980:14):

מִרְשָׁם: עִיּוּן בַּמִּלּוֹן, צֵיד שִׁיר

עִיּוּן בַּמִּלּוֹן לְאַחַר הֶתְקֵף תִּסְכּוּלִים
הוּא מִטּוּבֵי הַפֻּרְקָנִים. עֲדָרָיו
אֵינָן שֵׂיוֹת אוֹבְדוֹת בַּמִּדְרוֹן
אוֹ מְטַפְּסוֹת עַל גִּבְעוֹת־הַסְּתָם.
הֵן נָחוֹת בְּאֵיזֶה עֵמֶק הַשָּׁוֶה
כִּלְאַחַר סְעֻדָּה אֲדִישֵׁי אֲרָיוֹת.

אוּלָם כְּשֶׁהֵן יוֹצְאוֹת לְצֵיד שִׁיר
הֵן מְלֻוּוֹת חֻלְשַׁת־דַּעַת:
מְשֻׂגִּים אָז עוֹיְנִים זֶה אֶת זֶה
דִּמּוּיִים בּוֹעֲרִים בְּנִפְרָד. רַק
כְּשֶׁהַמִּבְנֶה עַל תָּאָיו נִשְׁלָם
וְהַפְּנִים מַאֲפִיל־מַזְהִיר חֲלִיפוֹת
נַעֲשֵׂית כָּל מִלָּה עֶצֶם נֶאֱמָנָה
מְחֻבֶּרֶת כִּמְבְּרֵאשִׁית לַחֲבֶרְתָּהּ.

שִׁלְגֵי סְבִיר כְּמוֹ נְמַסִּים אָז
בַּיָּם הַתִּיכוֹן, וְלֹא חָשׁוּב
אִם מַאֲרַב הַתִּסְכּוּלִים שׁוּב
מוּכָן לְזַנֵּק.

Prescription: Studying a Dictionary, Hunting a Poem

Studying a dictionary after an attack of frustration
offers the most potent release. Its flocks
are not lost lambs on a slope,
nor do they climb up meaningless hills.
They rest in a valley of equilibrium
as indifferent lions after a meal.

But when they set out for poem hunting
they are somewhat discouraged:
concepts then are hostile to each other,
similes burn in isolation. Only
when the structure with its cells has been completed
and the interior alternately darkens and brightens,
each word becomes a loyal bone
joined anew to its neighbor.

Then Siberian snows almost melt
in the Mediterranean, and it does not matter
whether the ambush of frustrations
is ready for another assault.

The charm of this poem stems from the "scrambling" of two unrelated (even foreign), semi-professional jargons, which are nonchalantly implanted in Preil's favorite metaphorical vision (his notorious reconciliation of discordants, as in "Siberian snows almost melt / in the Mediterranean"). On one hand, there is the witty attempt to analyze (rather than describe) the linguistic procedures involved in the poetic process. For that purpose the poet enlists metalinguistic vocabulary ("concepts," "similes," "structure"), thereby effecting the impression of a distanced scientific observation. However, this very vocabulary is whimsically embedded in an arch-metaphor, which is a paradox in itself: The dictionary entries, normally calm, passive like a herd of lambs, turn into wild (predatory) animals in the process of "hunting a poem." One can here detect distant echoes of an earlier metapoetic poem: "A first line of a poem / is a hawk holding on to its prey." The initial turbulence and traumas of the creative drive were similarly dissolved there in an "imagined arch of victory," as here the snows melt in the warm Mediterranean when "the structure with its cells is completed." But here the similarity ends. For while the earlier poem, "*Hesberah shel Shura Rishona*" (1968), is an allegedly "objective," self-referential poem, the later poem is an open acknowledgment of the therapeutic value of artistic creativity. Thus the playful analysis of the poetic process is framed by the admission that, if nothing else, the writing of a poem has saved its begetter from one frustration attack, enabling him to relax before the next sets in. The insight itself may not be new in Preil's verse, but the language is definitely so. The popular "psychological" frame of reference is felt not only in the explicit use of terminology ("frustration attack," "release"), but in the implicit "negative" translation of some popular idioms as well. The negative statements that open the metaphoric description of the dictionary entries may be read, for instance, as a mirror-image of the poet's emotional state. "They" are not lost lambs, but he may be "a lost soul"; they do not climb up insignificant hills, but he may be "climbing up the walls"; finally—they are resting in a "valley of equilibrium," precisely that idyllic state of affairs the poetic voice longs for but never reaches. In other words, the dictionary has a relaxation effect on the poet because there he finds his "ego-ideal"—all the qualities he yearns for, but has to do without. Yet the psychological insight does not stop here: Therapy is not a matter of passive observation. Nor is art a matter of spending energy formlessly. Creativity, claim art psychologists (see Noy, 1969), is a process of disciplined structuring. In the language arts this may mean jolting words out of their satiated rest ("de-automatizing" them, in the Russian Formalists' jargon), letting go of their old familiar meanings, and finally giving them new life by rejoining them harmoniously despite tensions and contradictions. (The myth of creation is connoted here by the use of "bone" and *mi-bereshit* [from the beginning, since Genesis].) That this sense of creating *ab novo* has been the declared *raison d'être* of all artistic innovators is only too obvious. What is less in agreement is the teleology of this practice or achievement. Can artistic creativity save the world—as some Romantics would claim? Or is it a world unto itself—as some "pure art" advocates declared (with Imagists and New Critics following suit in different degrees of adherence)?

In its own way the metapoetic verse of Gabriel Preil has spanned these two extreme positions "with all the transitions between them." The "valley of equilibrium" in which it has recently come to rest is the small intimate space between man and his personal sorrows. Paradoxically, the acceptance of this truth has released new resources in Preil's poetic persona. The wistful irony of his earlier verse has recently been replaced by forgiving humor. Playful and witty, his writing now constantly keeps returning to themes and figures of his former poems in order to reexamine them from the vantage point of here and now. The effect created by this recapitulation is often humorous, thereby deautomatizing our perceptions and habitual readings. Obvious examples of this new trend are the poems "*Ha-Tzorech: Haklata*" [The Need: Recording] and "*Mashma'ut ha-Chum*" [The Meaning of Brown], which are included in Preil's forthcoming collection (still in press while this is being written) under the title *Chamishim Shirim ba-Midbar* [Fifty Poems in the Wilderness]. These poems almost parody the earlier poems "*Muklatim*" [Recorded] and "*Gonei Chum*" [Nuances of Brown] (1980:23 and 1968:38, respectively). Less obvious, but perhaps more instructive, is the poem "*'Ir, Dumiyat Telefon*" [City, Telephone Silence], which actually reacts to the complaint of "*'Ulai Mavet*" [Death Perhaps] (1978:17) by an "original" solution: "It is better maybe to abstain / even from the tastiest of words / to bundle up as a hedgehog / and enjoy a wonderful sleep / one that would arouse the envy of kings."

The opposition between the "tastiest of words" and the "bundling up" for a royal sleep is paradigmatic of this latest stage in Preil's verse. It continues the trend of self-analysis and true autobiographic introspection we noticed earlier. The art of beautiful (= tasty) words is conceived of here as a substitute for a less productive escapist drive.[16] And both of these may be viewed as defenses against the dominant feelings of sinking, or drowning, in the "wilderness."[17] This insight is brought to its logical conclusion (and to its highest artistic point as well) in the whimsical, unusually long poem "*'Al Frost, Oblomov ve-'Alai*" [On Frost, Oblomov and Myself] (subtitled "From a Joyful Diary") (*Yediot 'Ahronot*, January 22, 1982, p. 8). Inspired, no doubt, by the masterful Russian cinematic reworking of Goncharov's *Oblomov* which was shown in New York in the summer of 1981, Preil here dived into the deep waters of his memories, this time not in order to draw an imagistic picture, but in an attempt to give a rather full account, almost a narrative, of the first critical reviews of his work. Predictably, these most cherished moments are totally intertwined with the memory of his mother, "an expert in languages, / and particularly in Chekhov's and Goncharov's stories." She is the one who allegedly nicknamed him "Oblomov," but even she "did not know how much I prefer / the nightly dive / the holding on to this bait. / Yes, her son is still an Oblomov." Furthermore, claims the poet today, by then he had already realized that the poets to whom he was compared (Frost, Whitman, and lately, Stevens) "are secondary / (at most) in my sleeping game." That this is not an earnest declaration is made clear in a recent metapoetic poem: "I am an American-style Oblomov / yet not all Oblomovs are alike. / There is an Oblomov who writes a poem / between the beginning and the end" ("*Ha-Struktura Chasera*" [The Structure is Missing]).

So this American Oblomov plays not only "sleeping games," but (as may be expected) "writing games" as well—as, for instance, in another semi-metapoetic poem, "*Yeriya, Te'imat Tapuach*" [A Shot, Tasting an Apple], which opens the new section of the forthcoming book. This long poem draws a humorous, detailed analogy between the poet and "a scientist from Oregon / whose job is to differentiate among / one hundred species of apples." The comparison concludes on a whimsical note:

לַמְסַפֵּר כָּאן צְלִיל כִּמְעַט־אִידִילִי
אוּלָם עֻבְדָּה שֶׁאֲנִי לְבַדִּי בַּחֶדֶר
וְהַגֶּשֶׁם לֹא פּוֹסֵק, לֹא פּוֹסֵק,
נִשְׁאָר לִי רַק לַעֲשׂוֹת מִשְׂחָק
עִם כְּתִיבַת שִׁירִים, לַעֲקֹב
אַחַר הַשִּׁיר הָאֶחָד
לְתָפְסוֹ בְּרֶשֶׁת אֲמִינָה
וּלְיַדֵּד אוֹתוֹ בִּמְכֻוָּן
(מַנִּיחַ שֶׁאֵין כָּאן אֹנֶס)
עִם הַתַּפּוּחַ הָאֶחָד...

This narrative sounds quite idyllic
but in fact I am alone in my room
and the rain doesn't cease, doesn't cease.
All I have left is to play the game
of writing poems, to track
the single poem down,
catch it in a credible net
and intentionally make it befriend
(assuming there is no compulsion [rape] here)
the single apple:...

The purpose of this game is not explicitly stated, although by now it may readily be guessed.[18] Preil, however, does not commit himself. In the title of the concluding poem, "*Sheyar ha-Shirim*,"[19] he wittingly brings together a classical Hebraic source, *Shir ha-Shirim (Song of Songs, Song of Solomon)* and the semantically contrasting but phonetically very close noun *sheyar* (something left over, a remnant, mostly devalued; in an unvocalized text *shir* and *sheyar* are spelled identically: *shin* [sh], *yod* [i], *reish* [r]). The butt of this pun is the aspiration which has been shared by romantics (and symbolists) of all times, to create the "absolute work of art," as Mallarmé put it.

שְׁיַר הַשִּׁירִים

אֲנִי יוֹשֵׁב מוּל הַנְּיָר הַמִּתְגָּרֶה בִּי
וְאוֹמֵר:
הַאֻמְנָם חָשַׁבְתִּי פַּעַם
שֶׁיִּפְרַח לִי שִׁיר מְסַכֵּם אֶחָד
לְלֹא הוֹתֵר מָקוֹם לַאֲחֵרִים
טוֹבִים וְכֵן גְּרוּעִים מִמֶּנּוּ?
אֵיזוֹ תְּמִימוּת מְשַׁטָּה.

וַדַּאי שֶׁאִי אֶפְשָׁר לְהִתְחָרוֹת
עִם שִׁיר הַשִּׁירִים — מֵעֵין
סִכּוּם הַמְקֻדָּשׁ, סִכּוּם הַמְחֻלָּן.
אֵיזוֹ יֻמְרָה הָיְתָה בִּי אָז
וּמַה כָּעֵת נִשְׁאָר?
מִשְׂחֲקֵי קוֹלוֹת הַצִּפֳּרִים
תּוֹךְ יָרֹק אַוְרִירִי
מִשְׂחֲקֵי אוֹר־וָצֵל בֵּין
רִבּוּעֵי הַמִּדְשָׁאָה.

נוֹסָף לָזֶה אֲנִי מְקַסֵּם לְעַצְמִי
רֵאשִׁית אֶת אַגָּדַת כַּרְמֵי עֵין־גֶּדִי
לְאַחַר מִכֵּן אֶת מַטָּעֵי הַתַּפּוּחִים וְטַלָּם
בְּמָקוֹם שֶׁאֵינֶנּוּ
גַּם אֶת נוֹפוֹ הַשָּׁקוּף שֶׁל אַנְדְּרוּ מַרְוֶל,
הַמְאַהֶבֶת הַהַסְסָנִית שֶׁלּוֹ.
כָּךְ טוֹב לִי. הַחֶשְׁבּוֹן כְּמוֹ בָּרוּר.
אַף צֵל שֶׁל סִכּוּם לֹא בָּא לִי.
אַךְ מֶה הָיוּ עוֹשׂוֹת
הַמִּלִּים הַנּוֹדְדוֹת
לוּ חָתַמְתִּי: סוֹף.

Remnants of Poems [Songs]

I sit, face the paper teasing me
and say:
Did I ever indeed think
that one final poem [song] will bloom for me
leaving no space for others,
better as well as worse?
What a beguiling naivety.

One cannot, of course, compete
with the Song of Songs—a kind of
summing up of the sacred, the mundane.
How pretentious I was then,
and what is now left?
Games of birds' voices
in the airy green,
games of light and shade among
squares of lawn.

In addition I conjure up for myself
first the legend of Ein Gedi vineyards,
afterwards the apple orchards and their dew
in a place that does not exist,
Andrew Marvell's luminous landscape too,
his coy mistress.
Thus I am at ease. The account seems clear.
Not a shade of summing up appears.
Still, what would the wandering words have done
had I signed: End.

Fusing the diametrically opposite connotations of "*Shir ha-Shirim*" (a model of perfection) and *sheyar* (the devalued remnant), the poet actually debunks the lofty aspirations he once held but now finds impossible to sustain. Instead, the poem (and the forthcoming collection) ends on a rather playful note. Giving up the old pretenses, the poet now admits that his poetic creativity is a matter between himself and language or previous texts. The once much deliberated question of priority between "life" and "art" seems to have been solved unequivocally. The birds (the ubiquitous symbol of the poet) have lost all metaphoric implication; with them, color has also disappeared from the painter's palette. There appears to exist a clear-cut distinction—the objective world out there, including the voices of concrete birds and real games of light and shade, and the purely subjective game of fantasy, of poetic magic. Curiously, the world of magic the poet conjures up for himself consists of the *narrative* referent analogous to the one signified by "*Shir ha-Shirim.*" "*'Agadat Karmei 'Ein Gedi*" [The Legend of Ein Gedi Vineyards] invokes a folk-tale version of the story dramatized poetically in the biblical Song of Solomon. Still, the use of a different signifier changes the whole perspective: It is not the hallowed perfection of Scripture, but rather the softer, more intimate tones of the folk-tale (the popular narrative about young Solomon and Shulamit, his pastoral beloved) that are evoked by the poet. This intimacy is further underlined by the recourse to one of the poet's favorite images, the "apple orchards" in his lost Garden of Eden, his Lithuanian childhood.[20] Finally, the nonchalant joining of the Hebraic pastoral with Andrew Marvell's almost sarcastic version of the very same genre ("To His Coy Mistress") clearly identifies the nature of this poetry: It is neither scriptural nor another model of perfection, nor a naive love idyll or childhood recollection, but rather the reflections of a "somber romantic" who feels at ease without grand summaries or conclusions.

Characteristically, this concluding metapoetic poem cuts across a variety of poetic modalities (romantic rhetoric; imagistic miniature; narrative-idyllic detail). It attests to Preil's refusal to hold on to any one form of artistic doctrine. The only "closure" this open-eyed romantic can finally allow himself is a rhetorical question, one that is not punctuated (and therefore also not intoned) as a question. Playfully ending this poem (and the collection) on the lexeme *sof* (end), the poet nevertheless denies the possibility of putting an end to his creative resources. Consequently, an open door is left for new games with "the wandering words." Such games may not be idyllic, nor may they be "effective" in the real world. Still, they may very well serve as sublimatory defenses against the threatening wilderness that constitutes the very real life experience of the begetter of this work.

Conclusion

This study began as a search for the sources of a unique breakthrough in Hebrew modernism achieved on American soil. Our findings led us to place this exilic modernism in a wider context—the particular "historical poetics" of Hebrew and the general theory of literary translation and cultural transfer. Preil's poetic modernism turned out to be paradigmatic of the Jewish bilingual tradition, at least as far as the modernizing transfer from Yiddish to Hebrew is concerned. No less paradigmatic was the "blind spot" of the critics who for a long time ignored Preil's bilingual connection, thereby preventing even the poet himself from getting in touch with his own sources. With this blockage recently removed, we could follow Preil's own efforts by tracing his roots in the poetic traditions of both Hebrew and Yiddish. Because a major divergence between the two traditions has been a generic one, we have concluded that Preil's unique achievement stems from the fertile conflict between his Hebraic romanticism and his Yiddish imagism. The ups and downs of this conflict were explored by a close look at the poet's formative years in general, and at his autotranslational enterprise in particular. There we discovered that, despite the strong resistance of the romantic norms of Hebrew verse, imagism finally took over, making Preil the modernist he is known to be. Under the pressure of both literary (critical) as well as extra-literary circumstances (World War II), romanticism, we concluded, seemed to fall from grace. But not for long. In one way or another, the subsequent evolution of Preil's poetics is the story of the different guises in which his original romantic impulses keep coming back, cleverly eating away at the imagist worldview while at the same time utilizing its technical achievements. Finally, the crucial tension between object and subject, which has always plagued Imagism (as well as other objectivist theories) has been solved in Preil's recent work. Wedding the most direct, at times almost scientific, language with his most personal metaphoric vision, and implanting them both in a relatively new narrative framework, his poetry now promises to continue his multifaceted games with "the wandering words," thereby crossing boundaries and categories as never before.

Notes

Introduction

1. "Literary multilingualism" or "polyglot writing" is used here interchangeably to denote a writer's use of more than one language for literary purposes, disregarding the question of the writer's degree of proficiency in each of them. Cf. Forster (1970:18), who traces the history of multilingual literature from the Middle Ages to modern times.

2. See Kenner, "The Invention of Language" (1971:94–120), and "Words Set Free" (1971:121–144); Sheppard, "The Crisis of Language" (1976).

3. This German concept and its English offshoots are described in Wellek's "The Concept of Romanticism," 1963:128–129, especially 153–154. Uitti traces the nationalistic attitude to language all the way back to Dante's *De vulgari eloquentia*, in which Dante proposes that "the 'vernacular' is inherently nobler than Latin" (1969:36–42). Cf. also Kenner, 1971:106–110; Steiner, 1972; Bradbury, 1976 (especially p. 101).

4. From 1880 on—the Revival period and the Israeli period. For literary histories see Sha'anan (1962, 1967, 1977). In English, Halkin, 1950; Silberschlag, 1973.

5. The term *diglossia* is borrowed from linguistics in order to draw a line between this condition and regular (complete) multilingualism. (The existence of the latter is actually denied by most scholars.)

6. For the history of Hebrew see W. Chomsky, 1966 (Hebrew ed., 1967); Bendavid, 1967; Rabin, 1972.

7. See, for instance, Klausner's *History of Modern Hebrew Literature*, 1930–1950, Vol. 6.

8. Sadan, 1962:9–66; 1965, 1970. Werses, 1971 (especially 61–62), 1977. Miron, 1973, 1979a. Shmeruk, 1978, 1979. Jewish literature in German and English is treated only in the work of Shaked (1983).

9. For lack of other terms, the word *style* is used throughout this work in two differentiated senses: the normative, as in "separation of styles" (high vs. low, etc.), and the descriptive, as in "realistic style" (roughly: 'the mode of expression'). The intricate issue of modern approaches to style is beyond the scope of this presentation. For contemporary theoretical and practical arguments, see, for instance, Sebeok (1960), Chatman (1971), and 'Style' and 'Stylistics' in Preminger (1974).

10. On the intimate ties between recent literary and semiotic work at Tel Aviv University and the theories of Russian neo-Formalists and their contemporary disciples, namely, Czech Structuralists and Soviet Semioticists, see my essay, "Poetics and Politics" (1985).

11. For an English translation, see Matejka and Pomorska, 1971:79–81. For a discussion of this "quasi-structuralist" last-minute attempt to revise Russian

Formalism (before it was stamped out by the Soviets), see Erlich (1955)1981:134–135. Cf. Fokkema, 1976 (especially, 163–169).

12. For the Russian Formalists' theory of literary evolution, see Striedter's survey, 1977, 1978. Tynjanov's seminal essay (1922) is translated into English in Matejka and Pomorska, 1971:66–78. Cf. also Erlich (1955) 1981:251–271; Wellek, 1963:47–50. For a comprehensive bibliography of recent research in theory and practice of the polysystem hypothesis, see Even-Zohar, 1979:305–310.

13. On the roots of the systemic view in twentieth-century development of natural philosophy (from atomistic to holistic), see Laszlo, 1972. On its debt to modern philosophies of language, see Uitti, 1969:107ff; Levy, 1976:16–50. Cf. Erlich (1981:277), who draws a comparison between the Formalists' *sistema* or *struktura* and the "organized whole" of *gestalt* psychology, which was contemporaneous with them.

14. On the difference between this approach and that of some of the New Critics, see Erlich, 1981:253; Wellek, 1963:310; Uitti, 1969:159; Striedter, 1978. For a critical account of "The Formalist Projection," see Jameson, 1972:43–100.

15. Since the Romantic Age, innovation or eccentricity and originality have been considered the essential features by the arbiters of canonized taste.

16. Frye, 1957:108. Elsewhere, Frye also agrees with the Formalists concerning the filial aspect of literary change—the preference of "sons" for their "grandparents" or "uncles" (p. 62), a point to which we will return later in our inquiry.

17. On the cultural implication of this premise, see Progoff, 1953, especially Part II:159–287.

18. This is Jung's definition of the psychic process of "individuation." (Progoff, 1953:143–45; Franz, 1964:157–254.)

19. On the implications of the condition of "dissociation," see Jung, 1964:6–9; 72–73.

20. For a historical review, see Even-Zohar's "Russian and Hebrew" and "Israeli Literature: A Historical Model" (1978:63–72).

Chapter I
The Revival Period (1880–1920): A Bilingual Symbiosis?

1. The generic models of Mendele's fiction, for example, were clearly Russian (Gogol, Saltykov-Schedrin). The linguistic techniques he used in realizing these models were transferred from Yiddish to Hebrew (more on this below).

2. Recent prominent studies include Werses, (1962)1971:60–87; Shaked, 1965, 1977; Miron, 1973, 1979a; Perry, 1968, 1981. Zeitlin's article (1943) deals merely with the linguistic effects of Mendele's bilingualism.

3. For a summary and bibliography, see Shaked, 1977:40–43, 491.

4. The emergence of Hebrew non-canonized literature (detective stories and children's literature) has been studied only recently (Shavit [Zohar and Yaacov], 1974).

5. The first attempt at such a transition can be traced to his first Hebrew novel (during the *first* period); however, his artistic intentions only partially materialized there. See Miron, 1979a:223–224.

6. " 'Yidele [little Jew], what do you have to say?' he [Abromovitz] used to ask whenever he had difficulties in finding the proper Yiddish expression." D. Eynhorn, "Mendele bay der Arbet" [Mendele at Work], in *Ale Verk fun Mendele*, Vol. XX:59. Quoted by Miron, 1973:67.

7. Obviously, Mendele was not the first to attempt such a fusion. In fact, he improved on the techniques of his teachers Zweifel and M. Lefin, but it was only with him that this technique was established as a normative method. In fact, the tension between "purists" and their opponents can be traced back to medieval Hebrew belles lettres in its various manifestations (cf. Barzilay, 1979).

8. For another aspect of Mendele's autotranslational transfer, see Perry, 1981.

9. "The individual's personal variety of the community language system" (Pei and Gaynor, n.d.:95).

10. The anti-*Nusach* revolt was initiated by M.Y. Berdichevsky and perpetuated by the "poetic" novelist U.N. Gnessin and the "naturalist" Y.H. Brenner. On the stylistic innovations of the last two, see Shaked, 1973, 1977:378–382, 413–418; Miron, 1979.

11. His linguistic appropriations follow the sequence of countries in which he lived—Russia, England, Palestine.

12. Here we again run into a convergence of sources, as in Mendele's case. Brenner's literary models are unquestionably Russian (Tolstoy, Dostoyevsky, Uspensky—see Bacon, 1973, 1975; Feldman, 1979a, 1984), but his linguistic model is probably (Russified) Yiddish (see Shaked, 1977:380–381; Bacon, 1972).

13. See, for instance, the section "Translators [talking] about Translation," in *Siman Kri'a* 8 (1978:306–311) or Hrushovski's translation of Sholem Aleikhem in *Siman Kri'a* 10 (1980).

14. The issue of realistic style and the vernacular in bilingual writing was raised as late as 1965, when Y.D. Berkowitz published his childhood memories, in Hebrew (*Moznayim*, 1964–1965) and Yiddish (*Di Goldene Keyt*, 1964–1966), simultaneously. When asked about his so-called translation from Hebrew into Yiddish, he said: "I don't translate; it is being written in Yiddish by itself: I used to speak and think in this language throughout my years in Slutzk." See Werses, 1977.

15. See Even-Zohar, 1978:63–75; Shmeruk, 1969; Shavit, 1978.

16. On the concept "Bialik's generation" and its poetic implications, see Miron, 1961. On Bialik's contemporary, Saul Tchernichowsky, see below.

17. On the biblical nature of the verse of Bialik's predecessors ("*Chibat Tziyon* poets") see Kartun-Blum, 1969:31. The earlier history of the theoretical debate is traced by Barzilay, 1979.

18. Interestingly enough, these external sources themselves adopted the image of the biblical poet. On the history of this identification in the European Romantic movements, see Abrams, 1953; Shroder, 1961; Erlich, 1964. Cf. Shmeruk, 1969.

19. Bialik, "Shiratenu ha-Tze'ira" [Our New (young) Poetry], 1974:150, 155. On the transition from neo-Classical norms of the preceding generation, see Kartun-Blum, 1969.

20. On the psychological and autobiographical elements of Bialik's romanticism, see Zemah, 1969; Har'el-Fish, 1975; Averbach, 1977. On the concreteness of his nature descriptions, see Ha'ephrati, 1976:20–21.

21. For a detailed description of the technique of the "Inverted Poem" see Perry, 1976. The ambiguities and contradictory implications created by the dense texture are described also in Ha'ephrati, 1976. Cf. the dramatic quality attributed to English Romantic verse by Brooks, 1947.

22. For the different metrical systems see Zhirmunskii [1922] 1966; Wellek and Warren [1942] 1977:158–174; Frye, 1957:251–281; Lotz and Chatman, in Sebeok, 1960:135–172; Gross, 1965:37–41; Fussel, 1979. On Hebrew prosody, see Bacon, 1968; Hrushovski, 1971; U. Shavit, 1983. On Bialik's prosody, see Benshalom, 1945; Shapira, 1966; Shavit, 1978.

23. Earlier verse was governed by *syllabic* meters, which resulted in mechanical (visual) symmetries. The first poet to recognize the need for change was, characteristically, a *bilingual* writer (A.B. Gottlober, 1811–1899). See Hrushovski, 1954:233; Kartun-Blum, 1969:32–34.

24. Shavit, 1978, claims that Bialik followed Y.L. Gordon in the tripartite division of his canon, but replaced the latter's "fables" by his folk-songs (p. 195).

25. The rather simplified strophe structure and the relative metric freedom of the pure accentual meter is described by Hrushovski, 1954:224, 233 and 1977.

26. In this he was, indeed, preceded by David Frishman, who followed German (Klopstock's) hymnal free rhythms in his poem "The Messiah" (Shavit, 1979). On German prosody, see Zhirmunskii, 1966:181–192.

27. The varieties of these "free rhythms" are described by Hrushovski (1954, 1960), who also suggests this term in place of the French-inspired *free verse*. Other reservations of the term and of the measure of freedom implied by it are voiced by Hough, 1960:97–107 and Gross, 1965:25, 97–99. (These contemporary writers have been preceded by Eliot's early "Reflections on *Vers Libre*," 1917.) On the interrelation between modernist poetics and these prosodic tendencies see "Free Verse," Williams, 1974.

Chapter II
Beyond the Bilingual Symbiosis: Between Russian and Central-European Modernist Models (1920–1940)

1. The poet Rachel (1890–1931) and A. Ben-Yitzhak, respectively. Also, the first poems of David Fogel (see below) were actually published before the war.

2. On Shlonsky, see Levin (1960); Yoffe (1966); A. Weiss (ed.), 1975 (bibliography); Miron, 1974/5, 1975/6.

3. On the gradual transition and its effect on Shlonsky's prosodic techniques, see Kagan, 1975:130–150. On the varieties of Hebrew pronunciation, see Morag, 1971, especially 1120–1130. Also Hrushovski, 1971:1229–1230.

4. For a documented review of the period and its underlying conflicts, see Z. Shavit, 1983, especially 173–185.

5. This artistry provoked his nickname (a pun based on an anagram of his name) *Shlonsky-Leshonsky*, roughly meaning "Shlonsky the tongue twister" or "the language virtuoso" (playing on the word *lashon* [tongue, language]).

6. Natan Alterman, 1910–1970; Lea Goldberg, 1911–1970; Bat-Miriam, 1901–1980; Ezra Zusman, 1900–1973; Eliyahu Tessler, 1901–1965. (On Lea Goldberg, see Alter,

1977:91–102). The only Russian-born exception was Rachel (1890–1931) who wrote in simple conversational Hebrew. In her case, the reason was a lack of thorough Hebrew education on the one hand, and a close reliance on the conversational Russian lyricist Anna Akhmatova on the other. Cf. Hrushovski, 1971:1232; Miron, 1974/75:71.

7. See Y. Friedlander (ed.), 1974, especially the introduction (pp. 7–30); Alter, 1977:103–118; Lindenbaum, 1984.

8. See Lindenbaum 1974:242–281; 1984; Hrushovski (tr.), 1979:103–143; (1970) 1978:26–27; Shmeruk, 1979.

9. His not-too-well-known Yiddish verse of those years was recently collected in the second volume of his *Gezamelte Verk* (Magnes, 1979). Cf. Shmeruk, 1979.

10. For a detailed prosodic analysis of his early verse, see Hrushovski, [1970] 1978.

11. We have here one more example of the Oedipus complex in its literary guise—the "Anxiety of Influence" in Harold Bloom's formulation (1973). But unlike poets of other cultures, the second generation of modern Hebrew poets did not have any model grandfathers (Frye, 1957:62) or uncles (Shklovsky, 1923; quoted in Erlich, 1981:260) to hark back to. This lacuna corrected itself by the next generation, and Israeli writers immediately followed the cultural-sociological patterns observed in other cultures (Striedter, 1978:7). See also below, the close of this chapter.

12. The inept literal translation is as follows: Nagging and boring: poems-water, sentiments-licorice; / Rhyming doggerels: love and strife, and heart with hurt, and I don't know what! / Lasses—dresses, angels—priests, crime and blind, and street-dogs. (From *Mefisto*, 1922:52, quoted by Lindenbaum, 1974:263).

13. The amphibrachic meter gives the impression of mechanical regularity because of the complete overlapping of the metrical units (the feet) with the semantic units (the words).

14. His identification with Brenner's enterprise is expressed in *Kelapei Tish'im ve-Tish'a*, 1928:19–21.

15. See Greenberg's desperate search for "Bialik of the Past," the prophetic seer whose voice had been silenced: "*Bialik, 'ayeka?*" (Bialik, where are you?, 1928:12–13). Cf. *Kelev Bayit*, 1929:84–86.

16. The manuscript was published in *Siman Kri'a* 3–4, 1973:387–392.

17. It is probably no accident that it was in the 1950s that Greenberg resumed his writing in Yiddish, after a break of two decades (see note 9, above).

18. Apparently not much has changed since Brenner's mournful insight: "Of life secretly flowing—there is not even a hint" (Brenner [1911], 1937:164).

19. "Yet if the only form of tradition, of handing down, consisted in following the ways of the immediate generation before us in a blind or timid adherence to its successes, 'tradition' should positively be discouraged." T.S. Eliot, "Tradition and the Individual Talent" (1919), in Eliot, 1975:38.

Chapter III
Preil's bilingualism: The Critical Reception

1. I have adopted here Jauss' concept of *Rezeptionsästhetik* as the interaction between a new literary form and the system into which it is received. See Jauss, 1974.

2. Throughout the years, only two reviewers claimed to detect in Preil's Hebrew "a

lack of natural vitality" (Pnueli, 1954) or "outmoded expressions" (Bar-Yaakov, 1961). On another level, the critic Yeshurun Keshet (1963) raised the question as to whether Hebrew governs all of Preil's psychic being or only his conscious, conceptual faculties. Natan Zach (1954) and S. Sandbank (1962), on the other hand, detected occasional archaisms in Preil's Hebrew but approved of them as stylistic factors contributing to the "modernistic expression" or the "deautomatization" of the text.

3. As early as 1938, Shlonsky was aware of the different "styles" that were being hatched in *Eretz-Yisra'el*: "Home and street styles, the spoken and the written—styles of students and of urchins, of clerks and of laborers..." (1960:178).

4. When the leader of the "new" Israeli poets, Natan Zach (b. 1930), delineated "The Stylistic Climate of Hebrew Verse in the 50's and 60's" (1966a), he included Preil among the representative "young" poets who broke the boundaries of the stanza, preferred short forms and organic compositions, and lowered the traditional high poetic diction.

5. The only reproach came from the American-turned-Israeli, S. Halkin, who earlier criticized the over-Americanism of the periodical *Niv*, which was the mouthpiece of a group of young Hebrew writers, including Preil (Halkin, 1937).

6. On a few occasions Preil admitted that when he began to write he was unaware of the inner tensions and undercurrents that were permeating Hebrew poetry at the time. His extensive reading in search of literary roots came only later.

7. For general overviews of Hebrew poetry in the United States, see Halkin, 1942:49, *et passim*; Silberschlag, 1944, 1973:249–328 [English]; Epstein, 1952; Miklishansky, 1967; Kabakoff, 1967, 1978. See also Preil's own essays, 1954, 1955.

8. See Epstein, 1952:142; Preil's essays on Bavli (1961) and Halkin (1947); Band (1978:200); Sandbank (1976:103–122).

9. Similarly, the first generation of immigrant poets (who arrived around 1890) kept writing verse in accordance with sentimental *Chibat Tziyon* norms, long after the dominance of these norms was superseded in the center. The tendency to preserve and petrify literary standards is typical of "the decline to periphery," and was also noticed in social and linguistic behaviors: A cohesive group of immigrants tends to stick to its old culture in its new place, while in its previous home norms change and centers decline (Even-Zohar, 1978:77).

10. For a correlation between poets listed here and Preil's translations from the English, see Appendix 1.

11. Only a few of those are extant, in the book *'Achi-Sefer* (1943), while the bulk of those early translations have been lost. See also Appendix 1. The *In Zikh* movement and its manifesto are discussed in chapter V below.

12. For a detailed discussion of the literary implication of these facts, see chapter IX below.

13. For Jakobson's definition of novelty as the shifting of emphasis among the diverse potential (aesthetic) organizing principles (=*Dominanta*), see Matejka and Pomorska, 1971:82–91. The *dominanta* of Modernist verse are discussed in more detail in chapters V and VIII below.

14. Zach unfolds his views in *Time and Rhythm in Bergson and in Modern Poetry*, 1966 (see also 1966a). For the counterattack, see mainly Golomb (1976) and Lavo (1977). For the English reader, some sense of Zach's poetic venture, which was

strongly influenced both in theory and practice by T.S. ELiot, may be gleaned from his collection of translated poems, *The Static Element* (1982).

15. Shabtay, 1962; D. Carmi, 1962; Avineri, 1963; Kremer, 1968; Bertini, 1971. Only one voice was raised against this unified chorus: Y. Keshet (1963) claimed that Preil was less American than the rest of his American peers; significantly, Keshet was also aware of Preil's Yiddish verse, although he touched upon it very gingerly.

16. It is also possible that this was triggered by the fact that Preil's first book had been published in New York in a limited edition and was soon out of print.

17. For the original, see Appendix 4.

18. Cf. the tragic tone of his closing lines:

זינגער, ס׳איז דיר לײַכט דײַן װעג,
װײַל ביסט אײביג און טויט —
האסט פֿארלוירן דײַן גוף.

Singer [Poet], your path [journey] is light [easy],
since you are eternal and dead...
you've lost your body.

19. At least two of these writers deserve notice: Mordechai Yoffe, who wrote about Yiddish letters in the Hebrew periodical *Ha-Do'ar* (1944) and later translated Hebrew verse into Yiddish (1951, 1960), and Moshe Starkman, who devoted an essay to the pioneering bilingualists in America (*Ha-Metzuda*, 1954). See also Leshchinsky, *ibid.* Preil himself gave credit to Jewish bilingual writers in two short reviews (1960, 1963).

20. In his insightful essay, Miron (1977) suggests that Preil's early Introspectivism stemmed from his ties with Yiddish Modernism. The following discussion significantly modifies this suggestion (see especially chapters V, IX and X).

21. A similar correlation between dual language loyalty and openness to innovative poetics is attested to by the intriguing work of the (currently) "senior" Israeli poet, Avot Yeshurun. Born as Yechiel-Alter Perlmutter in the Ukraine (1904), he migrated to Palestine in 1925. Although he had attempted writing verse (in Yiddish!) in his youth, and was well read in both Yiddish and Hebrew literature, he did not publish his first book of verse until 1942. Like Preil, he was a late bloomer, and probably for similar reasons (see chapter IV). Like him, he also gained his fame in the 1960s, with the publication of his second book of verse (1961), which coincided with the Modernist shift in the poetic taste of the "young" writers. For more details, see the bilingual edition of his verse, *The Syrian-African Rift and Other Poems* (1980).

An analogous case may be suggested by the pioneering free verse of Amir Gilboa' (1917–1984). Although identified with the *Palmach* generation, and considered one of the first Israeli poets to deviate from Alterman's versification, Gilboa' was, in fact, also born in the Ukraine (né Feldman), and had written Yiddish verse before migrating to Israel in 1937.

Chapter IV
A Family Romance: Preil's Exilic Hebraism

1. Preil (1976:11). Unless otherwise stated, poems are cited by the publication date and the page number in the volume in which they appeared; if incorporated into the 1972 collection, this reference is given too. The translations aspire to be literal renditions of the originals to the extent that English structures permit this. Transcriptions of Hebrew poems will be offered only when the poems are subjected to phonetic or prosodic analysis. In the case of Yiddish, however, transcriptions are offered for the sake of readers who may have passive comprehension of the language, with no active reading facility.

2. "*Le-Zecher ha-'Av ha-Me'ushar*" [In Memory of the Happy Father] written in 1937 (1944:18; 1972:212); and "*Shelosha Shirim la-'Em*" [Three Poems for a Mother] written in 1941 (1944:69; 1972:232). "*Sichat Savim ba-Ya'ar 'al ha-Shachmat*" [Grandfathers' Conversation Over Chess] (1954:79,97), and "*Sava ve-Tidhar*" [Grandfather and an Elm Tree] (1954:97).

3. This was a clear departure from the tradition beginning with Bialik and continuing with U. Z. Greenberg, Shlonsky, and even Fogel, who regarded their biography as a part of their poetic utterance and as a manifestation of poetic truths. On the Romantic origins of this tendency and on the issue of biography and literature in general, see Tomashevskii, 1971:47–55; Lotman, 1976:82,103–106.

4. See, for example, "*Ba-Hoveh ha-Temidi*" [In the Eternal Present] (1976:49); "Mother's uncle was a physician to the Persian Shah..." For a full analysis of this poem, see Miron, 1977.

5. Rabbi Joshua-Joseph Preil (ca. 1850–1890) was a rabbinical scholar and a man of letters. In addition to a book of commentary, *'Eglei Tal* [*Drops of Dew*], his collected essays were posthumously published in New York (1924). They include "A Chapter on Verse"—an evaluation of the work of the leading poet of the time, Y. L. Gordon (1830–1892). Though a pious leader of a small community, he contributed to the "Enlightened" Hebrew periodical *Ha-Melitz*, polemicizing about contemporary national issues (against the *Chibat Tziyon* movement). His premature death was eulogized by the Talmudist Rav Tza'ir (Chaim Tchernowitz), who also mentions him in his autobiography (1954:143).

6. On parallelism as a basic poetic device, see Jakobson, 1958; Austerlitz, 1958:45–65; Shapiro, 1976:79–85. Most pertinent in this case is Lotman's suggestion of "situational rhymes" (1976:196; also 88–90).

7. Literally, "a problem," but mainly used as a technical term for a subject of study in the legal deliberations of the Talmud.

8. Regelson in 1947, and Halkin—who encouraged Preil's Hebrew writing and whose friendship was of particular significance to the young poet (see a poem dedicated to Halkin, 1954:33; 1972:148)—in 1949. (This was Halkin's second *aliya*; he had immigrated to Palestine in 1932 and returned to the U.S. in 1939. Efros migrated later, in 1955.)

9. 1961:84, 106–111; 1972:118, 132, 133, 134. Also a smaller group appeared earlier, in *Ner mul Kochavim*, 1954:100–102, 1972:204.

10. In constructing his irony, the poet utilizes two kinds of allusions. One is to

Solomon Ibn Gabirol (ca. 1021–1053), a leading Hebrew poet in medieval Spain, famous for his tempestuous soul as well as for his poem on this topic, "*'Ani ha'Ish*" [I Am the Man] (Shirman, [3]1971, vol. I:186). The second is a linguistic allusion to contemporary Zionist sociolect. The expression "planting trees," which implies a will for self-immortalization (its Zionist implications notwithstanding), is repressed here and replaced by "planting books"—a poet's version of the will for immortality. In order to understand the urgency of this wish, one should perhaps remember that Preil has never married and had been living throughout the years with his mother and stepfather, who were both sympathetic to and encouraging of his poetic career. With the death of his stepfather in the 1960s, the shelter must have been disrupted. By the 1970s, the poet was, no doubt, experiencing concern for his aging mother and his own solitary future. (His mother died in 1977, shortly after the publication of the poems under discussion here.) Cf. poems about his mother in *Shirim mi-Shenei ha-Ketzavot*, pp. 50–51.

11. For the concept of a "generating nucleus," see Riffaterre's "Matrix," 1978:19–21, *et passim*. For further discussion, see below, chapter VI.

12. English is powerless to render the grammatical pun by which Preil juxtaposes reality and invention or imagination. The word for reality (*metzi'ut*) derives from the root *m.tz.'*., which in its basic form means "to find," hence *reality* = what one finds, what is there; however, in the causative, the same root yields the verb "to invent, to make up" (*le-hamtzi*), which Preil uses in the sense of "invent" or "imagine."

13. Cf. Cohen (1982), who claims that Michal himself was aware that his (and his contemporaries') utopian attitude to the Land of Israel was possible only as long as an actual encounter did not take place (p. 205).

14. *Chibat Tziyon*, literally "love of Zion," was a pre-Zionist national-cultural movement.

15. Faivl Shraga Preil (ca. 1880–1921) was an "enlightened" young Hebraist, who inherited his father's pen and zeal for Hebrew, without his rabbinic proclivity. An ardent Zionist, he was the head of *Tze'irei Tziyon* ("The Youths of Zion," a non-Marxist Zionist-Socialist party) of the small Lithuanian town of Krakes, while struggling to make a living as the local druggist and banker. Clara Preil (ca. 1888–1977) was also versed in Hebrew (in addition to her familiarity with Russian and German literature) and later played an important role in providing her son with the space and freedom he needed for pursuing his poetic vocation.

On some of the other relatives, see the poems, "*Ba-Hoveh ha-Temidi*" [In the Eternal Present] (1976:49), and "*Ha-Doda, ha-Dod va-'Ani*" [My Aunt, Uncle and Myself] (1980:41).

16. Helman Kushner (ca. 1890–1965) was a graduate of the famous Telz Yeshiva and taught Talmud at the Rambam Yeshiva in Brooklyn. He seems to have shared his wife's enthusiasm for his stepson's poetic career. See the poems dedicated to him, "*Rambam: Vinter 1964*" (*Lider*, 1966:68); "*Zo ha-Pa'am ha-Rishona*" [This is the First Time] (1968:41).

17. These first three poems, "Frost," "Landscape" [*Peyzazh*], and "Wonder Mirror" [*Vunder-Shpigl*] were later incorporated into *Lider*, 1966:14,42,53.

18. The "Objectivists" were a later offshoot of the earlier American Imagists. They are described by Kenner, 1975:158–193, and Alter, 1977:119–136. On the Imagists

and their poetic principles, see Coffman, 1951; Hough, 1960:3–83, especially 12–16, 35, 80; Pratt, 1963:11–39, especially 18, 22; Gross, 1965:100–168, especially 105, 119–120; Kenner, 1971:173–191, 397–406; Juhasz, 1974:13–39; Harmer, 1975; Zach, 1976.

Chapter V
The Return of the Suppressed: Preil's Yiddish Sources (*In Zikh*)

1. The nature of *In Zikh* (1920–1940) and its introspectivistic manifesto is discussed below. For the cultural background of its inception and the prior stages of the modernization of Yiddish verse in America (the *Yunge* in particular), see Howe and Greenberg, 1969:25–55; Liptzin, 1972:311–332; Wisse, 1976:265–276. Glatstein's poetic oeuvre was recently described in Hadda, 1980. See also the introduction to the collection of English translations of his poems, R. Whitman, 1972:11–26. In Hebrew, Sadan, 1970:120–140; Hrushovski, tr., 1978a:79–100; Shenhod, tr., 1964.

2. The autobiographical genre had been so excessively used by Yiddish poets that Glatstein already parodied it (see his "*Oytobiyografie*," published in *Kredos*, 1929, and reprinted in his collection, *Fun Mayn Gantser Mi*, 1956:323).

On the function of the title in arousing false expectations (generic and others) and on its role as an interpreting marker, see Riffaterre, 1978:99–114.

3. *Of Time and Place* (*Mi-Toch Zeman ve-Nof*) is the title of Preil's collected poems (1972).

4. On semantic oppositions and their function in constructing the meaning of a text, see Greimas, 1970:40; Leech, 1974:106; Lotman, 1976:72–87; Riffaterre, 1978:43–44, *et passim*.

5. Cf. Harold Bloom's notion of "misreading" or "misprision," attributed by him to the reading of 'strong poets' of all ages, including Hebrew Kabbalists (1975, 1976:103–105, 117, 123).

6. Of the disagreement among critics concerning the continuity or discontinuity of Glatstein's oeuvre, see Sadan, 1970; Hadda, 1980:22–27.

7. On the heated debate concerning this issue, see Niger, 1925, and 1925a; Leyeles, 1925; Minkoff, 1942; and later Glatstein, 1971. There is no doubt, however, that the *Inzikhistn* were influenced by the Modernist trends of their time. In fact, the mere publication of a manifesto was itself a sure sign of Modernism (cf. Bradbury and McFarlane, 1976:192–205). For more on this issue, see Feldman, 1985. My thanks to Avraham Nowersztern for bringing this debate to my attention.

8. Cf. Miron, 1977:172; Roskies, 1980:353; Feldman, 1985.

9. Cf. Hadda, 1980:28–41, 56–58, 64–70.

10. Glatstein's encouragement of Preil can be attested to by the several reviews he devoted to him. As early as 1940 he dubbed the young poet the *mezinek* (youngest son) of *both* Hebrew and Yiddish in America. He saw him as "a symbol of our twin languages that can dwell together in one poet without a conflict." Two decades later Glatstein continued this train of thought when he suggested a bilingual edition of Preil's poems (1961). His last review of Preil's verse is included in his posthumous collection, 1972.

11. Teller's poetic career may serve as an intriguing test case for the inherent limits of the Imagist/Objectivist poem. Characteristically, he moved from purely imagist poems to "poems of the time" (1940), and from these to essayistic treatment of historico-political problems: *Scapegoat of Revolution* (1954); *The Kremlin, the Jews and the Middle East* (1957); *The Jews: Biography of a People* (1966), etc. Cf. my (Hebrew) essay (1983a) and my "Tribute to Y.L. Teller," *Midstream*, Dec. (1983b).

12. This narrative style seems unexpected only against the background of Preil's recent work. It is actually a return to one of the modes he had tried in his earliest stages (see chapter VI, below).

13. This style is also reminiscent of the "Objectivism" of the 1930s, although Preil, at least, denies any familiarity with it. See chapter IV, note 15, for references.

14. See Teller's critique on the rhetorical poetics of Zalman Shne'ur, below. Cf. Frye, 1957:60–61.

15. "In the Imagist poem human content is implied rather than stated." "Imagist poems differ from other poems in leaving more to the reader to interpret" (Pratt, 1963:30). Cf. Smith, 1968:254–255. On the dangers inherent in this technique, see Hough, 1960:83; Gross, 1965:107. In this tendency toward "dehumanization," Imagism participated in a Modernist process that reached its zenith in the later movements of Dadaism and Surrealism (cf. Balakian, 1947:106, 132; R. Short, 1976).

16. Zalman Shne'ur (1887–1959) joined Bialik's circle in Odessa at the age of thirteen and subsequently lived in Warsaw, Vilna, Paris, and Berlin. After an unsuccessful attempt to settle in *Eretz Yisra'el* (1925) he returned to Paris from which he barely escaped in 1941. He then settled in New York, where he had been contributing to Yiddish periodicals since 1926. While in New York, he published a long epic in Hebrew and translated his Yiddish novels into Hebrew. He migrated to Israel in 1951. See Klausner, 1947; Sha'anan, IV, 1967. More on this in chapter VII.

17. For a detailed discussion of (auto)translational strategies, see chapter IX.

18. For a detailed discussion of both Shne'ur's rhetoric and the Imagists' "poetics of hardness," see chapters VII and VIII, respectively.

19. Most of the Yiddish reviewers applauded Preil's bilingual creativity without any further comments. One of them (Starkman, 1966) even noticed a touch of Hebraism in Preil's Yiddish images (this applies, of course, to a later stage in Preil's writing, when he was translating from Hebrew into Yiddish).

Chapter VI
Romanticism Revisited: The Early Hebrew Verse

1. Shaked, 1976:13–42. Cf. Band, 1968:38–53. On Agnon's noncommittal irony, see my essays (Feldman, 1983, 1985b).

2. This process is even more restrictive for the readers of Preil's verse in translation. His English translators exhibit a marked preference for the imagistic miniatures and ignore his earlier work or even the later longer narrative or "romantic poems" (cf. my "Tribute to Y.L. Teller," 1983b). The bilingual edition of Preil's verse, *Sunset Possibilities and Other Poems* (1985, the Hebrew–English poetry series of the Jewish Publication Society), includes *no* poems from the 1944 volume and only three poems from the 1954 volume. Although these translations were prepared by

Robert Friend, Preil's chief translator, similar biases characterize most other translations, including *Autumn Music*, 1979, ed. by Howard Schwartz).

3. This kind of poem, which had been phased out of Preil's subsequent work, has made a comeback in poems published most recently. See his later book *'Adiv le-'Atzmi* [*Courteous to Myself*], 1980, and the poem "Yehuda Leib Teller," discussed above, chapter V, pp. 62–66.

4. For the question of the freedom of *vers libre* see Eliot, "Reflections on *Vers Libre*" (1917) in 1975:31–36; Hrushovski, 1954, 1960; Hough, 1960:84–107; Gross, 1965:99, 111, 176, *et passim*; Herrenstein-Smith, 1968:84–87; Williams, 1974.

5. The count depends on whether or not the initial *sheva* is considered a phonetically independent syllable (as in the prefixes *ve-* [and], *be-* [in], *le-* [to]). Cf. Bacon, 1968:67–77 and Kagan, 1975:144–149.

6. The chief characteristic of colloquial Hebrew structure is the rejection of the biblical order of VSO (predicate + subject). However, when this order is retained in modern Hebrew, it automatically signals an elevated style, as we shall presently see.

7. This reader-oriented version of the Romantic organicist approach derives from Roman Ingarden's phenomenology of reading (1931, 1937; quoted by Wellek, 1963:278–279). His theory of "schematized views" (cf. Iser, 1971) was elaborated (sometimes in divergent ways) by Riffaterre, 1967, 1967a, 1974, 1978; Smith, 1968; Eco, 1976; Todorov, 1969; Fish, 1970, 1980; Iser, 1971, 1974; Lotman, 1976. Cf. Culler, 1975:98–103, 113–160, *et passim*; Tompkins, 1980.

8. It is the last point that is so vehemently opposed by current "deconstructionist" literary criticism. Following Derrida's assault on the "metaphysics" of meaning, Barthes modified his earlier position and called for the deference of closure and the plurality of reading (1974:15–16), while Fish argued *against* "coming to the point,... [against] the need to simplify and close" (1970:148). Cf. Culler, 1975:241–254; Harari, 1979, especially 17–120.

9. See Bialik [3]1973:32, 176, 204, 240, 316.

10. The literal meaning of *sofer* is "one who counts." The scribe was supposed to count the letters and dots so as not to miss any of them while copying. For another use of the term (i.e., an official in charge of conscription to the army), see de Vaux, 1961:225–251.

11. Cf. *'ad she-titmaleh pegimatah* in Talmud Yerushalmi, Berachot 13:4.

12. It may recall the ancient ritualistic sacrifice that took place in the Temple on the Day of Atonement. The Talmudic directives for the ceremony use the verb *'era* (a perfective form of the same verb, *le-'arot*), in describing the handling of the blood of the sacrifices (Yoma 5:4).

13. "...and the writing was God's writing, engraved (*charut*) on the tablets" (Exodus 32:16); this is the only use of the verb in the Bible, a fact which strengthens its association.

14. See *Michtav Katan Li Chatava* [She Wrote Me a Brief Letter], Bialik, 1973:64.

15. The term was suggested in Riffaterre (1978:139) to describe one of the periphrastic rules generating the surface level of the text from two subtexts or hypograms.

16. On the element of surprise as a stylistic marker see Riffaterre, 1967:467.

17. This equivalence also offers a syntactic justification for the use of the definite

article before *zemirim*. For a similar device in Baudelaire's *Les Chats*, see Riffaterre, 1970:210.

18. The term was widely used by Shlonsky and Greenberg. See, for example, Shlonsky, 1978:23, 29, 31, 142; Greenberg, 1929:30, 79, 84.

19. Cf. Preil's poem "The Nineteenth Century" cited on p. 51, chapter IV, above. In another poem the *zamir* is coupled with Bialik's cricket:

> ...And at midnight I heard
> the tune of a cricket
> repeating its refrain
> until the hour was wrapped in shades of sapphire
> and from the grove
> the voice of the nightingale
> shone.
>
> "*Deyokan 'Atzmi*" [Self-Portrait] (1968:54).

20. The image of the sacred parchment was also used by Shlonsky and Greenberg, but never in its cosmic-mythic aspect (cf. *Bereshit Rabba*, 1:a; *Genesis Midrash Rabba*, 1939:1).

21. On the problematic conflict between scribal loyalty and personal concerns, see Agnon's " 'Agadat ha-Sofer" [The Tale of the Scribe], 1974, V.II, 131–145.

22. The abrupt transition is signaled also by the syntax. The enjambment between lines 2 and 3 separates the tenor of the scribal image from its vehicle, which introduces the theme of the tragic dichotomy of life/death. The same holds true for the only other enjambment (lines 12–13). A detailed prosodic analysis is given below.

23. In the descriptive elements of the sun imagery one could detect a faint echo of Wordsworth's *Prelude*, Book II, 11:368–370): "An auxiliary light/Came from my mind which on the setting sun / bestowed new splendour..." (Wordsworth, 1920:647). However, Preil handles the analogous elements in a more mythologized fashion.

24. The poet's central position in the Romantic worldview was presented in Shelley's "A Defence of Poetry" (1951:1023–1055). Cf. Abrams, 1953:99. As for the Promethean image, see Shroder's summary (1961:98): "the Romantics interpreted the tale of Prometheus as a myth of revolt... The name of Prometheus was linked with that myth of human progress which runs through much of Romanticism." Cf. also Balakian, 1947:105.

25. On the poetics of the literary allusion, see Ben-Porat, 1976; C. Perri, 1978; Riffaterre, 1978.

26. See Bialik's "*Megilat ha-'Esh*" [The Fire Scroll] 1973:408.

27. "The Fall of Hyperion," Canto I, 11:188–190 (Keats and Shelley, n.d.:357).

28. It is probably based on the old identification of blood=soul (Deuteronomy 12:23). Unfortunately, this idiom is still a relevant one in modern Israeli sociolect. It is often used in military memorial ceremonies.

29. This is clearly in the tradition of Russian Romantic poetry; cf. Erlich, 1964, Cf. the "fall of Icarus" as another Romantic metaphor, in Shroder, 1961:217.

30. Preil openly identifies with Bialik in a later poem (1961:10, 1972:82), in which he uses a composite of Bialik's motifs including his "rock." Cf. also "when I knock my head/against the poem's rock" (1968:75, 1972:56).

31. Again, the Romantic grounding of this image may be reinforced by an association with an English source. The juxtaposition between the lyric nightingale and the bereaved eagle echoes Shelley's elegy for Keats, *Adonais*, stanza XVII (1951:552). Shelley's mourning eagle, in its turn, recalls Aeschylus' use of the same image in *Agamemnon*: "...as eagles stricken in agony / for young perished..." (Act I, II, 49–50). (For this intertext I am indebted to the generous reading of Prof. Robert Belknap.) However, Preil's exact verbal expression has its antecedents in biblical sources (cf. Zephaniah, 1:14: *Mar tzoreach sham gibor*) which were also used by Bialik to describe a lonely eagle, although in a different context (1973:182).

32. It should perhaps be noted that in Yiddish the word *soyfer* has not undergone a similar shift; it still retains only the older meaning (scribe), while a modern author is designated by words of German origin. (See, for instance, Glatstein's poem, *Der Bratslaver tsu Zayn Soyfer*, 1956:160).

33. The centrality of this motif in Preil's later work and its different guises are discussed in chapters IV and V above.

34. This supports Eco's definition of "art" as ambiguously organized messages which follow a precise design that is *the same* on all levels (or systems) of the text (1976:271).

35. The broad distance between stresses which these clusters create is described by Hrushovski (1954:240–246) as one of the traits of *Yiddish*, which in this respect was under the sway of Eastern Slavic tongues. Since a clear preference for this device is typical of the bilingual poet U.Z. Greenberg (see chap. II, section 2), it is possible that Preil, too, transferred this feature from Yiddish to Hebrew.

36. The prominence of constructs is definitely significant: There are ten (hyphenated) occurrences in our thirteen-line poem: *'atik-yomin* (line 1), *rig'ei-chayim* (line 3), *be-chaf-yadam* (line 12), etc. Examples for syndetic combinations are *'otiyot ve-tagim* (line 2), *'argaman ve-shachor* (line 9), and *mi-dor le-dor* (line 11). Other groupings consist of prepositional phrases—*parus lefanai* (line 1), compound predicates—*bati lechadesh* (line 5), and adjectival phrases—*libam ha-mefarper* (line 12).

37. On the relationship between rhythm and syntax, see Brik, 1971; Gross, 1965:38; Hough, 1960:103–104; Hrushovski, 1960:179–181; Smith, 1968:85. On the term *rhythmo-syntactic figures*, see also Zhirmunskii, 1966:158–170. On the significance of syntactic consideration in the production of poetic utterance, see Nowottny, 1962:9, 19, *et passim.*

38. The second and third strophes are almost identical in their structure; the first and the fourth are marked by parallel enjambments.

39. On the anaphora as a rhythmic factor, particularly in the free verse of Whitman and his followers, see Willy, 1929; Allen, 1975:225–227; Hrushovski, 1978:36. Gross (1965) mentions the effect of Whitman's syntactic parallelism (p. 86), stating that "Whitman's basic contribution was the substitution of syntax for meter" (p. 85).

40. Cf. Keats' "Ode to a Nightingale" and "Ode on a Grecian Urn," Shelley's "Ode to the West Wind," and Wordsworth's "Ode on Intimations of Immortality."

41. For the term and its applicability to Yiddish free verse, see Hrushovski, 1954:253–257. On the tension between meter and syntax, see Zhirmunskii, 1966:23, 158–170; Wellek and Warren, [1942] 1977:158–173; Lotman, 1976:46. The lack of this

tension is considered by Hough (1960:104) as the rhythmical disadvantage of free verse. Cf. Gross, 1965:84.

42. These later culminated in Preil's unprecedented endeavor to render Sandburg's *Prairie* into Hebrew (1949). For a list of Preil's translations, see Appendix 1. Cf. his essay on Sandburg on the occasion of the latter's seventy-fifth birthday (Preil, 1953/54).

Chapter VII
Toward a Poetics of Despair: The Budding of Hebrew Modernism

1. *Bitzaron*, vol. 40 (New York: 1949), p. 19.

2. The fact that Shne'ur's claim has been recently refuted (on the grounds of its *Ashkenazi* metric grid—see Shavit, 1981) does not detract from the significance of his conscious intention to create a new rhythmic option in Hebrew, even if, in fact, he failed to do so. (Cf. the "unmasking" of U.Z. Greenberg's "free rhythms" by Hrushovski (1970), referred to in chap. II, section 2).

3. Curiously enough, in the earliest version of the poem (*Gilyonot*, 1939) the second line ended with the normative form *'agaleh*, thus consisting of twelve syllables. By replacing it with the short biblical form *'agal* (consistently in the 1944 book as well as in the 1972 collection), the poet added to the elevated tone of the opening and to the rhythmical symmetry of the couplet.

4.

5. אוּלָם לֹא אֵדַע אֵיךְ אָכִיל כָּל דִּמְעָה נִשְׁפְּכָה
6. מִיּוֹם בָּאָה לָאָדָם, — טַל־נֶחָמָה בְּאֶבְלוֹ,
7. פְּנִינַת־יְקָר בְּשִׁמְמוֹנוֹ כָּבֵד;
8. אֵיךְ אָבִין הַצְּחוֹק מִדַּרְדֵּר תָּמִים
9. בְּצֵל עֵץ־דֻּבְדְּבָן מַשְׁלִיג נֹגַהּ בְּמִשְׁעוֹל,
10. אוֹ בֵּין חוֹמוֹת יִתְגַּלְגֵּל עַרְמוּמִי וְנִקְשֶׁה.
11. וְהֵן גַּם זֹאת אֵדַע:
12. דִּמְעָתִי־יְתוֹמָה נֹאדוֹתַי מְלֵאִים שֶׁלִּי לֹא תּוּכַל דְּלוֹת
13. וּצְחוֹקִי נָדִיר לֹא יְעוֹרֵר רֶנֶן פַּעֲמוֹנֵי־כֶסֶף לִי.

But I don't know how I can contain all the tears shed
since Man's beginning—a comforting dew in Man's mourning,
a precious pearl in his deep desolation;
how I can understand the innocent laughter rolling out
in the shade of a cherry tree snowing lustre on the path,
or shewdly and harshly rolling among walls.
But also this I know:
My orphan-tear is unable to exhaust my *own* full jugs
and my rare laughter would not arouse a tune of silver bells for me.

5.

20. בְּשָׂרִי יָחוּשׁ הַשְּׁכוֹל פָּרַשׂ מִכְמֹרֶת, הַשֵּׁן הַנִּנְעֶצֶת,
21. לִי עוֹד יַזְהִירוּ טַל־נֶחָמָה שֶׁיָּבַשׁ, פְּנִינָה שֶׁכָּהֲתָה;
22. וְרַק אֲנִי לְבַדִּי — שׁוֹמֵר נֶאֱמָן לַשִּׂמְחָה שֶׁשָּׁקְעָה.

My flesh senses bereavement spreading a net, the penetrating tooth;
the dried-out comforting dew, the darkened pearl, still shimmer for me;
I alone am the faithful guard of the joy that expired.

6. See T.S. Eliot's "The Metaphysical Poets," 1975:59–68; Preminger, 1974:195, 196.

7. Similarly, the third part of *Ner mul Kochavim* [Candle Against Stars] (1954), entitled "*Mi-Derech Leil 'el Yom*" [From Night-Road to Day], includes poems which touch upon the Holocaust. Their pathos, however, is greatly toned down.

8. The poem was originally published in 1940, in *Niv*, New York.

9. The tight formal net of anaphoras and parallel lines, both synonymous and antithetic, can be clearly perceived even in translation.

10. The changes that have taken place in Preil's use of the "birds" code are among the clearest indicators of his evolution. The imperial eagle never appears again; nightingales make occasional appearances, but the poet is mostly represented as "just [another] bird, hopping on a greyish thread" (*'eizo tzipor* [*revi'it*] *menateret 'al chut 'afarpar*), in "*Shalosh Tziporim ve-'Achat*" [Three Birds and (Another) One], 1968:60; 1972:50. Clearly, this difference in metaphorical representation signals a transition in the poet's self-perception from the heroic to the ironic, from pathos to understatement. For a detailed analysis, see below, chapter X.

11. The title is based on the widely used idiom *'azelat yad* (Deuteronomy 32:36), "(the) hand is gone," namely "powerless." Preil's original usage, conveying the lack of *words*, may have been inspired by the collocation of *'azelat yad* with the lack of *prayer* in Bialik's earlier version of an elegy-turned-wrath poem. Cf. "*'Al ha-Shechita*" [On the Slaughter], Bialik, 1973:152:

לִבִּי מֵת. אֵין עוֹד תְּפִלָּה עַל שְׂפָתַי.
וּכְבָר אָזְלַת יָד, אַף אֵין תִּקְוָה עוֹד.

My heart is dead, there is no more prayer on my lips.
The hand [power] is gone, nor is there any hope left.

As in the poem "Notes on an Ancient Parchment" (see chap. VI, above), it is possible that another of Bialik's poems obliquely inspired the imagery of this poem. In "*Levadi*" [Alone], a broken wing represents the motherly figure of the impoverished Divine Presence (*ha-shechina*); when the shelter she offers becomes too "narrow" (*tzar*), she tries to "shelter" and/or "fence in" (*sacha*) her last devotee under her broken wing. Although Preil replaces *kanaf* (wing) by its poetic synonym *gaf*, both *tzar* and *sacha* are lexically represented in his phrase *ke-suka tzarat kir va-gag* (line 4). (*Sacha* and *suka* derive from related roots.)

Some typically elegiac expressions seem to point to Isaiah 22, one in a series of oracles of doom. It opens with the loaded noun *masa* (oracle) (line 5) and continues with a well-known threnodic verse (22:4) which is represented in our text by three vocables: *meni* (from me) (line 1), *shod* (violence) (line 3), and *'ami* (my people) (line 2). The connotations of doom are intensified by other intertextual ties of *shod*. The phrase *shod va-shever* (calamity) is often used by both Isaiah and Jeremiah. Also strongly associated with Jeremiah's elegies is the word *nehi*, (lament) (line 5), and the word *tzori* (balm) (line 2). (Less obvious, though contextually relevant, are the sources of *hachil* (contain, hold) (line 5) in Jeremiah 6:11; 2:13). The interjection *'Alelai* (Woe to me) (line 2) is from Job (10:15), which is also the main biblical source of *mila* (word) (line 1). This intertext is particularly clear because throughout the Bible the older synonym is used, *davar* (cf. *diber*, "spoke"). The rare form *meni* (instead of *mimeni*, "from me") is another marker of the special diction and rhetoric of Job.

12. In the famous opening of his poem "*Ha-Matmid*" [The Yeshiva Student], Bialik says: "God has let survive / A burning coal in the ashes." However, *gachelet* can also stir up connotations of prophetic calling and the word of God, because it belongs to the same paradigm as *ritzpa*, the "glowing coal" of Isaiah's sanctification (Isaiah 6:6).

13. The morpheme *niv* is easily recalled, because the most frequently used form of the verb is its causative, *yanivu* (will bear fruit). The affinity between "fruit" and "utterance" is based on Isaiah 57:19, where "utterance" is conceived as the "fruit of the lips" (*niv sefatayim*).

14. Cf. "The Idea of the Modern" in Howe, 1967: "For the modernist writer the universe is a speechless presence..." (p. 21). Hassan extends the notion of "silence" to what he terms "*Post* modernism," (1982).

15. The odd meter, composed wholly of paeons, is, in fact, a foreshadowing of the fate of dipodic feet in modern Hebrew verse. Since the majority of Hebrew words are polysyllabic and the stress ratio is 1:3, dipodic meters tend either to skip certain tonic accents, mostly first and third (the melodious "Russian" school of Shlonsky-Alterman) or to dissolve its paeons—a trend that had begun with U.Z. Greenberg and continued later with the young poets in the 1950s and 1960s (see chapter I, above). Preil was one of the pioneers in this respect. Cf. Hrushovski, 1971, 1978:33–35.

16. The similarity between Preil's elegiac rhythm and that of Lamentations can be demonstrated by the following charts, which illustrate the tension between two concurrent rhythmic systems in Lamentations 1:1,2; syntactically there are three units in each verse (I), but the cantillation marks dictate a binary division (II).

The arrows in these charts mark chiastic parallelism (on all levels—semantic, syntactical, and morphological) which variegate the perfect symmetry of the accents in hemistichs b+c of each verse. The cantillation rhythm cancels that effect completely in verse 1 and changes its proportion in verse 2.

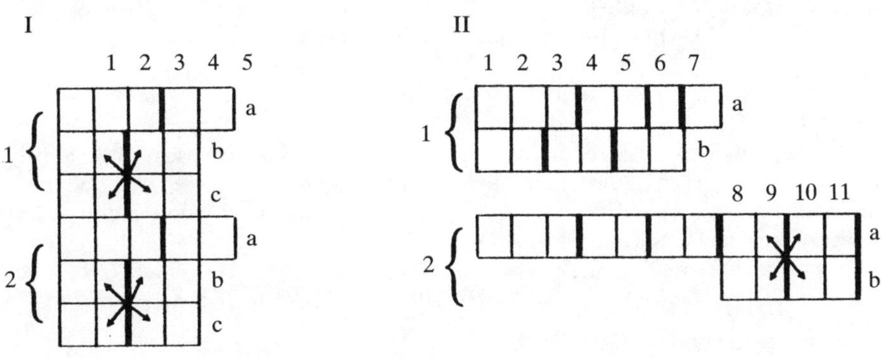

17. On the catalogue (enumeration) as a rhythmic device, see Gross, 1965:87; Smith, 1968:98–109; Allen, 224–230; Fussel, 1979:76–89.

Chapter VIII
Yiddish Beginnings: Études in Imagism (1935–1936)

1. Except for one poem, "*Oktober*," all Yiddish poems were incorporated into *Lider* (New York, 1966) and will be cited herein by their page number in this book.

2. However, when rendered into Hebrew, these poems constituted a change in the horizon of expectations held by the Hebrew literary circles in New York (see chap. IX).

3. Cf. Juhasz' chapter "Definition as Example" (1974:40–49). However, it should be noticed that a more direct metaphor was developed by the Imagists by omitting the copula altogether. Pound's famous lines: "The apparition of these faces in the crowd: / Petals on a wet, black bough" are a case in point. Hugh Kenner (*loc. cit.*, especially 197) convincingly argues that this technique evolved from an initial "misreading" of the nature of Chinese ideograms, which Pound took to represent static images (cf. Frye, 1957:123). Needless to say, the transfer to English of what he (Pound) perceived as a peculiar stylistic feature of Chinese must have created totally different effects in the target language due to the syntactic choices involved. The lack of copula is stylistically significant in English, whereas in Chinese it is simply a traditional feature of the language. (See Yip's highly informative essay [1974].) In this respect Yiddish resembles English, and the omitted copula is felt as a stylistic marker, signaling a more direct treatment. This option was used by Teller (see, for instance, the second strophe of "Heat," translated in Appendix 2), but not by Preil. Curiously, Preil does avail himself of this device when writing/translating in Hebrew, as we shall have the opportunity to see later.

4. See, for example, "*Hesberah shel Shura Rishona*" [Explaining a First Line] (1968:9, 1972:25): "A first line of a poem / is a hawk . . . / or a lightning-stricken forest / . . . "; or, in "*Perusho shel Shir*" [The Meaning of a Poem] (1968:10, 1972:25): "The Poem is the only stable ground / is a prayer renewing its colors like butterflies" (cf. also note 6 below).

5. See, for instance, "The day was translucent / as a painting by Monet", or "Van Gogh: Williamsburg" (1968:80, 42; 1972:40, 59). Van Gogh is alluded to several times in *Mapat 'Erev* (1960:27, 55) which is the most "painterly" of his books (cf. Miron, 1977:172). Other painters occasionaly mentioned are Rembrandt and El Greco.

It should be noted that in Hebrew verse Preil was preceded by the "colorists" Ben-Yitzhak and Fogel. His Yiddish predecessor, Teller, showed more interest in the effects of light. This predilection manifested itself in his extensive use of the Yiddish equivalents of glitter, glow, shine, and so on (exploiting the wide range of their different derivatives) and in the frequent use of mirrors and window panes in his imagery (see translated samples in Appendix 2).

6. For a similar construction in a later Hebrew poem see "Three Birds and [Another] One" (1968:60; 1972:50), discussed in detail in chapter X below:

Three birds	tenor:concrete
were three notes of music	metaphor: sound
were three drops of paint	metaphor: sight
on a greyish	
telephone line	complement: concrete
conducting voice from maze to maze	metaphor: sound
from an abstract view to the land of the inane.	metaphor: sight

Both Yiddish and Hebrew examples demonstrate how far removed Preil's nature imagery is from its Romantic counterpart; the metaphoric materials are *not* drawn from the same source as the tenor (cf. Wimsatt, 1954:103–118).

7. This subjective element, as well as the reconstructable chain of associations it implies (snow flakes may *look* like question marks; question marks *conceptually* evoke riddles; riddles are associated with secrets, unknown destiny, and so forth), is in accordance with the principles of *In Zikh* (see chap. V, pp. 59–60).

8. The part of the chart that deals with sounds has been omitted here because it is not relevant to our case. Gombrich's diagram is a simplification of C.E. Osgood's three-dimensional "semantic space," as presented in "The Measurement of Meaning," Urbana, 1957 (quoted by Gombrich, *ibid.*).

9. In fact, Teller's technique is much closer than Preil's to the Chinese-inspired "poetics of discontinuity" (cf. Yip, 1974; Yu, 1979; Bock, 1979), detected also in Imagism and Objectivism. Preil's need to round out his presentation (often very subtly) is much stronger, as was already argued (although from another point of view) by Perry (1972, 1979).

10. This freedom of selection, which is nevertheless determined by the constraints of the text itself, is aptly described by Lotman (1976:85): "The poetic world has thus not only its vocabulary, but its own systems of synonyms and antonyms. Thus, in some texts 'love' can be a synonym of 'life,' whereas in others, it is a synonym of 'death'... A word in poetry may not equal itself and may even be its own antonym." Cf. Tynjanov (1924) 1971:136–145; Ullmann, 1971.

11. If Frye's statement that "charm" is an etymological descendent of "chant" (*carmen*) is correct (1957:278), it is fascinating to observe how semantic ties are recreated even without obvious derivative or etymological affinities. *Gezang* and *kameyes* preserve the same connotations of incantation as do their English counterparts.

12. For the suggestion that the act of reading is an experience or a temporal event, and that the question by which meaning is extracted should be "What does a sentence do?" rather than "What does a sentence mean?", see Fish, 1970.

13. Characteristically, the bird associated with the magical chanting is not the Romantic nightingale or eagle, but a modest whispering swallow, probably the precursor of the plain "birds" of Preil's later Hebrew verse (see chap. X).

14. The prevalence of the mirror (or window panes) in the verse of both Teller and Preil may remind us that the anti-Romantic revolt is often considered a return to mimetic art. Frye argues, for instance, that the different phenomena of twentieth-century modernism "are all in a way part of a reversion to high mimetic standards" (1957:63), and that the modern poet "thinks of himself more as a

craftsman than as a creator or unacknowledged legislator...hence...the kind of non-didactic revelation implied in such terms as *symbolisme* and imagism" (*op. cit.*, pp. 60–61).

15. This early formulation of Imagism by its founder T.E. Hulme is reported by F.S. Flint in "History of Imagism," written for the *Egoist* magazine in 1915.

16. Cf. the differences between this poem and Teller's "*Vint*," outlined in chap. V above.

17. The semantic constituent of negation is realized in the following words which all have privative connotations: *op-grunt* derives from the German *Abgrund* (literally "*off*-ground"), *farvorlozt* implies *un*doing former ties, *nekhtens* evokes a past which is *no* more (particularly in view of the idiom a *nekhtiger tog*, roughly connoting "bygones"), and *besalmens* (cemetery) stands for death, the ultimate negation.

18. It is perhaps interesting to note that the idea of intertextuality so prevalent nowadays in literary criticism has earlier roots in the discipline of art history. In 1943, Wolfflin claimed that "every picture owes more to other pictures painted before, than it owes to nature." Quoted by Gombrich in "André Malraux and the Crisis of Expressionism" (1978:82) and elaborated in other essays and in his book *Art and Illusion*, 1960.

19. "The only way of expressing emotion in the form of art is by finding an 'objective correlative'; in other words, a set of objects, a situation, a chain of events which shall be the formula of that *particular* emotion; such that when the external facts, which must terminate in sensory experience, are given, the emotion is immediately evoked." ("Hamlet" in Eliot, 1975:48).

20. "A work of literature...creates an (at least one) Internal Field of Reference [IFR]... At the same time, however, many sentences in a literary text may refer to an External Field of Reference [ExFR]... Many generalizations... refer to both inside and outside. The reader judges such statements both from the values of the IFR and from the values of the ExFR (the real world)"—Hrushovski, 1979a:373; cf. Even-Zohar, 1980.

Chapter IX
Autotranslation as Literary Transfer

1. See, for instance, his letter to A. Shlonsky, for many years one of Israel's leading translators (July 28, 1965, Genazim 55928): "...I'll be very grateful to you for informing me of your present work on translation. I am highly preoccupied with the problems involved in translation; the interest they arouse in me is endless." For the original, see Appendix 4.

2. Since the 1960s, Preil's autotranslations have reversed their direction—he now translates from Hebrew to Yiddish only. This reversal may very well signify the general shift that has been taking place in the Hebrew–Yiddish diglossia. Unavoidably, Yiddish has been losing its status as a folk language, while Hebrew is gaining the vitality of the vernacular, at the probable expense of its classical status. Obviously, there is room to examine the effects of this complementary transfer on contemporary *Yiddish* verse, but such an examination lies beyond the scope of the present study.

3. "It is for this reason that we oppose the cosmic poet, who seems to us to shirk the real difficulties of his art" (Pound, 1915).

4. The term *semichut hamchasha* was suggested by Dan Pagis to denote this figure of speech which is common in the poetry of the medieval poet Moses Ibn Ezra (1970:69–70). A similar device in English poetry is described by Frye, 1957:280–281.

5. I suspect, although I have no way of substantiating this, that Preil may have been inspired by Glatstein's political satire "*Shpigl Ksav*" (1956:328, originally published in *Kredos*, 1929), in which the political connotations of red and black function as a central device: "*O, shtey oyf, o, shtey oyf, o, shtey oyf / tsum kamf vos iz royt. / .... Mit der fon vos iz royt / mit der hemd vos iz shvarts / shvartsroyt roytshvarts / tsumershtn, tsum tsvelftn, tsum viftn – / un der troyer iz zayn noentster korev.*"

Preil himself makes use of these two kinds of palettes in the poem "*Nyu Hempshayr Meydl*" (*Lider*:137), which was also published in *In Zikh* (1938) but was never translated into Hebrew. In this poem, the girl is described in "pastel" colors (white face, green eyes), whereas the threatening world is "dressed in *scarlet* and *black* / and every third man is his brother's hangman..."

6. On the gender of the metaphor as a specific problem in translation see Jakobson (1959), Dagut (1976), and Van der Broeck (1981). Cf. Feldman, 1982.

7. The subject of love or *eros* is rarely dealt with by Preil. The only other poem that was never translated is also a love poem, "*Nyu Hempshayr Meydl*" (see note 5, above). Here, the night/light dichotomy of *Kontrast Motiv* is transposed to the opposition winter/summer. The poet is described as a dreamer seeking refuge, but the girl's wintry face and lips block the way to her "sealed summer."

8. Curiously enough, Preil's penchant for contrasts and polarities manifests itself even in his essayistic writing. The title of his article on Agnon resembles the Hebrew title of "*Kontrast Motiv*": "*Mashehu 'al Yesodot ve-Nigudim be-Sipurei 'Agnon*" (1966). A few years later he finds elements of verbal surprise in the poetry of Yehuda Amichai. This is characteristically defined by him as a fusion of "cool irony" and "spicy warmth" (1970).

9. If the following English renditions sound somewhat awkward, it is because I tried to stay as close as possible to the original, as the only way to render the stylistic differences between the Hebrew and Yiddish versions.

10. The recently coined term *realemes* pertains to "items of reality" which, when used in verbal utterances, "constitute items of *cultural* reality, the repertory of realia..." (Even-Zohar, 1980:67). The relevance of this term to the issue of translation is strongly argued: "Various replacements of realemes, partial delections, as well as amplifications are normal translational procedures" (p. 68).

11. The Hebrew expression *tel-'afar* often connotes a grave, thus totally changing the "neutral" meaning of the Yiddish *bergl.* For this comment I am indebted to the careful reading of Gideon Toury.

12. Since the Hebrew alphabet has numerical values, the Hebrew calendar uses letters instead of numbers. Occasionally, a sequence of letters would form a meaningful verbal unit. The symbol תרצ"ח for the year 1938 appropriately means "you will murder [kill]," and it is this meaning that is operative in the content of this Holocaust poem.

13. The shift from the Yiddish *shvalbn* (swallows) to *ankorim* (sparrows) may be

seen as the beginning of Preil's employment of the image of the undistinguished grey bird (see chap. X). My thanks to Gideon Toury for calling my attention to the "unfaithful" translation.

14. It took Preil about three decades to be able to write "Chinese-style" without seeking elevation of his subject matter (see his dainty reworking of the motif in "A Chinese Drawing" [1968:25, 1972:33]). However, his interest in this topic dates from his early contacts with the Inzikhists, with whom Chinese motifs were very popular (see Preil's translation of Glatstein's "Chinese Theatre," *'Achi-Sefer*, 1943:551–555).

15. The single-strophe structure and the prepositional anaphoras are reinforced by the *ve-* (and) in line 7, which counteracts the sense of surprise effected by "suddenly."

16. This is possible because many Hebrew adjectives are formally present-tense verbs; for example, *mishtokeket* (eager) actually means desires or yearns to; *mitholel* (wild) means behaves wildly, gets out of hand, etc.

17. Syntax also contributes in creating the effect of activity: The literary VS order is manipulated here without the effect of literariness. The fact that five of the seven syntactic units *open* with a verb somehow stresses the line of action, rather than functioning as a stylistic sign. This is achieved by the use of compound sentences; in fact, only in two cases (*pirperu ha-mayim* and *kasam shikui*) do we have a real reversal of syntactic order; in the others, the verbs simply relate to former subjects.

18. The analogous evolution of Hebrew modernism on the two peripheries calls for further investigation. Pomerantz was probably inspired by Polish and Yiddish expressionism. In one of his works he declares that he recites his poems to pine trees and discusses them with his pets, since "they do not demand that I pour my blood / into isometric shining glasses" (1966:140).

19. Cf. Preil's Yiddish review (1953) which, rather surprisingly, explains the Israeli literary scene from a socio-political point of view.

20. Preil often jokingly says that he feels closest to the three "P"s of Hebrew poetry: Fogel (Hebrew *f* is an allophone of *p*), Pomerantz, and Dan Pagis (a younger contemporary, b. 1930). Of these three, Fogel's poetics resembles his own the most, especially in the "discontinuity" and use of colors (cf. Schwartz, 1972). However, Fogel's imagism is much more stylized; the reality he conjures up never attains the concreteness of Preil's later urban and country scenes (cf. Miron, 1977). A poem such as "*Le-yad ha-Bayit ha-Yashan*" (1944:13), for example, is reminiscent of Fogel's mood and use of language (cf. Fogel, 1966:75, 115). Interestingly, it was only in his English essay (1959) that Preil openly related Ben-Yitzhak, Fogel, and Lea Goldberg (!) to the Imagism of Fletcher and Amy Lowell (p. 9).

Chapter X
Metapoetics: To Imagism and Back

1. We should remember that there is hardly any other Hebrew poet in whom art and life so fully overlap (see chap. IV, note 9, in particular, for the biographic circumstances inspiring this condition). Cf. Kartun-Blum, 1982 (p. 6), which was brought to my attention after the completion of this chapter.

2. Cf. the opening of "The Pond": "I know a forest / and in the forest I know a humble [chaste, hidden] pond / ...and no one knows what there is in its [her] heart..."

Later on the phrase "Who knows" ("...perhaps she secretly dreams," etc.) is repeated four times (pp. 361–366).

3. See, for example, "*Ba-Sheki'a ha-Tzehuba*" [In the Yellow Sunset] (1960:39; 1982:93): "*Bi-Fshot ha-Tav'era*" [Upon the Fire's Spread] (1960:27; 1972:87); "Stav *ba-Gan ha-Merkazi*" [Fall in Central Park] (1960:23; 1972:127), "*Mis'ada Avtomatit*" [An Automatic Restaurant] (1960:23; 1972:127). See also references to painters in this volume, particularly Van Gogh (pp. 27, 55) and Rembrandt (p. 50)—quite an intriguing choice in its polarity.

4. Cf. Preil's later poem "*Perusho shel Shir*" [The Interpretation of a Poem] (1968:16; 1972:25): "How will I defend myself, how will I explain / that the poem is the only stable ground..."

5. Admittedly, such pure objectivism is rare in Preil's Hebrew work. In most of the imagistic poems the speaking subject is *not* obliterated. See, for example, "*Nofah shel Shura*" and "*Shurot Boker va-'Erev*" in this book (1968:12, 15). Only very few poems are as "objective" as the poem "*Gonei Chum*" [Nuances of Brown] (1968:32), which was, I believe, one of the poems responsible for establishing Preil's fame as an "imagist." For Preil, then, pure Imagism is mostly reduced to a technique, rather than constituting a comprehensive poetics.

6. Cf. chap. VIII, note 6.

7. Summer has a derogative connotation in Preil's idiolect. He often prefers the cool weather, the clouds, and the snow.

8. For an in-depth analysis, see my Hebrew article, Feldman, 1979.

9. There are at least fifteen occurrences of the color grey or its derivatives in *Ha-'Esh ve-ha-Demama* (1968), in contrast to both earlier and later volumes. For more on the use of colors in Preil's recent verse, see Treinin (1981) and Toker (1981).

10. See, for example, the poem "*Ta'arucha*" [The Exhibition] (translated in Feldman, 1981), in which the romantic code of "the poet as a bird" is used to contrast past and present in terms of colorfulness vs. greyness: "But, the poetess kept silent: / Only her letters / speaking mutely / behind the glass / almost proved / that all has been said / and grey is the backdrop of things— / even though once / a garden was mentioned / and she was among the trees / a bird / colorful even in despair" (1968:92; 1972:65). For an earlier version of this same contrast, see "*Tzayar 'Ivri*" [A Hebrew Painter] (1960:111), quoted in chap. IV above. For a Yiddish antecedent of "a grey bird" see the poem "*Frost*," chapter VIII, especially note 13.

11. See "*'Arim she-Bi*" [Cities within Me] and "*Gan ha-'Andartot*" [The Garden of Statues] (1968:85, 91; 1972:62, 65, respectively).

12. See, for example, "a grey joy" in "*Deyokan 'Atzmi* [Self-Portrait] (54); "*Be-Siman ha-Piyus ve-ha-Geshem*" [Under the Sign of Appeasement and Rain] (111); "*'Izun u-Mikreh*" [Balance and Accident] (45); and "*Ha-Ribua' ha-Memutan*" [The Moderate Square], in "*Gramercy Park*" (1972:19).

13. However, for the admirers of Preil's imagism these volumes feature such lucid miniatures as "*Halicha Geshuma*" [A Rainy Walk] (1976:27), "*Taklit*" [A Record], and "*'Adiv le-'Atzmi*" [Courteous to Myself] (1980:15, 22).

14. "No one would ever believe if I told / of such a sunset. They would say / outworn phrases were kindled / in my mind, / the complicator of things came / and made me a poeticizing immature youth" (1976:24). And cf. "*Sheki'at ha-Chama*"

[Sunset] in 1980:45: "This time it is not a pretext / for a scientific classification of nuances, placing it / in the mythology of this or that people, / nor for the play of languages that once were, / nor even for a title of a young poet's / first book."

15. Cf. also "*Zemani Ka'et*" [My Time Now] (1980:47):

כָּעֵת עִם עֵמֶק שִׁלְגָּהּ שֶׁל הָאֵם, עִם
הָעַלְוָה הַמַּחְלִידָה הַנֶּאֱחֶזֶת בִּי, עוֹד
לֹא הִסְפַּקְתִּי לִלְמֹד פֶּרֶק פִּכָּחוֹן, וְתוּר
וְכֵן לְהָבִין שֶׁאֶתְגָּר הוֹפֵךְ לְקֶרַח.

עִם זֹאת מַה־מִּסַּעַר מַרְעִיד אֶת שָׁרָשַׁי —
וְחָשׂוּף אֲנִי נִמְשָׁךְ לַחֲזָרָה מְסֻפֶּקֶת
לְעוֹנוֹת חֲלוֹמִיּוֹת פְּקוּחוֹת עַיִן.

Now, with mother's valley of snow,
with the rusty foliage seizing me,
I have not managed to learn a lesson
of sobriety, of acceptance,
nor to understand that challenges
turn to ice.

Still, something stormy stirs my roots,—
and exposed, I am drawn to a dubious return
to open-eyed seasons of dream.—

Similarly, see "*Shir Sho'el Katan*" [A Brief Questioning Poem] (1981:47): "There was an unfathomed romanticism / experienced by youths / at the turn of the century. / Mother was young then / and father loved her flowing hair..."

16. Cf. another poem from the same collection, "*Ba-Chanut ha-Sfarim*" [At the Bookstore]: "I could add, of course / that she is one of the poems / but such things went to sleep / bundled up like me / in the waking spring..."

17. See, for example, "You sink. No question. / You don't wish for a thing. / A woman is a dying flame / A book is closed with no comfort" (*'Al ha-She'elot* [On Questions]); or: "I am not in New York / I am enclosed in the *shtetl* across the sea / drowning in mud, sinking in oddities, / a bachelor playing his petty games / ...My former geography, / doubling itself / in the mirror of a sunset now, / grows more and more familiar. / Soon I'll run into / Gnessin in the rain. / I am not in New York. / Tomorrow, perhaps, for the sake of a balance / I'll take up a pen / and write a few words / to a friend in the Promised Land." ("*Chipus ha-'Izun*" [Search for a Balance]).

18. Cf. "Only in the poem he finds his city. / Even if it grows as white as Athens / it is all aflame in Jerusalem. / This is how at times he calms down" ("*'Ir ha-Shir, Shenei 'Anashim*" [The Poem's City, Two People]).

19. See *Siman-Kri'a* 16–17, April 1983: p. 127.

20. See, for example, "The Lithuanian autumn is not a youth anymore / having smiling apples dance in his basket" ("*Zichron Setavim ba-'Aviv*" [Remembering Autumns in Spring], 1968:29).

Appendix 1

Preil's Translations into Hebrew

From Yiddish (poems by Jacob Glatstein):

"*Te'atron Sini*" [Chinese Theatre]. *'Achi-Sefer*, New York:1943, pp. 551–555.

"*Avishag*" [Abishag]. *Op. cit.*, pp. 555–556.

"*Leil Menucha, 'Olam*" [Good Night, World]. *Darom*, Argentina: 1944, p. 122.

"*La-'Achot ba-Merchakim*" [To a Sister Far Away]. *Ha-Doar*, 6/21/1946, p. 737.

"*Nigun*" [A Melody]. *Ha-Doar*, 4/12/1946, p. 562.

"*Dorenu*" [Our Generation]. *Ha-Doar*, 1/17/1947, p. 291.

"*Sheva' 'Esreh Levanot*" [Seventeen Moons]. *Ha-Doar,* 2/28/1947, p. 435.

From English:

Frost, Robert:

" *'Etz 'al-yad Chaloni"* [Tree at My Window]. *Ha-Doar*, 4/20/1945, p. 486.

"*Temunat Mechonit*" [Picture of an Automobile]. *Ha-Doar*, 5/28/1950, p. 964.

H.D. [=Hilda Doolitle]: " *'Etz 'Agas*" [Pear Tree]. *Ha-Doar*, 8/24/1945, p. 806.

Jeffers, Robinson: "*Tzohorayim*" [Noontime]. *Riv'on Katan* (Summer, 1944); pp. 219–220.

Sandburg, Carl:

"*Shir Ruach*" [Wind Song]. *Op. cit.*, pp. 221–222.

"*Siflei Kafeh*" [Cups of Coffee]. *Molad* 3, 1949, p. 241.

" *'Arava*" [Prairie]. *Sefer ha-Shana Li-Yehudei 'Amerika*, 1949, pp. 249–256.

" *'Ikar be-'Ilinoi*" [A Farmer in Illinois]. *Ha-Doar*, 9/21/1951, p. 768.

Stephans, James: "*Dirdere*" [Deirdre]. *Niv* (April, 1937), p. 37.

Whitman, Walt: "*Demumot Tihyena ha-Machanot ha-Yom*" [Hush'd Be the Camps Today]. *Ha-Doar*, 4/24/1945, p. 405.

Wylie, Elinor: "*Ben Kastilia*" [Castilian]. *Riv'on Katan* (Spring, 1944), pp. 108-110.

Appendix 2

Y.L. Teller: *Miniatures*, 1934

(Selections)*

First Frost (p. 6)

The sun is high. The light
strikes sharp like hail.
It smells of distant noise,
of first frost.

Girls walk small
shaggy dogs;
boys wheel about
in spinning circles.

The air is raw.
Birds glitter nearby.
Cold and distant fumes.

ערשטער פראָסט

די זון איז הויך. דאָס ליכט
שלאָגט שאַרף ווי האָגל.
סע שמעקט מיט ווייטן רעש,
מיט ערשטן פראָסט.

מיידלעך פירן קליינע,
קודלעוואַטע הינט;
יינגען רעדלען אום
אין שווינדלדיקע קרייזן.

די לופט איז רוי.
פייגל בלענדן נאָענט.
קעלט און ווייטע רויכן.

Figure (p. 8)

Winds will break trunks
around slender girl-walk;
the face will tear itself
as through webs;
sun will shudder
and panes will clatter in light;
who will thaw the joy
of hard and pointed nipples?

פיגור

ווינטן וועלן ברעכן שטאַמען
אַרום שלאַנקען מיידל־גאַנג;
דאָס פנים וועט זיך רייסן
ווי דורך נעצן;
זון וועט שוידערן
און שויבן וועלן בראַזגען אונטער ליכט;
ווער וועט אויפטאַיען די פרייד
אין האַרטע און שפּיציקע נאָפּלען?

* The spelling of the Yiddish follows the original as it was published in 1934.

Snow Shovelers (p. 43)

Small people with glittering
shovels
speak white language
in the night.

Miles of voices,
spades and snow.
Streetcars ring
through the lit tumult.

In the fog bodies glow
like panes.
Breath steams up
all the stars.

שניי־שאַרער

מענטשעלעך מיט בלאַנקענדיקע
שופליעס
רעדן ווייסן לשון
אין דער נאַכט.

שטרעקעס מיט קולות,
רידלען און שניי.
טראַמווייען קלינגען
דורך ליכטיקן טומל.

אין נעפל גליען לייבער
ווי שויבן.
אָטעם פאַרהויכט
אַלע שטערן.

⁂ (p. 10)

Autumn. Boys
unfurl snakes in the air;
windows bloom
like orchards.
Days of dull sun
and hot colors.
Riders bridle their horses;
speeding over blazing cities
as through storms.

⁂

האַרבסט. יינגלעך
לאָזן שלאַנגען אין דער לופט;
פענצטער צעבליען
ווי סעדער.
טעג פון מאַטער זון
און הייסע פאַרבן.
רייטער צוימען זייערע פערד;
יאָגן איבער צעצונדענע שטעט,
ווי דורך שטורעמס.

Autumn (p. 13)

My eyes darken
from flying birds.
The sun is far in the sky
and warm at the feet.
The earth is homey
and dry;
Limbs are awake
like nerves.

האַרבסט

מיינע אויגן טונקלען
פון פליענדיקע פייגל;
די זון איז ווייט אין הימל
און וואַרעם ביי די פיס;
די ערד איז היימיש
און טרוקן;
גלידער זענען וואַך
ווי נערוון.

Heat (p. 14)

June. You are limp
from the shine.

The air—light [weightless],
glittering planes.
Windows—near and distant
and blind in the sun.

Houses move from the banks,
and like on the water
it strikes with lustre.

היץ

יוני. דו ביזט שלאַף
פון שיין.

די לופט — לייכטע,
בלאַנקענדיקע פלאַכן.
פענצטער — נאָענט־ווייט
און שטאַר פון זון.

הייזער רירן פון די ברעגן,
און ווי אויפן וואַסער
שלאָגט מיט בליאַסקען.

From the Forest (p. 11)

The noisy rush of streams
like the fall of heavy weights;
shimmer of hatches and splinters—
flying foam
over swaying trees.
Small birds glitter
like drops in the sun.

פון וואַלד

דאָס ראַשיקע לויפן פון שטראָמען
ווי דאָס פאַלן פון שווערע געוויכטן;
בלענד פון העק און שפּענער —
פליענדיקער שוים
איבער וואַקלענדיקע ביימער.
קליינע פייגל פינקלען
ווי טראָפּנס קעגן זון.

A Town Street (p. 20)

The wind drives signs
like waves over our heads;
the sun clatters, like glass,
and there is a cold glitter
among the trees.

Shimmers are caught in a wildweb.
Automobiles float
with impetus, as if gliding.

It darkens. Windows are open,
and from radios night shrieks
with hot voices.

שטאָט־שאָסיי

דער ווינט טרייבט שילדן
ווי כוואַליעס איבער אונדזערע קעפּ;
די זון בראַזגעט, ווי גלאָז,
און איז אַ קאַלטע בלענדעניש
צווישן די ביימער.

שיינען פאַרכאַפּן אין ווילדוועב;
אַוטאָמאָבילן טראָגן זיך
מיט אימפּעט, ווי אויף גליטש.

ס׳טונקלט. פענצטער זענען אָפן,
און פון ראַדיאָ שרייט די נאַכט
מיט הייסע קולות.

Appendix 3

Prosodic Charts of

"He'arot 'al Gevil 'Atik Yomin."

I. Ashkenazi syllabo-tonic scanning

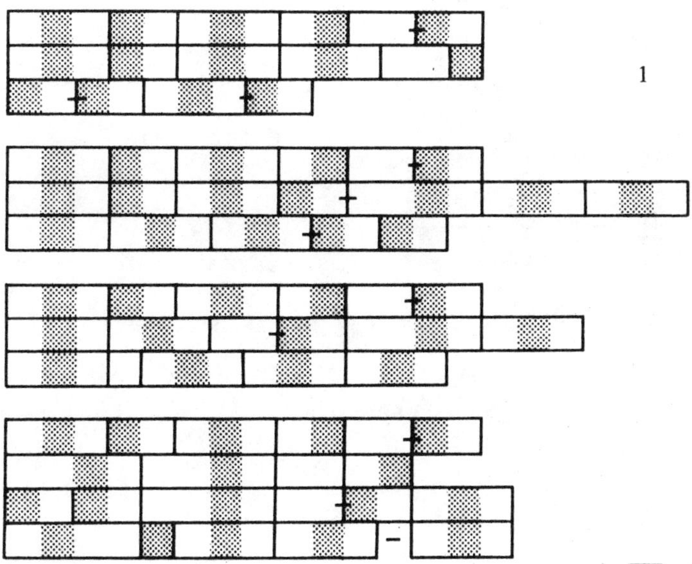

Line	*anap.*	*amph.*	*iamb.*	*tro.*	*paeon*
1		2	1	1	1
2	1	3		1	
3		1		3	
4		2	1	1	1
5		4		2	1
6		3		2	
7		2	1	1	1
8		3			2
9		3			1
10		2	1	1	1
11					3
12		1		2	·2
13		3	1		1
	1	29	5	14	14

Rubrics represent words; hyphens represent constructs.

II. Sephardi syllabo-tonic scanning

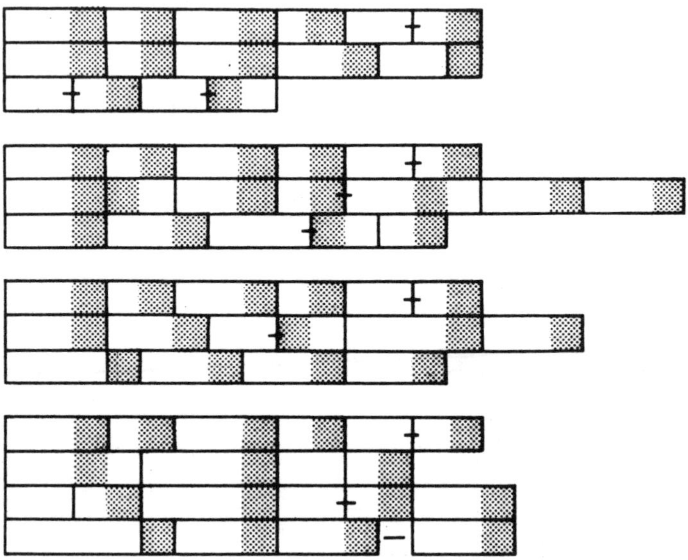

	anap.	*iamb.*	*tro.*	*paeon*
1	2	2		1
2	4	1		
3				2
4	2	2		1
5	4	1	1	1
6	3			1
7	2	2		1
8	3			2
9	3			1
10	2	2		1
11				3
12	1			3
13	2			2
	28	10	1	19

Rubrics represent words; hyphens represent constructs.

III. Sephardi accentual scanning

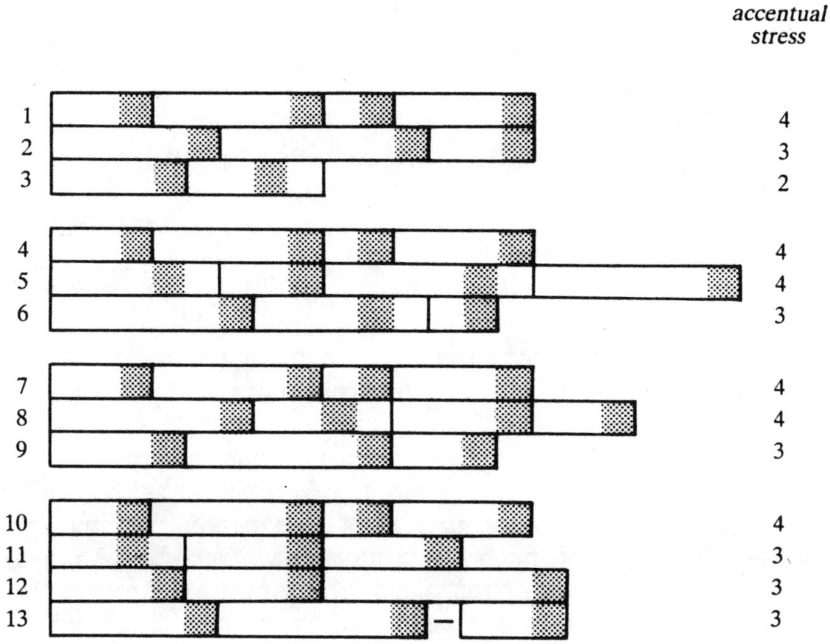

Appendix 4

Letters to A. Broides and A. Shlonsky*

I. To A. Broides (September 21, 1966)

21 בספטמבר, 1966

אברהם ברוידס יקירי,

זה עכשיו קיבלתי את מכתבך הנלבב כ״כ וברצוני להודות לך: איש־בשורה טובה אתה לי ותבורך על כך. מרחוק גם אני מרים כוס לחיינו, והעיקר — לחיי הספרות העברית.
אם לא קיבלת עדיין את ספר שירי האידי — מי יודע אולי אבד בדרך — אל תצטער: אשתדל באלה הימים לשלוח לך העתק נוסף.
חבל שלא כתבת לי יותר חדשות. אמנם עומד אני בקשר עם סופרים ותיקים וצעירים בארץ ומובן מאליו שאני קורא בעיון רב את הפריודיקה שלנו — אך מוצא אני בדבריך עפעס וואָס קנאַקט, משהו שמעיד על חיות רבה. — ו״אגב״ חשוב: מלאו שבעים שנה למשורר האידי המפורסם יעקב גלטשטיין ולא מצאתי בשום מקום אפילו ציון העובדא גרידא! (ובאותה שעה מרבים אצלנו לקשור כתרים לראשיהם של כל מיני סופרים לועזיים ממדרגה לא־ראשונה) אינני מבין את היחס הזה לספרות האידית — הלא שלנו היא וקרובה יותר מן ההוטנטוטים והבשיבזוקים שמעסיקים את כתבי העת והעתונים שלנו.
מזמן לזמן פוקדים אותנו אורחים מישראל: אני שומע ששטיינמן מתעתד לבוא; עכשו נמצא פה יהודה עמיחי; לפני זמן מה היה בניו־יורק גורי — וכן שמיר. כולם נזקקים, כנראה, לקצת התרעננות. אשר לי, לא יכולתי הקיץ לצאת אפילו לשבוע שלם. אמא שלי שתחי׳ חולה ואינני יכול להתבדר התבדרות ממשית, ארוכה. ומזה תסיק, שלצערי יש לי עכשיו נימוק ״הגון״ מאד לדחות את נסיעתי לארץ.
נו, אסיים בברכת גמר חתימה טובה — לך וללאה הטובה.

ובידידות תמיד,
גבריאל פרייל

[1] My thanks to Mr. Dov Ben-Yaakov and his staff in the literary archives of Genazim for allowing the use and publication of these letters (Genazim #93111/1 and 55928). Special thanks go to Mrs. Devorah Zissi for her generous help.

II. To A. Shlonsky (July 28, 1965)

28 ביולי, 1965

אברהם שלונסקי יקירי —

מה שלומך? אינני יודע מי ״חייב״ כתיבה למי. אך לא חשוב בעצם. העיקר שאני הוגה בך תכופות ומתוך געגועים.
מה נשמע? אצלי — הזקינה אמי ואינה מרגישה כדבעי. אני עצמי ג״כ הולך ו״מתקשש״. תפילתי האחת היא ששירי ישארו צעירים, לכהפ״ח לזמן־מה.
בינתיים ודאי שידוע לך שהופיעה האנתולוגיה של בורנשו, כרמי, שפייזהנדלר. דומני שזהו ספר חשוב באמת, מאמץ ראשון במינו ויש לאמר ״הן״ לחיובי שבו. ודאי שישנם חסרונות ואפשר להצביע על מספר מגרעות, אך אין זה מן היושר לבקש ולמצוא רק פסול ופגם. קראתי, אגב, את מאמרו של אהרן מגד ב״משא״ וסבור אני שקלע, פחות או יותר, למטרה.
כ״כ מרובים העניינים שרציתי לדון בהם — לו ישבנו יחד בבית־קפה ובהרחבת הדעת. אך מזלי גרם שגם השנה, כנראה, לא אוכל לנסוע לישראל — וזה כואב לי מאד. הלא מרגיש אני את עצמי כחלק אינטגרלי של שירתנו בארץ — וכך רואים אותי אנשים גם בה — ועם זאת כאילו נדון אני להיות תלוי על בלימה בנוף זר אם־גם מגרה.
נו, אני מכין לדפוס קובץ רביעי של שירי. יחד עם זאת אני כבר חושב על אוסף כללי של דברי: די צייט שלאָפט ניט. וכיוון שכתבתי ארבע מלים באידיש — כך יצאו להן אלו מחוד עטי — עלי להודיעך, שספר שירים משלי עומד לצאת בלשון זו עצמה.
אסיר תודה אהיה לך אם תבשרני מה על עבודותיך בתירגום כעת. הבעיות הכרוכות בתירגומים מעסיקות אותי מאד ואין סוף לעניין שהן מעוררות בי. דרוש בשלומה הטוב של מירה ומסור לה את מיטב ברכותי.

והריני שלך בידידות רבה,
גבריאל פרייל

Bibliography

1. *Gabriel Preil's Works*

Verse:

1944. *Nof Shemesh u-Chefor* [Landscape of Sun and Frost]. New York: Ohel.
1954. *Ner mul Kochavim* [Candle against Stars]. Jerusalem: Bialik Institute.
1960. *Mapat 'Erev* [Map of Evening]. Tel Aviv: Dvir.
1966. *Lider* [Poems]. New York: World Congress for Yiddish Culture. (Yiddish)
1968. *Ha-'Esh ve-ha-Demama* [Fire and Silence]. Tel Aviv: Massada.
1972. *Mi-toch Zeman ve-Nof: Shirim Mekubatzim* [Of Time and Place: Collected Poems]. Jerusalem: Bialik Institute.
1976. *Shirim mi-Shenei ha-Ketzavot* [Poems from End to End]. Tel Aviv: Schocken.
1980. *'Adiv le-'Atzmi* [Courteous to Myself]. Tel Aviv: Ha-Kibbutz ha-Me'uchad.
1986. *Chamishim Shirim ba-Midbar* [Fifty Poems in the Wilderness]. Part of a forthcoming collection (1972–1985), still untitled. Tel Aviv: Ha-Kibbutz ha-Me'uchad and Sifriyat Po'alim.

Prose:

1937. "Le-Yovelo shel Zalman Shne'ur" [For Zalman Shne'ur's Jubilee]. *Niv*, 2, no. 1 (November): 4–5.
1940. "Shirei Dov Pomerantz" [The Poems of Ber Pomerantz]. *Ha-Doar* (24 May):471–472.
1947. " 'Al Shirato shel Halkin" [On Halkin's Poetry]. *Ha-Doar* (7 Nov.):18.
1951. "Be-Shulei Sifro ha-'Angli shel S. Halkin 'al ha-Sifrut ha-'Ivrit ha-Modernit" [Marginalia to S. Halkin's English Book on Modern Hebrew Literature]. *Bitzaron*, 23 (Dec.–Jan.):196–200.
1953. "Karl Sandburg ben 75" [Carl Sandburg is 75]. *Mabua'*, 2:232–233.
1953. "Hebreishe Poezye in Eretz Yisrael" [Hebrew Poetry in Israel]. *Di Tsukunft* (September):372–375. (Yiddish)
1954. "Nusach 'Amerika ba-Shira ha-'Ivrit" [The American Style in Hebrew Poetry]. *Ha-Metzudah*, 7:497–504.

1955. "Di Hebreishe Literatur in Amerika" [Hebrew Literature in America]. *Di Tsukunft* (October):369–371. (Yiddish)
1956. "'Al Ya'akov Glatshtein: Bi-Melot lo Shishim Shana" [For Jacob Glatstein's Sixtieth Birthday]. *Ha-Doar* (9 Nov.):28.
1959. *Israeli Poetry in Peace and War*. New York: Herzl Institute, Pamphlet no. 13.
1960. " 'Asara Meshorerim Yisre'eliyim be-Targum 'Idi" [Ten Israeli Poets in Yiddish Translation]. *Ha-Doar* (1 April):379.
1961. " 'Al ha-'Amerikaniyut shel Hillel Bavli" [On Bavli's Americanism]. *Bitzaron* 45 (Dec.–Jan.):76–77.
1962. "Der Yokh un di Monung fun a Lid" [The Yoke and the Demands of a Poem]. *Sevive* 5 (Feb.):23–25. (Yiddish)
1962a. "Arum *Di Freyd fun Yidishn Vort* (Glatshteyn's Lider-Bukh)" [About Glatstein's Book of Verse *The Joy of the Yiddish Word*]. *Sevive* 7 (Sept.):53–55. (Yiddish)
1963. "Meshorerah shel Kentaki (Y.Y. Shwartz) [The Poet of Kentucky]. *Ha-Doar* (7 June):546.
1964. "Yidish un Universal in Poezye" [Yiddish and Universal (Elements, Aspects) in Poetry]. *Sevive* 12 (April):40–42. (Yiddish)
1966. "Mashehu 'al Yesodot ve-Nigudim be-Sipurei Agnon" [Something About Elements and Contrasts in Agnon's Stories]. *Bitzaron* 55 (Nov.–Dec.):94–97.
1970. "Vegn Kritik un 'Nit Kritik'" [Concerning Criticism and 'Non-Criticism']. *Sevive* 30 (Jan.):3–5. (Yiddish)
1970a. "Mashehu 'al Yehuda 'Amichai" [Something About Yehuda Amichai]. *Ha-Doar* (8 May):416.

English Translations:

1979. *Autumn Music: Selected Poems of Gabriel Preil.* Ed. Howard Schwartz. St. Louis: Cauldron Press.
1985. *Sunset Possibilities and Other Poems.* Tr. Robert Friend. Philadelphia: Jewish Publication Society.

2. *Selected Writings on Preil*

Alter, Robert. 1965. "Lakes" (an interpretation). *The Modern Hebrew Poem Itself.* Ed. Stanley Burnshaw, T. Carmi, and Ezra Spicehandler. New York, Chicago, San Francisco: Holt, Rinehart and Winston.
Avineri, Shraga. 1963. " 'Al ha-Dimuyim be-Shirei Gavriel Preil" [The Images in Preil's Poems]. *Carmelit* 9:201–214. Reprinted in his *Sheneim-'Asar Meshorerim* [12 Poets]. Tel Aviv: Yavneh, 1969, pp. 174–181.

Bar-Yaakov, M. 1961. "Meshorer Mevusam Nofim" [A Poet Intoxicated with Landscapes]. *Ma'ariv* (5 May).
Barka'i, Adah. 1977. "Shirat Shenei ha-Ketzavot shel Gavriel Preil" [Preil's Verse of Two Ends]. *Moznayim* 44 (Dec.):37–40.
———. 1978. "Meshorer shel Zeman ve-Nof" [A Poet of Time and Place]. *'Al ha-Mishmar* (30 June):6–7.
Barzel, Avivah. 1976. "Shirim mi-Shenei ha-Ketzavot me'et Gavriel Preil" [Poems from End to End by Gabriel Preil]. *Ha-Doar* (1 Oct.):661–662.
Bass, Shmuel. 1946. "Nof Shemesh u-Chefor" [Landscape of Sun and Frost]. *Gilyonot* 18 (Winter):295.
Bavli, Hillel. 1943. "Shirei Gavriel Preil." *Ha-Doar* (17 Jan.):252.
Ben-Shaul, Moshe. 1977. "Zehav Tiras 'Afil" [Golden Late Corn]. *'Al ha-Mishmar* (4 Nov.):6.
Bertini, K.A. 1961. "Mapat 'Erev" [Map of Evening]. *Moznayim* 13 (July–Aug.):294–295.
———. 1971. "Paitan 'Ivri be-'Amerika" [A Hebrew Poet in America]. *'Al ha-Mishmar* (20 Aug.):6–7.
Carmi, D. 1962. "Shirei Gavriel Preil" [Preil's Poems]. *Pi ha-'Aton* (16 Jan.):3.
Dor, Moshe. 1968. "The Fire and the Silence." *Hebrew Book Review* (Fall):1–4.
Epstein, Abraham. 1943. "Gavriel Preil's Hebreishe Lider" [Preil's Hebrew Poems]. *Di Tsukunft* (April):243–245. (Yiddish)
———. 1944. [1952]. "Gavriel Preil." In his *Mi-Karov u-me-Rachok*. New York: Ohel, pp. 202–207. Reprinted in his *Soferim 'Ivriyim be-'Amerika*, 2 vols. Tel Aviv: Dvir, 1952, vol. 1, pp. 229–236.
Feldman, Yael S. 1979. "Ha-Tzipor ha-'Afora" [The Grey Bird]. *Ha-Sifrut/Literature* 28 (April):113–117.
———. 1980. "Gabriel Preil: American Hebrew Poet". *Jewish Book Annual* 38 (New York):133–140.
———. 1981. "At the Exhibition" (trans. of Preil's "*Ta'arucha*"). *Midstream* 3 (March):16.
Friedland, Eliezer. 1960. "Shirat ha-'Ani be-Chivshono shel ha-Zeman" [The Verse of the "I" in the Mysteries of Time]. *Bitzaron* 43 (Sept.–Oct.):42–47.
Glatstein, Jacob. 1940. "Prost un Poshut" [Plain and Simple—a literary column]. *Nyu York Morgn Zhurnal* (18 Feb.). (Yiddish)
———. 1961. "Gavriel Preil." *Der Yidisher Kemfer* (27 Oct.). Reprinted in his *Mit Mayne Fartog Bikher: Eseyen* [With my Diaries: Essays]. Tel Aviv: I.L. Peretz Publishing House, 1963, pp. 545–548. (Yiddish)
———. 1972. "Gavriel Preil." *In Der Velt Mit Yidish: Eseyen* [In the World

with Yiddish: Essays]. New York: World Congress of Jewish Culture, pp. 129–133. (Yiddish)

Goldberg, Lea. 1949. "Deyokena'ot be-Shiratenu ha-Chadasha: Gavriel Preil" [Portraits in Our New Poetry: Gabriel Preil]. *Ba-Sha'ar* (24 March):5–6.

Halkin, Simon. 1937. "Le-'Achim Tze'irim be-'Amerika" [To Young Brothers in America] *Gilyonot* 5 (Adar–Nissan):182–184. (Signed Sh.H.)

Hanaami, Moshe. 1965. "Shira Mefukacha" [Sober Poetry]. *Bitzaron* 52 (April):17–24.

———. 1965. "Pegisha 'im Gavriel Preil" [An Interview with Gabriel Preil]. *Masa* (28 Aug.).

———. 1969. " 'Or 'Achar 'Or" [Skin After Skin]. *Bitzaron* 61 (Sept.–Oct.):20–24.

———. 1977. "Shakua' bi-Setavo ha-Perati [Immersed in His Private Autumn]. *Yedi'ot 'Ahronot* (19 Aug.).

Ivry, Yitzhak. 1955. "Shirat Preil" [Preil's Verse]. *Ha-Doar* (10 June):568.

Keshet, Yeshurun. 1963. " 'Al Shirat Gavriel Preil" [On The Verse of Gabriel Preil]. *Moznayim* 17 (June–July):95–102. Reprinted in his *'Amadot*. Jerusalem: Shalem, 1970, pp. 161–168.

Komem, Aharon. 1977. "Le-Mahuto shel ha-Shir ha-Tziyuri ha-Moderni" [On the Essence of the Modern Painterly Poem]. *Yedi'ot 'Ahronot* (21 Jan.).

Kremer, Shalom. 1968. "Pegisha 'im Gavriel Preil ve-Shirato" [A Meeting with Gabriel Preil and His Verse]. *Moznayim* 28 (Dec.):15–19.

Lander, Pinchas. 1955. "Ner Mul Kochavim" [Candle Against Stars]. *Ha-Po'el ha-Tza'ir* (22 Feb.):12–13.

———. 1955. "Shirei Gavriel Preil" [Gabriel Preil's Poems]. *Ha-'Aretz* (14 Oct.).

Leyeles [Glantz], Aharon. 1966. "Dikhterisher Intelektualism" [Poetic Intellectualism]. *Tog-Morgn Zhurnal* (20 Nov.). (Yiddish)

Lubin, Ayah and Tuvia Shlonsky. 1958. "Shirato shel Gavriel Preil" [Gabriel Preil's Poetry], in *Ma 'Ekra*. Ed. Zvi Adar, 2 vols. Jerusalem: The Hebrew University, School of Education, vol. 2, p. 179.

Margoshes, Shmuel, 1966. "Gavriel Preil's Lid" [Gabriel Preil's Poem]. *Tog* (15 Oct.). (Yiddish)

Martan, Avraham. 1966. "Ha-Bikoret ha-'Ivrit 'al Gavriel Preil" [Critical Reviews on Preil]. *Bitzaron* 54 (Sept.):163–167.

Miron, Dan. 1977. "Shirei Zeman 'Acher: Hirhurim 'al Shirat Preil ha-Me'ucheret" [Poems of Another (Different) Time: Ruminations on Preil's Later Verse]. *Bitzaron* 68 (April–May):168–181, 202.

Moked, Gabriel. 1961. "Shenei Meshorerim 'Ivriyim me-'Artzot ha-Berit" [Two Hebrew Poets from the United States]. *Yedi'ot 'Ahronot* (26 May):6.

Perry, Menachem. 1972. " 'Eineiha Mimul: 'Al Shiro shel Gavriel Preil 'Pereida' ve-'al 'Aspekt 'Echad shel Shirato" [On Preil's Poem 'Parting' and on One Aspect of His Verse]. *Siman Kri'a* 1 (Sept.):255–263.

———. 1979. "Ha-'Ona ha-Me'uzenet: 'Al Mivneh ha-'Omek shel Shirei Preil" [The Balanced Season: The Deep Structure of Preil's Poems]. *Siman Kri'a* 9 (July):369–378, 453–461.

Pnueli, S.Y. 1954. "Shira 'Ivrit be-Makom she-'Ein 'Oznayim 'Ivriyot" [Hebrew Poetry Where There Are No Hebrew Ears]. *Zemanim* (6 Aug.).

Rabinowitz, Yeshayahu. 1969. "Darko shel Gavriel Preil ba-Shira" [Gabriel Preil's Way in Verse]. *Ha-Doar* (28 March):354–358.

Ravitch, Melekh. 1967. "A Hebreisher Poet – Vos Shraybt Yidish" [A Hebrew Poet Who Writes Yiddish]. *Di Goldene Keyt* 59:224–226. (Yiddish)

Ribalow, Menachem. 1943. "Ha-Sifrut ha-'Ivrit be-'Amerika" [Hebrew Literature in America], in *'Achi-Sefer*, eds. Samuel Niger and Menachem Ribalow. New York: Louis Lamed Foundation, pp. 93–182.

Sandbank, Shimon. 1962. "Ha-'Ish she-ba-Shir" [The Person in the Poem]. *'Amot* 7 (July–Aug.):88–89.

Shabtay, Aharon. 1962. "Shirei Gavriel Preil" [Gabriel Preil's Poems]. *'Al ha-Mishmar* (6 April).

———. 1965. "Kavim le-Shirato shel Gavriel Preil" [Some Features of Preil's Verse], in *Mivchar Shirim u-Devarim 'al Yetzirato shel Gavriel Preil* [Selected Poems of Gabriel Preil], introduction by Aharon Shabtay. Tel Aviv: Machbarot le-Shira, pp. 5–11.

Shalom, Shin. 1945. "Be-Ma'arechet ha-Yetzira—*Nof Shemesh u-Chefor* le-Gavriel Preil" [On Gabriel Preil's *Landscape of Sun and Frost*]. *Davar* (n.d.).

———. 1960. "Beracha le-Gavriel Preil" [Congratuations to Gabriel Preil]. *Bitzaron* 43 (Sept.–Oct.):36.

Shamir, Moshe. 1954. "Bein Shir le-Shura" [Between a Poem and a Line]. *Davar* (6 Aug.).

Sharoni, Edna G. 1981–82. "Weary Singer of Exile." *Modern Hebrew Literature*, Vol. 1–2 (Winter):50–55.

Silberschlag, Eisig. 1943. "Ha-Shira ha-'Ivrit ba-'Olam he-Chadash" [Hebrew Verse in The New World], in *'Achi-Sefer*. Ed. Samuel Niger and Menachem Ribalow. New York: Louis Lamed Foundation, pp. 216–245.

———. 1962. "Gavriel Preil, Meshorer ha-'Uvdot" [Gabriel Preil, The Poet of Facts]. *Ha-Doar* (2 March):281–282.

Starkman, Moshe. 1944. "Vegn Bikher un Menshn" [About Books and People – on Preil's translations]. *Tog* (7 May). (Yiddish)

———. 1966. "A Molerisher Liriker" [A Painterly Lyricist]. *Sevive* 21 (Dec.):44–46. (Yiddish)

Stavi, Zissi. 1977. "Gavriel Preil ve-ha-Meshulash Lita, New York, Yerushalayim" [Gabriel Preil and the Triangle Lithuania, New York, Jerusalem – an interview with the poet]. *Yedi'ot 'Ahronot* (21 Oct.).

Teller, J. L. 1945. "Dos Ershte Bukh fun Hebreish-Yidishn Dikhter Gavriel Preil. *Getseltn* 4 (July–August):135–136. (Yiddish)

Toker, Naftali. 1981. "Ha-Romantikan ha-Mefukach" [The Sober Romantic]. *Moznayim* (Aug.–Sept.):245–249.

Treinin, Avner. 1981. "Zechuchit li Tavhir ha-Choshech She-be-Lev Tsohorayim" [A Glass Lightens Up the Darkness at Noontime]. *Yedi'ot 'Ahronot* (13 Feb.):21.

Yoffe, Mordechai. 1950. "Hebreishe Velt: Der Amerikaner Motiv" [Hebrew World: The American Motif]. *Nyu York Morgn Zhurnal* (7 May). (Yiddish)

———. 1955. "Tikun 'Ivri le-Noseh 'Amerika'i" [A Hebrew Rendition of an American Theme – a brief version of his Yiddish article]. *Davar* (25 Feb.).

Yonatan, Natan. 1968. "Be-Chevel ha-Migdalim ha-'Aforim" [In the Region of the Grey Castles], in his *'Ad Sof ha-Kayitz ha-'Indiyani* [To the End of the Indian Summer]. Merhavia: Sifriyat Po'alim, pp. 64–68.

Zach, Natan. 1954. " 'Aklim Perati" [Private Climate]. *'Al ha-Mishmar*, Literary Supplement (2 Jan.):5.

———. 1959. "Mivchano shel ha-Shir" [The Test of a Poem]. *La-Merhav* (4 Oct.).

———. 1961. "Be-Siman ha-Sha'a ha-Mefuyeset" [Under the Sign of the Reconciled Hour]. *Molad* 19 (March–April):187–189.

Zeitlin, Aharon. 1960. "Ha-Nof ve-ha-Nefesh: 'al Shirei Gavriel Preil" [The Landscape and the Soul: On the Poems of Gabriel Preil]. *Bitzaron* 43 (Sept.–Oct.):37–41.

3. *Related Works*

Abrams, M.H. 1953. *The Mirror and the Lamp: Romantic Theory and the Critical Tradition.* London, Oxford, New York: Oxford University Press.

Abramowitsch, Shalom Jacob. 1958. *Susati* [The Mare]. *Kol Kitvei Mendele Mocher Sefarim.* Tel Aviv: Dvir, pp. 307–350.

'Achi-Sefer. 1943. See Niger.

Aeschylus. 1942. *Agamemnon.* Ed. David Grene and Richmond Lattimore. New York: The Modern Library, pp. 41–105.

Agnon, Shmuel Yosef. 1974. " 'Agadat ha-Sofer" [The Tale of the Scribe]. *'Elu ve-'Elu*, vol. 2 of *Kol Kitvei 'Agnon.* Jerusalem and Tel Aviv: Schocken, pp. 131–145.

Allen, Gay Willson, 1975. *The New Walt Whitman Handbook*. New York: New York University Press.

Alter, Robert. 1977. *Defenses of the Imagination: Jewish Writers and Modern Historical Crisis*. Philadephia: Jewish Publication Society of America.

Auerbach, Erich. (1946) 1953. *Mimesis: The Representation of Reality in Western Literature*. Trans. W.R. Trask. Princeton: Princeton University Press.

Austerlitz, Robert. 1958. *Ob–Ugric Metrics: The Metrical Structure of Ostyak and Vogul Folk-Poetry*. Folklore Fellows Communications No. 174. Helsinki: Suomalainen Tiedeakatemia, Academia Scientiarum Fennica.

Averbach, David. 1977. "Wordsworth u-Bialik: Shirat ha-Yaldut" [The Poetry of Childhood]. *Moznayim* 45 (July):102–112.

Bacon, Yitzhak. 1968. *Perakim be-Hitpatechut ha-Mishkal shel ha-Shira ha-'Ivrit* [Stages in the Development of Meter in Hebrew Poetry]. Tel Aviv: Mif'al ha-Shichpul.

———. 1972. "Be-Shulei Targumo shel Brenner mitoch *Tuvia ha-Chalban*" [Marginalia to Brenner's translation of *Tevie the Milkman*]. *Siman Kri'a* 1:211–222.

———. 1973. "Ha-Ma'amad 'al ha-Gesher" [The Scene on the Bridge]. *Ha-Sifrut/Literature* (April):275–281.

———. 1975. *Brenner ha-Tza'ir* [The Young Brenner], vol. 1. Tel Aviv: Ha-Kibbutz ha-Me'uchad.

Balakian, Anna. 1947. *Literary Origins of Surrealism*. New York: King's Crown Press.

Band, Abraham. 1978. "Mapat Derachim" [Road Atlas – on Halkin's essayistic writings], in *Sh. Halkin: Mivchar Ma'amarim*. Ed. Dan La'or. Tel Aviv: Am Oved, pp. 198–203.

———, Arnold (Abraham). 1968. *Nostalgia and Nightmare*. Los Angeles: University of California Press.

Barthes, Roland. 1974. *S/Z: An Essay*. Trans. Richard Miller. New York: Hill and Wang.

Barzilay, Isaac. 1979. "From Purism to Expansionism: A Chapter in the Early History of Modern Hebrew." *Near East Studies in Memory of M.M. Bravman = Journal of Ancient Near Eastern Society of Columbia University*, 11:3–15.

Bendavid, Abba. 1967. *Leshon Mikra u-Leshon Chachamim* [Biblical and Mishnaic Hebrew]. 2 vols, Tel Aviv: Dvir.

Ben-Porat, Zivah. 1976. "The Poetics of Literary Allusion." *PLT* 1:579–587.

Benshalom, Benzion. 1945. *Mishkalav shel H.N. Bialik* [Bialik's Meters]. Tel Aviv: Gazit.

Ben Yitzhak, Avraham. 1958. *Shirim* [Poems]. With an essay by Benzion Benshalom. Jerusalem: Tarshish.

Bialik, H.N. [8]1973. *Shirim* [Poems]. Tel Aviv: Dvir La'am.

———. [6]1974. *Divrei Sifrut* [Literary Essays]. Tel Aviv: Dvir La'am.

Bloom, Harold. 1973. *The Anxiety of Influence: A Theory of Poetry*. New York: Oxford University Press.

———. 1975. *A Map of Misreading*. New York: Oxford University Press.

———. 1976. *Kabbala and Criticism*. New York: Seaburg Press.

Bock, L.A. 1979. "Trakl and Chinese Poetry." Letters to the Editor. *PMLA* 94 (Oct.):955–957.

Bradbury, Malcolm and James McFarlane, eds. 1976. *Modernism: 1890–1930*. New York: Penguin.

Brenner, Y.H. (1911) 1937. "Ha-Zhaner ha-'Eretz Yisre'eli va-'Avizarehu" [The Paraphernalia of the Literary Genre of Eretz-Israel]. *Kol Kitvei Brenner*, vol. 8, book 1. Tel Aviv: Shtibel, pp. 160–166.

Brik, Osip. (1927) 1971. "Contributions to the Study of Verse Language," in *Readings in Russian Poetics*. Ed. Ladislav Matejka and Krystina Pomorska, pp. 117–125.

Broeck, Raymond Van den. 1981. "The Limits of Translatability Exemplified by Metaphor Translation," *Poetics Today* 2:4, 73–88.

Brook-Rose, Christine. 1965. *A Grammar of Metaphor*. London: Secker and Warburg.

Brooks, Cleanth. 1947. *The Well Wrought Urn: Studies in the Structure of Poetry*. New York: Harcourt, Brace & World, Inc.

Cahn, Eric. 1976. "Revolt, Conservatism and Reaction in Paris 1905–25," in Bradbury and McFarlane, pp. 162–171.

Chatman, Seymour. 1960. "Comparing Metrical Styles," in *Style in Language*, ed. Thomas A. Sebeok, pp. 149–172.

———. 1971. "On Defining 'Form'." *New Literary History* II, 2 (Winter):217–228.

Chomsky, William (Ze'ev). 1966. *Hebrew: The Eternal Language*. Philadelphia: Jewish Publication Society.

———. 1967. *Ha-Lashon ha-'Ivrit be-Darchei Hitpatechutah* [The Evolution of Hebrew]. Jerusalem: Rubin Mass.

Coffman, Stanley. 1951. *Imagism: A Chapter for the History of Modern Poetry*. Norman: Oklahoma University Press.

Cohen, Tova. 1982. *Me-Chalom li-Metzi'ut: 'Eretz Yisra'el be-Sifrut ha-Haskala*. [From Dream to Reality: The Land of Israel in the (Hebrew) Enlightenment Literature]. Ramat Gan: Bar-Ilan University Press.

Culler, Jonathan. 1975. *Structuralist Poetics: Structuralism, Linguistics and the Study of Literature.* Ithaca, New York: Cornell University Press.

Dagut, M.B. 1976. "Can Metaphor Be Translated?" *Babel* XII:21–33.

de Vaux, Roland. 1961. *Ancient Israel.* Tr. John McHugh. New York: McGraw Hill.

Eco, Umberto. 1976. *A Theory of Semiotics.* Bloomington: Indiana University Press.

Eliot, T. S. 1975. *Selected Prose.* Ed. Frank Kermode. New York: Harcourt Brace Jovanovich; Farrar, Strauss and Giroux.

Epstein, Abraham. 1952. *Soferim 'Ivriyim be-'Amerika* [Hebrew Writers in America]. 2 vols. Tel Aviv: Dvir.

Erlich, Victor. (1955) [3]1969. *Russian Formalism: History–Doctrine.* The Hague, Paris: Mouton.

———. 1964. *The Double Image: The Concept of the Poet in Slavic Literatures.* Baltimore: Johns Hopkins University Press.

Even-Shoshan, Abraham. 1977. *Ha-Milon he-Chadash* [New Hebrew Dictionary]. 3 vols. Jerusalem: Kiryat-Sefer.

Even-Zohar, Itamar. 1970. "The Function of the Literary Polysystem in the History of Literature." Presented to the Tel Aviv Symposium on the Theory of Literary History, Tel Aviv University, Feb. 2, 1970. Reprinted in Even-Zohar 1978:11–13.

———. 1970a. "Le-Verur Mahutah ve-Tifkudah shel ha-Lashon ha-Yafa be-Diglosya" [The Nature and Function of the Language of Literature in Diglossia]. *Ha-Sifrut/Literature* II, 2:286–303. [English Summary:443–446].

———. 1975. "Bodler be-Targum Lea Goldberg" [Baudelaire Translated by L. Goldberg]. *Ha-Sifrut/Literature* 21:32–45.

———. 1978. *Papers in Historical Poetics.* Tel Aviv: The Porter Institute for Poetics and Semiotics, Tel Aviv University (= Papers on Poetics and Semiotics 8).

———. 1979. "Polysystem Theory." *Poetics Today*, vol. 1:1–2, pp. 287–361.

———. 1980. "Constraints of Realeme Insertability in Narrative." *Poetics Today*, vol. 1:3, pp. 65–74.

———. 1981. "Translation Theory Today." *Poetics Today*, vol. 2:4, pp. 1–8.

Feldman, Yael S. 1979a. "From Dostoyevsky to Brenner." *Hebrew Annual Review* 3:91–104.

———. 1982. "Ha-Lashon ve-ha-Mitos" [Myth in Language: Is it Translatable?] *Ha-Doar* (May):369–371.

———. 1983. "Bein Mafteach le-Man'ul" [Between a Key and a Lock]. *Ha-Sifrut* 32 (June 82):148–154.

———. 1983a. "Y.L. Teller u-Masoret ha-'Imagism ha-'Idi" [Y.L. Teller and the Tradition of Yiddish Imagism]. *Moznayim* 57,4 (Oct.):36–37.

———. 1983b. "A Tribute to Y.L. Teller." *Midstream* (Dec.):52–53.

———. 1984. "Bein ha-Miti le-vein ha-Teragi" [Between the Mythic and the Tragic]. *Machbarot Brenner* 3–4 (Tel Aviv: Ha-Kibbutz ha-Me'uchad), pp. 217–238.

———. 1985. "Jewish Literary Modernism and Language Identity: The Case of *In Zikh*." *Yiddish*, vol. 6:1, pp. 44–54.

———. 1985a. "Poetics and Politics: Israeli Literary Criticism Between East and West." *Proceedings of the American Academy for Jewish Research*, vol. 52, pp. 9–35.

———. 1985b. "How Does a Convention Mean? A Semiotic Reading of a Bilingual Key-Irony in Agnon's *A Guest for the Night." Hebrew Union College Annual*, vol. LVI, pp. 251–269.

Fish, Stanley E. 1970. "Literature in the Reader: Affective Stylistics." *New Literary History*, vol. 2:1, pp. 123–161.

Fleischer, Ezra. 1975. *Shirat ha-Kodesh ha-'Ivrit bi-Yemei he-Beinayim* [Hebrew Liturgical Verse in the Middle Ages]. Jerusalem: Keter.

Flint, F.S. 1913. "*Imagisme*." *Poetry* I (March):6.

Fogel, David. 1966. *Kol Shirei D. Fogel* [All His Poems]. Machbarot le-Sifrut.

———. 1974. "Lashon ve-Signon be-Sifrutenu ha-Tze'ira" [Language and Style in Our Young Literature]. *Siman Kri'a* 3–4:387–392.

Fokkema, D.W. 1976. "Continuity and Change in Russian Formalism, Czech Structuralism and Soviet Semiotics," *PTL* 1:153–196.

Forster, Leonard Wilson. 1970. *The Poet's Tongues: Multilingualism in Literature*. Cambridge University Press, in association with University of Otago Press.

von Franz, M.–L. 1964. "The Process of Individuation," in *Man and His Symbols*. Ed. C.G. Jung and M.–L. von Franz. New York: Dell, pp. 157–254.

Friedlander, Yehuda, ed. 1974. *U.Z. Greenberg: Mivchar Ma'amarim* [Selected Critical Essays on Greenberg's Oeuvre]. Tel Aviv: Am Oved.

Frye, Northrop. 1957. *Anatomy of Critcism: Four Essays*. Princeton: Princeton University Press.

———. 1963. *The Well-Tempered Critic*. Bloomington and London: Indiana University Press.

Fussel, Paul. (1965) 1979. *Poetic Meter and Poetic Form*. New York: Random House.

Genesis Midrash Rabba. 1939. Tr. H. Freedman. London: Soncino.

Glatstein, Jacob, Aharon Leyeles, and N.B. Minkov. 1920. "Introspectivism". *In-Zikh: A Zamlung Introspektive Lider* [Introspectivist Anthology]. New York: Mayzel Farlag, pp. 5–27. (Yiddish)

Glatstein, Jacob. 1944. "Leyendik dem Akhiseyfer" [On Reading *'Achi-Sefer*]. *Sevive* 7 (April–May):25–29. Reprinted in his *Shtralndike Yidn*. New York: Farlag Matones, 1946:70–78. (Yiddish)

———. 1956. *Fun Mayn Gantser Mi* [Of All My Labour: Collected Poems, 1919–1956]. New York: no publisher. (Yiddish)

———. 1971. "Tsuriktrakhtungen" [Thinking Back], in his *Gezangen fun Rekhts tsu Links*, New York, pp. 11–18. (Yiddish)

Golomb, Haray. 1976. "Yareach be-Or Zach" [A Moon in Clear (Zach's) Light]. *Ha-Sifrut/Literature* 23:7–22.

Gombrich, E.H. 1956. *Korot ha-'Omanut* [The Story of Art]. Trans. Hanokh Kalay and Arie Lerner. Tel Aviv: Am Oved.

———. 1960. *Art and Illusion: A Study in the Psychology of Pictorial Representation*. New York: Pantheon Books.

———. (1963) 1978. *Meditations on a Hobby Horse and Other Essays on the Theory of Art*. London and New York: Phaidon.

Greenberg, Uri Zvi. 1926. *Ha-Gavrut ha-'Ola* [Ascending Virility. Poems]. Tel Aviv: Sadan.

———. 1928. *Kelapei Tish'im ve-Tish'a* [Against the Ninety-Nine]. Tel Aviv: Sadan.

———. 1929. *Kelev Bayit* [A House Dog. Poems]. Tel Aviv: Hedim.

Greimas, A.J. 1970. *Du sens: essais sémiotiques*. Paris: Seuil.

Gross, Harvey. 1965. *Sound and Form in Modern Poetry: A Study of Prosody from Thomas Hardy to Robert Lowell*. Ann Arbor: University of Michigan Press.

Hadda, Janet R. 1976. "Language Experimentations in the Early Poetry of Yankev Glatshteyn." *Working papers in Yiddish and East European Jewish Studies*, no. 19. New York: YIVO.

———. 1980. *Yankev Glatshteyn*. Boston: Twayne Publishers, a division of G.K. Hall & Co.

Ha'ephrati, Joseph. 1976. *Ha-Mar'ot ve-ha-Lashon* [The Presented World: Evolution of the Poetic Language of Nature Description in Hebrew Poetry]. Tel Aviv: The Israeli Institute for Poetics and Semiotics, Tel Aviv University (= Literature, Meaning, Culture 1).

Halkin, Simon. 1942. *'Arai ve-Keva'* [Temporariness and Permanence: Literary Essays]. New York: Ohel.

———. 1950. *Modern Hebrew Literature (Trends and Values)*. New York: Schocken.

———. 1969. *Derachim ve-Tzidei Derachim ba-Sifrut* [Mainroads and Side Paths in Literature]. 3 vols. Jerusalem: Academon.

Har'el-Fish, A. 1975. "Ha-Tavnit ha-Romantit shel 'Ha-Berecha' " [The Romantic Structure of (Bialik's) 'The Pond']. *Moznayim* 41 (July):83–89.

Harari, Josué V. ed. 1979. *Textual Strategies: Perspectives in Post-Structuralist Criticism.* Ithaca: Cornell University Press.

Harmer, J.B. 1975. *Victory in Limbo: Imagism 1908–1917.* London: Secker & Warburg.

Hassan, Ihab. (1971) ²1982. *The Dismemberment of Orpheus: Toward a Post Modern Literature.* Madison: University of Wisconsin Press.

Hemshekh Antologye. 1945. See Starkman. (Yiddish)

Holmes, James S. 1971. "The Cross-Temporal Factor in Verse Translation." *Slavica Slovaca* 6:326–334.

Homburger, Eric. 1976. "Chicago and New York: Two Versions of American Modernism," in Bradbury & McFarlane, pp. 51–61.

Hough, Graham. 1960. *Image and Experience: Studies in a Literary Revolution.* London: Duckworth.

Howe, Irving, ed. 1967. *The Idea of the Modern.* New York: Horizon Press.

——— and Eliezer Greenburg. 1969. *A Treasury of Yiddish Poetry.* New York, Chicago, San Francisco: Holt, Rinehart & Winston.

Hrushovski, Benjamin. 1954. "Free Rhythms in Modern Yiddish Poetry," in *The Field of Yiddish: Studies in Yiddish Language, Folklore and Literature.* Ed. Uriel Weinreich. New York: Publications of the Linguistic Circle of New York. No. 3, pp. 219–266.

———. 1960. "On Free Rhythms in Modern Poetry," in *Style in Language.* Ed. Thomas A. Sebeok. Cambridge, Mass.: M.I.T. Press, pp. 173–190.

———. 1968. "Ha-'im Yesh la-Tzelil Mashma'ut?" [Are Sounds Meaningful?]. *Ha-Sifrut/Literature* 2 (Summer): 410–420.

———. (1970) 1978. *Ritmus ha-Rachavut be-Shirat U.Z. Greenberg* [The Theory and Practice of Rhythm in the Expressionist Poetry of U.Z. Greenberg]. Tel Aviv: The Porter Institute for Poetics and Semiotics, Tel Aviv University.

———. 1971. "Prosody, Hebrew." *Encyclopedia Judaica*, Vol. 13, pp. 1195–1240.

———. 1977. "Ha-Bayit ha-Tipusi be-Shir ha-'Am ha-'Idi" [The Typical Strophic Structure of Yiddish Folksongs], in *Sefer Dov Sadan.* Eds. Shmuel Werses, Natan Rotenstreich and Chone Shmeruk. Jerusalem: Hakibbutz Hameuchad, pp. 111–128.

———. tr. 1978. "Introspectivism" and a selection of the early poems of Jacob Glatstein, in *Siman Kri'a* 8:75–100. (Signed H. Benjamin).

———. tr. 1979. Poetry and Prose from U.Z. Greenberg's *The Albatross*, in *Siman Kri'a* 9:103–143. (Signed H. Benjamin).

———. 1979a. "The Structure of Semiotic Objects: A Three-Dimensional Model." *Poetics Today*, 1:1–2, pp. 363–376.

In Zikh, 1920. See Glatstein, Leyeles and Minkov.

Iser, Wolfgang. 1971. "Indeterminacy and the Reader's Response," in *Aspects of Narrative*. Ed. J. Hillis Miller. New York: Columbia University Press, pp. 1–45.

———. 1974. "The Reading Process: A Phenomenological Approach," in his *The Implied Reader: Patterns of Communication in Prose Fiction from Bunyan to Beckett*. Baltimore and London: Johns Hopkins University Press, pp. 274–294.

Ivir, Vladimir, 1981. "Formal Correspondence vs. Translation Equivalence Revisited." *Poetics Today* 4:2, pp. 51–60.

Jakobson, Roman. 1958. "Concluding Statement: Linguistics and Poetics," in *Style in Language*. Ed. Thomas A. Sebeok, Cambridge, Mass.: M.I.T. Press, pp. 350–377.

———. 1959. "On Linguistic Aspects of Translation," in *On Translation*. Ed. R.A. Brower, New York: Oxford University Press, pp. 232–239.

———. 1971. "The Dominant," in *Readings in Russian Poetics*. Ed. Ladislav Matejka and Krystina Pomorska, pp. 82–87.

Jameson, Frederic. 1972. *The Prison-House of Language*. Princeton, New Jersey: Princeton University Press.

Jauss, Hans R. 1974. "Literary History as a Challenge to Literary Theory," in *New Directions in Literary History*. Ed. Ralph Cohen. Baltimore: Johns Hopkins University Press, pp. 11–41.

Juhasz, Susan. 1974. *Metaphor and the Poetry of Williams, Pound and Stevens*. Lewisburg, PA: Bucknell University Press.

Jung, Carl G. 1964. "Approaching the Unconscious," in *Man and His Symbols*. Ed. C.G. Jung and M.-L. von Franz. New York: Dell, pp. 3–94.

Kabakoff, Jacob. 1967. *Chalutzei ha-Sifrut ha-'Ivrit be-'Amerika* [The Pioneers of Hebrew Literature in America]. Tel Aviv: Yavneh.

———. 1978. *Shocharim ve-Ne'emanim* [Seekers and Stalwarts: Essays and Studies on American Hebrew Literature and Culture]. Jerusalem: Rubin Mass.

Kagan, Eliezer. 1975. " 'Iyun ba-Fonetika shel Shlonsky" [On Shlonsky's Phonetics], in *Avraham Shlonsky: Mivchar Ma'amarim*. Ed. Aviezer Weiss. Tel Aviv: Am Oved, pp. 130–149.

Kartun-Blum, Ruth. 1969. *Ha-Shira ha-'Ivrit bi-Tekufat Chibat-Tziyon*. [Hebrew Poetry of the Chibat-Tziyon Period]. Jerusalem: Bialik Institute.

———. 1982. *Shira bi-Re'i 'Atzmah* [Poetry as Its Own Mirror: An Anthology]. Tel Aviv: Hakibbutz Hameuchad.

Keats, John and P.B. Shelley. n.d. *Complete Poetical Works*. New York: The Modern Library.

Kenner, Hugh. 1971. *The Pound Era.* Berkeley and Los Angeles: University of California Press.

———. 1975. *A Homemade World: The American Modernist Writers.* New York: Alfred A. Knopf.

Klausner, Joseph. 1947. *Zalman Shne'ur* [A Monograph—Hebrew]. Tel Aviv: Yavneh.

———. 1930–50. *Historya shel ha-Sifrut ha-'Ivrit ha-Chadasha* [History of Modern Hebrew Literature]. Jerusalem: Ahiasaf, vol. 6.

Lavo, Shulamit. 1977. " 'Al 'Itzuv ha-Melodiyut shel Shirei Alterman ve-'al 'Ofnei Kelitatah" [Perception of the Rhythmic Structures of Alterman's Verse], in *'Al Shira ve-Siporet* [On Poetry and Prose]. Ed. Zvi Mal'achi. Tel Aviv: Katz Institute, Tel Aviv University.

Laszlo, Ervin, 1972. *The Systems View of the World: The Natural Philosophy of the New Development in the Sciences.* New York: George Brazilier.

Leech, Geoffrey. 1974. *Semantics.* New York: Penguin Books.

Lefevere, André. 1981. "Beyond the Process: Literary Translation in Literature and Literary Theory." *Translation Spectrum.* Ed. Marilyn Gaddis Rose. Buffalo: State University of New York Press, pp. 52–59.

Leksikon fun der Nayer Yidisher Literature [Biographical Dictionary of Modern Yiddish Literature], 1956–. Ed. Ephraim Auerbach, Jacob Birnenbaum, Eliyahu Shulman, and Moshe Starkman. New York: World Congress for Jewish Culture. (Yiddish)

Lemon, Lee T. and Marion J. Reis, eds. 1965. *Russian Formalist Criticism.* Lincoln, Nebraska: University of Nebraska Press.

Leshchinsky, Shmuel. 1954. "Perakim be-Sifrut Yidish be-'Amerika" [Chapters of Yiddish Literature in America], in *Ha-Metzuda* VII. London and Waltham, Mass.: Ararat, pp. 532–555.

Levenston, A.E. 1965. "The Translation–Paradigm: A Technique for Contrastive Syntax." *IRAL*, III:3 (August), 221–225.

Levin, Israel. 1960. *Bein Gedi ve-Sa'ar.* Merhavia: Sifriyat Poalim.

Levy, Ze'ev. 1976. *Strukturalism bein Metod u-Temunat Olam* [Structuralism, Method and Theory]. Tel Aviv: Sifriyat Po'alim.

Leyeles, (Glantz) A. 1925. "An Ofener Briv tsu Sh. Niger" [An Open Letter to S. Niger], *Freie Arbeiter Stimme* (Feb. 20).

Lindenbaum, Shalom. 1974. "Shirat U.Z. Greenberg be-Yidish ve-Yachas ha-Bikoret 'Eleiha ve-'Elav" [U.Z. Greenberg's Yiddish Verse and the Critical Approaches to It], in *U.Z. Greenberg, Mivchar Ma'amarim.* Ed. Yehuda Friedlander, pp. 242–281.

———. 1984. *Shirat U.Z. Greenberg: Kavei Mit'ar.* [Greenberg's Hebrew and Yiddish Verse: An Outline]. Tel Aviv: Hadar.

Liptzin, Sol. 1972. *A History of Yiddish Literature*. Middle Village, New York: Jonathan David.

Lotman, Yury. 1976. *Analysis of the Poetic Text*. Ed. and trans. D.B. Johnson. Ann Arbor: Ardis.

Lotz, John. 1960. "Metric Typology," in *Style in Language*. Ed. Thomas A. Sebeok, pp. 135–148.

Mack, Maynard, Leonard Dean, and William Frost, eds. [2]1964. *Modern Poetry*, vol. 2 of *English Masterpieces*. Ed. Maynard Mack. Englewood Cliffs, NJ: Prentice-Hall Inc.

Mandelkern, Solomon. [10]1977. *Old Testament Concordance* (Hebrew). Tel Aviv: Schocken.

Matejka, Ladislav and Krystyna Pomorska, eds. 1971. *Readings in Russian Poetics*. Cambridge, Mass.: M.I.T. Press.

Mendele Mokher Seforim. 1958. See Abramowitsch.

Miklishansky, J.K. 1967. *Toledot ha-Sifrut ha-'Ivrit be-'Amerika* [History of Hebrew Literature in America]. New York: Ogen.

Minkoff, N.B. 1942. "Algemeyne Tendentsn in der Moderner Yidisher Literatur" [General Tendencies in Modern Yiddish Literature]. *Der Yidisher Kemfer* (22 May):90. (Yiddish)

Miron, Dan. 1961. " 'Al ha-Musag 'Doro shel Bialik' " [On the Concept 'Bialik's generation']. *Moznayim* 13:206–213.

———. 1961a. "Ha-Sifrut ha-'Ivrit be-Reshit ha-Me'a ha-'Esrim" [Hebrew Literature At the Turn of the Century]. *Me'asef* 2:436–466.

———. 1973. *A Traveller Disguised: The Rise and Evolution of the Yiddish Novel in the Nineteenth Century*. New York: Schocken.

———. 1974/5. "He'arot Chadashot le-Machloket Yeshana" [New Comments on an Old Controversy]. *'Achshav* 29–30:63–84.

———. 1975/6. "'Avnei-Bohu le-A. Shlonsky—Shirat ha-Hafshatot" [Shlonsky's Poetry of Abstractions]. *'Achshav* 31–32:63–91.

———. 1979. *Kivun 'Orot: Tachanot ba-Siporet ha-'Ivrit ha-Modernit* [Back to Focus: Studies in Modern Hebrew Fiction]. Tel Aviv: Schocken.

———. 1979a. *Bein Chazon la-'Emet: Nitzanei ha-Roman ha-'Ivri ve-ha-'Idi* [From Romance to the Novel: Studies in the Emergence of the Hebrew and Yiddish Novel in the Nineteenth Century]. Jerusalem: Bialik Institute.

———. 1980. "Darko shel Alterman 'el ha-Shira ha-Le'umit" [Alterman's Way to National Poetry]. *Ha-Doar* 21 (28 May):337–339, 358–359; (4 June):373–374.

———. ed. 1983. *Bialik: Shirim 1880–1898*. [Bialik: An Academic Edition, part I]. Tel Aviv: Tel Aviv University and Dvir.

Morag, Shlomo. 1971. "The Pronunciation of Hebrew." *Encyclopedia Judaica*. Vol. 13, pp. 1120–1146.

Nabokov, Vladimir. 1964. *Notes on Prosody*. Bollingen Series. Princeton: Princeton University Press.

Niger, Samuel. 1925. "Nit Altz Geshribn in Kurtze Shures Is Poezye" [Not Everything Written in Short Lines is Poetry]. *Tog* (Feb. 15). (Yiddish)

———. 1925a. "An Entfer A. Leyeles'n" [An Answer to Leyeles]. *Freie Arbeiter Stimme* (Feb. 27). (Yiddish)

Niger, Samuel and Menachem Ribalow, eds. 1943. *'Achi-Sefer* [Achisefer: Studies in the Literatures and Languages of the Jews, Short Stories and Translations from Jewish Poetry]. New York: Louis Lamed Foundation for the Advancement of Hebrew and Yiddish Literature.

Nims, John Frederic, ed. 1965. *Ovid's Metamorphoses: The Arthur Golding Translation (1567)*. New York: The Macmillan Company.

Nowottny, Winifred. (1962)1975. *The Language Poets Use*. London: Athlone Press.

Noy, Pinchas. 1969. "The Revision of the Psychoanalytic Theory of the Primary Process." *International Journal of Psycho-Analysis* 50:165–178.

Ovid's Metamorphoses. See Nims, 1965.

Pagis, Dan. 1966. "Mavo," in *Kol Shirei David Fogel* ["Introduction" to *The Works of David Fogel*]. Tel Aviv: Machbarot le-Sifrut, pp. 7–70.

———. 1970. *Shirat ha-Chol ve-Torat ha-Shir le-Mosheh Ibn 'Ezra u-Venei Doro* [Secular Poetry and Poetic Theory: Moses ibn Ezra and His Contemporaries]. Jerusalem: Bialik Institute.

———. 1981. *Points of Departure*. Tr. Stephen Mitchell. Introduction by Robert Alter. Philadelphia: Jewish Publication Society.

Pei, Mario and Frank Gaynor. n.d. *Dictionary of Linguistics*. New York: Philosophical Library.

Perri, Carmela. 1978. "On Alluding." *Poetics* 7:3 (September): 289–307.

Perry, Menachem. 1968. "Ha-Analogya u-Mekomah be-Mivneh ha-Roman shel Mendele Mokher Sefarim" [The Role of Analogy in the Structure of Mendele's Novels]. *Ha-Sifrut/Literature* 1:1, pp. 65–100.

———. 1976. *Ha-Mivneh ha-Semanti shel Shirei Bialik* [Semantic Dynamics in Poetry: The Theory of Semantic Change in the Text Continuum of a Poem, especially in the Hebrew Poetry of H.N. Bialik]. Tel Aviv: The Israeli Institute for Poetics and Semiotics. Tel Aviv University, Siman Kri'a Books and Ha-Sifrut.

———. 1981. "Thematic and Structural Shifts in Autotranslation by Bilingual Hebrew-Yiddish Writers." *Poetics Today* 2,4:181–191.

Persky, Daniel. 1943. "Yesodot 'Idiyim bi-Yetzirat Bialik" [Yiddish Elements in Bialik's Writings], in 'Achi-Sefer. Ed. Samuel Niger and Menachem Ribalow, pp. 81–90.

Pomerantz, Ber. 1966. *Shirim* [Poems]. Compiled and introduced by Noah Peniel. Israel: Massada.

Popovič, Anton. 1968. "Translation Analysis and Literary History." *Babel* XIV:68–76.

———. 1977. "Translation as Communication," in *Torat ha-Targum* [Translation Theory]. Gideon Toury, ed. Tel Aviv University, 1983, pp. 45–62.

Pound, Ezra. 1913. "A Few Don'ts by an Imagiste." *Poetry* I (March):6.

———. 1914. "Vorticism." *The Fortnightly Review*, XCVI (1 Sept.):461–471.

———. 1915. "Affirmations IV: As for Imagisme." *The New Age*, XVI (Jan. 28):13.

———. 1957. *Selected Poems of Ezra Pound.* New York: A New Directions Paperback.

Pratt, William C. 1963. *The Imagist Poem*. New York: Dutton.

Preil, Joseph Joshua. 1924. "Perek be-Shir" [A Chapter on the Poetry of Y.L. Gordon], in *Ketavim Nivcharim.* Ed. Eleazar Meir Preil. New York, pp. 1–15.

Preminger, Alex, F.J. Warnke and O.B. Hardison, Jr. [2]1974. *Princeton Encyclopedia of Poetry and Poetics.* Princeton: Princeton University Press.

Progoff, Ira. 1953. *Jung's Psychology and Its Social Meaning.* New York: Grove Press.

Rabin, Chaim. 1972. *'Ikarei Toledot ha-Lashon ha-'Ivrit* [Main Lines of the History of the Hebrew Language]. Jerusalem: The Jewish Agency.

———. 1983. "The National Idea and the Revival of Hebrew." *Studies in Zionism.* Tel Aviv: Tel Aviv University Press.

Riffaterre, Michael. 1967. "Criteria for Style Analysis," in *Essays on the Language of Literature.* Eds. Seymour Chatman and Samuel R. Levin. Boston: Houghton Mifflin, pp. 412–430. Reprinted from *Word* 15 (April 1959):1.

———. 1967a. "Stylistic Context," in *Essays on the Language of Literature.* Eds. Seymour Chatman and Samuel R. Levin. Boston: Houghton Mifflin, pp. 431–434. Reprinted from *Word* 16 (August, 1960):2.

———. 1973. "The Self-sufficient Text." *Diacritics* 3:39–45.

———. 1974. "The Stylistic Approach to Literary History," in *New Directions in Literary History.* Ed. Ralph Cohen. Baltimore: Johns Hopkins University Press, pp. 147–164. Reprinted from *New Literary History* 2:39–55, 1970.

———. 1978. *Semiotics of Poetry.* Bloomington and London: Indiana University Press.

Roskies, David G. 1980. "The Achievement of American Yiddish Modernism," in *Go and Study: Essays and Studies in Honor of Alfred*

Jospe. Ed. Raphael Jospe and Samuel Z. Fishman. Washington, DC: B'nai B'rith Hillel Foundations, pp. 353–368.

Sadan, Dov. 1982. *'Avnei Bedek* [Essays on Jewish Writers]. Tel Aviv: Ha-Kibbutz ha-Me'uchad.

———. 1965. *Sugyat Yidish be-Masechet Bialik* [Yiddish in Bialik's Oeuvre]. Jerusalem: Academon.

———. 1970. *'Avnei Miftan*, vol. 2 [Threshold Stones: Essays on Yiddish Writers]. Tel Aviv: Peretz Publishing House.

Sandbank, Shimon. 1976. *Shetei Berechot ba-Ya'ar* [Two Pools in the Wood: Hebrew Poetry and the European Tradition]. Tel Aviv: Ha-Kibbutz ha-Me'uchad and Katz Institute, Tel Aviv University.

Schwartz, Yael. 1972. "Kol Birkei ha-Tziv'onim" [All the (Colorful) Tulips' Glitter], *Siman Kri'a* 1:76–102.

———. 1979. " 'Al 'Ekronot ha-Tizmur shel ha-Muchashi ba-Sifrut" [On the Orchestration of the Concrete in Literature]. *Ha-Sifrut/Literature* 28:76–88.

Sebeok, Thomas A., ed. 1960. *Style in Language*. Cambridge, Mass.: M.I.T. Press.

Sha'anan, Avraham. 1962, 1967. *Ha-Sifrut ha-'Ivrit ha-Chadasha li-Zerameiha* [Trends in Modern Hebrew Literature]. 4 vols. Tel Aviv: Massada.

Shaked, Gershon. 1965. *Bein Tzechok le-Dema'* [Between Laughter and Tears: Studies in the Works of Mendele Mokher Sefarim]. Tel Aviv: Massada.

———. 1973. *Le-Lo Motza* [No Exit]. Tel Aviv: Ha-Kibbutz ha-Me'uchad.

———. 1976. *'Omanut ha-Sippur shel 'Agnon* [Agnon's Narrative Art]. Merhavya: Sifriyat Poalim.

———. 1977. *Ha-Siporet ha-'Ivrit, 1880–1970*. [Hebrew Narrative Fiction, 1880–1970], vol. 1: *Ba-Gola* [In Exile]. Israel: Ha-Kibbutz ha-Me'uchad and Keter Publishing Houses Ltd.

———. 1983. *'Ein Makom 'Acher* [No Other Place]. Tel Aviv: Ha-Kibbutz ha-Me'uchad.

Shapira, Zusha. 1966. *Ritmim be-Shirat Bialik* [Rhythms in Bialik's Verse]. Tel Aviv: Emesh.

Shapiro, Michael. 1976. *Asymmetry: An Inquiry into the Linguistic Structures of Poetry*. Amsterdam and New York: North Holland Publishers.

Shavit, Uzzi. 1978. "Levatim ve-Hitpatechuyot be-Shitot Mishkal u-Negina bi-Yetzirat Bialik" [Evolution and Revolution in the Development of Bialik's Prosody]. Dissertation, Tel Aviv University.

———. 1979. "Reshit ha-Ritmus ha-Chofshi ba-Shira ha-'Ivrit ha-Chadasha" [The Beginning of Free Verse in Modern Hebrew Poetry]. *Siman Kri'a* 9:461–466.

———. 1983. *Ha-Mahpecha ha-Ritmit* [The Rhythmic Revolution]. Tel Aviv: Ha-Kibbutz ha-Me'uchad and Katz Institute (Tel Aviv University).

Shavit, Zohar. 1983. *Ha-Chayim ha-Sifrutiyim be-'Eretz Yisra'el: 1910–33* [Literary Life in Palestine, 1910–33]. Tel Aviv: Porter Institute and Ha-Kibbutz ha-Me'uchad.

——— and Jacob. 1974. "Le-Toledot Sipur ha-Pesha' ha-'Ivri be-'Eretz Yisra'el" [Hebrew Crime Stories During the 1930s in Palestine]. *Ha-Sifrut/Literature* 18–19:30–73.

Shelley, P.B. 1951. *Shelley: Selected Poetry, Prose and Letters*. Ed. A.S.B. Glover. London: The Nonesuch Press.

Shenhod, Shlomo, trans. 1964. *Mi-Kol 'Amali* [Of All My Labor] by Jacob Glatstein. Jerusalem: Bialik Institute.

Sheppard, Richard. 1976. "The Crisis of Language," in Bradbury and McFarlane, pp. 323–337.

Shirman, Hayim. [3]1974. *Ha-Shira ha-'Ivrit bi-Sefarad u-vi-Perovans* [Hebrew Verse in Spain and Provence]. 4 vols. Jerusalem and Tel Aviv: Bialik Institution and Dvir.

Shklovsky, Victor. (1917)1965. "Art as Technique," in *Russian Formalist Criticism: Four Essays*. Trans. with an introduction by Lee T. Lemon and Marion J. Reis. Lincoln, Nebraska: University of Nebraska Press, pp. 3–24.

Shlonsky, Avraham. 1923. "Ha-Melitza" [The Flowery Trope]. *Hedim* 1: 189–190.

———. 1931. " 'Al 'Re'itichem Shuv be-Kotzer Yedchem' " [On Bialik's poem]. *Ketuvim*, 6 (Nov. 4):6.

———. 1960. *Yalkut 'Eshel* [Selected Essays]. Merhavia: Sifriyat Poalim.

———. 1978. *Yalkut Shirim* [Selected Poems]. With an introduction by A.B. Yoffe. Israel: Yachdav and 'Agudat ha-Soferim.

Shmeruk, Chone. 1969. "*Ha-Keri'a la-Navi*" [The Call to the Prophet: Shne'ur, Bialik, Peretz, Nadson]. *Ha-Sifrut/Literature*, 2:1, pp. 241–244. English summary:251.

———. 1978. *Sifrut Yidish: Perakim le-Toledoteiha* [Chapters in the History of Yiddish Literature, vol. 1]. Tel Aviv: Porter Institute for Poetics and Semiotics, Tel Aviv University.

———. 1979. "Yetzirato shel U.Z. Greenberg be-Yidish be-'Eretz Yisra'el u-ve-Polin be-Sof Shenot ha-'Esrim u-vi-Shenot ha-Sheloshim" [U.Z. Greenberg's Yiddish Works in Palestine and in Poland in the Twenties and in the Early Thirties]. *Ha-Sifrut/Literature* 29:82–89.

Shne'ur, Zalman. 1951. *Po'emot* [Epic Poems], vol. 2 of *Shirei Z. Shne'ur* [The Works of Z. Sh.]. Tel Aviv: Am Oved.

———. 1952. *Shirim* [Lyrical Poems]. vol. 1 of *Shirei Z. Shne'ur*. Tel Aviv: Am Oved.

Short, Robert. 1976. "Dada and Surrealism," in Bradbury and McFarlane, pp. 292–308.

Shroder, Maurice Z. 1961. *Icarus: The Image of the Artist in French Romanticism.* Cambridge, Mass.: Harvard University Press.

Silberschlag, Eisig. 1973. *From Renaissance to Renaissance: Hebrew Literature 1492–1970*, vol. 1. New York: Ktav Publishing House.

Smith, Barbara Herrenstein. 1968. *Poetic Closure: A Study of How Poems End.* Chicago-London: University of Chicago Press.

Spitzer, Leo. (1948) 1967. *Linguistics and Literary History: Essays in Stylistics.* Princeton: Princeton University Press.

Starkman, Moshe, ed. 1945. *Hemshekh Antologye fun Amerikaner-Yidisher Dikhtung 1918–1943* [Anthology of American Yiddish Verse]. New York: Farlag Hemshekh. (Yiddish)

———. 1954. " 'Ivrim ka-Chalutzei Yidish be-'Amerika" [Hebrew Writers as Pioneers of Yiddish in America]. *Ha-Metzuda* VII:505–531.

Steiner, George. 1975. *After Babel.* New York: Oxford University Press.

Striedter, Yuri. 1977. "The Russian Formalist Theory of Prose." *PTL* 2:3, pp. 429–469.

———. 1978. "The Russian Formalist Theory of Literary Evolution." *PTL* 3:1, pp. 1–23.

T. (Tcharny) Carmi. 1945. "Nof Shemesh u-Chefor" [Landscape of Sun and Frost]. *Niv* 3:23–27.

Tchernichowsky, Saul. [3]1967. *Mivchar Shirim* [Selected Poems]. Tel Aviv: Dvir La'am.

Tchernowitz, Chaim [Rav Tza'ir]. 1954. *Pirkei Chayim* [Autobiography]. New York: Bitzaron.

Teller, Yehuda Leib. 1930. *Simboln* [Symbols: Poems]. New York: Biderman. (Yiddish)

———. 1934. *Miniaturn* [Miniatures: Poems]. New York. (Yiddish)

———. 1975. *Durkh Yidishn Gemit* [In the Spirit of Yiddish: Poems]. Tel Aviv: Publishing House Israel Book. (Yiddish)

Todorov, Tzvetan. 1969. "How to Read?" in his *The Poetics of Prose.* Trans. Richard Howard. Ithaca. New York: Cornell University Press. 1977, pp. 234–246.

Tomashevskii, Boris. 1971 (1923). "Literature and Biography," in *Readings in Russian Poetics.* Ed. Ladislav Matejka and Krystina Pomorska, pp. 47–55.

Tompkins, Jane, ed. 1980. *Reader–Response Criticism.* Baltimore: Johns Hopkins University Press.

Toury, Gideon. 1974. "Li-Be'ayot ha-Sifrut ke-Rav Ma'arechet [On Literature as Polysystem]. *Ha-Sifrut/Literature*, 18–19:1–19.

———. 1977. "Equivalentzya ve-Choser Equivalentzya be-Targum Ke-

Funktzya shel Normot" [Translational Equivalence and Its Absence as the Function of Norms]. *Ha-Sifrut* 25, 33–39.

———. 1977a. *Normot shel Targum ve-ha-Targum ha-Sifruti le-'Ivrit ba-Shanim 1930–1945* [Translation Norms and Literary Translation into Hebrew in 1930–1945]. Tel Aviv: Porter Institute.

———. 1981. "Translated Literature: System, Norm, Performance." *Poetics Today* 2:4,9–28.

———. 1982. "A Rationale for Descriptive Translation Studies." *Disposition* 19–20–21, pp. 23–39.

Tynjanov, J.N. (1924) 1971. "The Meaning of the Word in Verse," in *Readings in Russian Poetics.* Ed. Ladislav Matejka and Krystina Pomorska, pp. 136–145.

———. (1927) 1971. "On Literary Evolution," in *Readings in Russian Poetics.* Ed. Ladislav Matejka and Krystina Pomorska, pp. 66–78.

——— and Roman Jakobson. (1928) 1971. "Problems in the Study of Literature and Language," in *Readings in Russian Poetics.* Ed. Ladislav Matejka and Krystina Pomorska, pp. 79–81.

Uitti, Karl D. 1969. *Linguistics and Literary Theory.* New York: W.W. Norton.

Ullmann, Stephen. 1971. "Stylistics and Semantics," in *Literary Style: A Symposium.* Ed. Seymour Chatman. London and New York: Oxford University Press, pp. 133–152.

Weinreich, Uriel. 1953. *Languages in Contact.* New York: Publication of the Linguistic Circle of New York, No. 1.

———. 1968. *Modern English–Yiddish, Yiddish–English Dictionary.* New York: McGraw–Hill.

Weiss, Aviezer, ed. 1975. *Mivchar Ma'amarim 'al Yetzirat Avraham Shlonsky* [Selected Critical Essays on Shlonsky's Works]. Tel Aviv: Am Oved.

Wellek, René. 1963. *Concepts of Criticism.* New Haven and London: Yale University Press.

——— and Austin Warren. (1942) [3]1977. *Theory of Literature.* New York and London: Harcourt Brace Jovanovich.

Werses, Shmuel. 1971. *Sipur ve-Shorsho* [Story and Source]. Ramat-Gan: Massada.

———. 1977. "Y.D. Berkowitz be-Yalduto" [Y.D. Berkowitz in His Childhood]. *Moznayim* 45:5 (Nov.):382–390.

Whitman, Ruth. 1972. *The Selected Poems of Jacob Glatstein.* New York: October House, Inc.

Whitman, Walt. n.d. *Leaves of Grass (1850–1881).* New York: Universal Library, Grosset & Dunlap.

Williams, William Carlos. 1962. *Pictures from Brueghel and Other Poems.*

New York: A New Directions Paperback.

———. (1965) 1974. "Free Verse," in *Princeton Encyclopedia of Poetry and Poetics*. Ed. Alex Preminger, pp. 288–290.

Willy, Autrey Nell. 1929. "Reiterative Devices in 'Leaves of Grass'." *American Literature* 1 (May):161–170.

Wimsatt, W.K. Jr., in collaboration with Monroe C. Beardsley, 1954. *The Verbal Icon: Studies in the Meaning of Poetry*. Lexington: University of Kentucky Press.

Wisse, Ruth R. 1976. "*Di Yunge* and the Problem of Jewish Aestheticism." *Jewish Social Studies* 38:265–276.

Wordsworth, William. 1920. *The Poetical Works of W. Wordsworth*. Ed. Thomas Hutchinson, M.A. London: Oxford University Press.

Yeshurun, Avot. 1980. *The Syrian–African Rift & Other Poems*. Trans. Harold Schimmel. Philadelphia: Jewish Publication Society.

Yip, Wai–Lim. 1974. "Classical Chinese and Modern Anglo-American Poetry: Convergence of Languages and Poetry." *Comparative Literature Studies*, vol. 11,1 (March):21–47.

Yoffe, A.B. 1966. *A. Shlonsky, ha-Meshorer u-Zemano* [A. Shlonsky, the Poet and His Times]. Merhavia: Sifriyat Po'alim.

Yoffe, Mordechai. 1941. "Mi-Masechet ha-Zeman: 'Esrim Shenot Sifrut 'Idit be-'Amerika" [Twenty Years of Yiddish Literature in America]. *Ha-Doar* (30 July):524–526.

———. 1951. *Antologye fun der Hebreishe Poezye* [Anthology of Hebrew Poetry]. New York: Cyco Bikher Farlag. (Yiddish)

Yu, Pauline. 1979. "The Poetics of Discontinuity: East–West Correspondences in Lyric Poetry." *PMLA* 94:261–274.

Zach, Natan. 1966. *Zeman ve-Ritmus 'Etzel Bergson u-va-Shira ha-Modernit* [Time and Rhythm in Bergson and in Modern Poetry]. Tel Aviv: Aleph.

———. 1966a. "Le-'Akliman ha-Signoni shel Shenot ha-Chamishim-Shishim be-Shiratenu" [The Stylistic Climate of the Fifties and Sixties in Our Poetry]. *Ha-'Aretz* (28 July).

———. 1976. "Imagism and Vorticism," in Bradbury and McFarlane, pp. 228–242.

———. 1982. *The Static Element: Selected Poems*. Trans. Peter Everwine and Shulamit Yasny-Starkman. New York: Atheneum.

Zeitlin, Aharon. 1943. "Mendele ha-Mekarev" [Mendele the Mediator], in *'Achi-Sefer*. Ed. Samuel Niger and Menachem Ribalow, pp. 74–81.

Zemah, Eddi. 1969. *Ha-Lavi ha-Mistater* [The Hiding Lion]. Jerusalem: Kiryat Sefer.

Zhirmunskii, Victor. 1966 (1922). *Introduction to Metrics: The Theory of Verse*. Trans. from the Russian C.F. Brown. Ed. E. Stankiewicz and W.N. Vickery. The Hague: Mouton.

Index